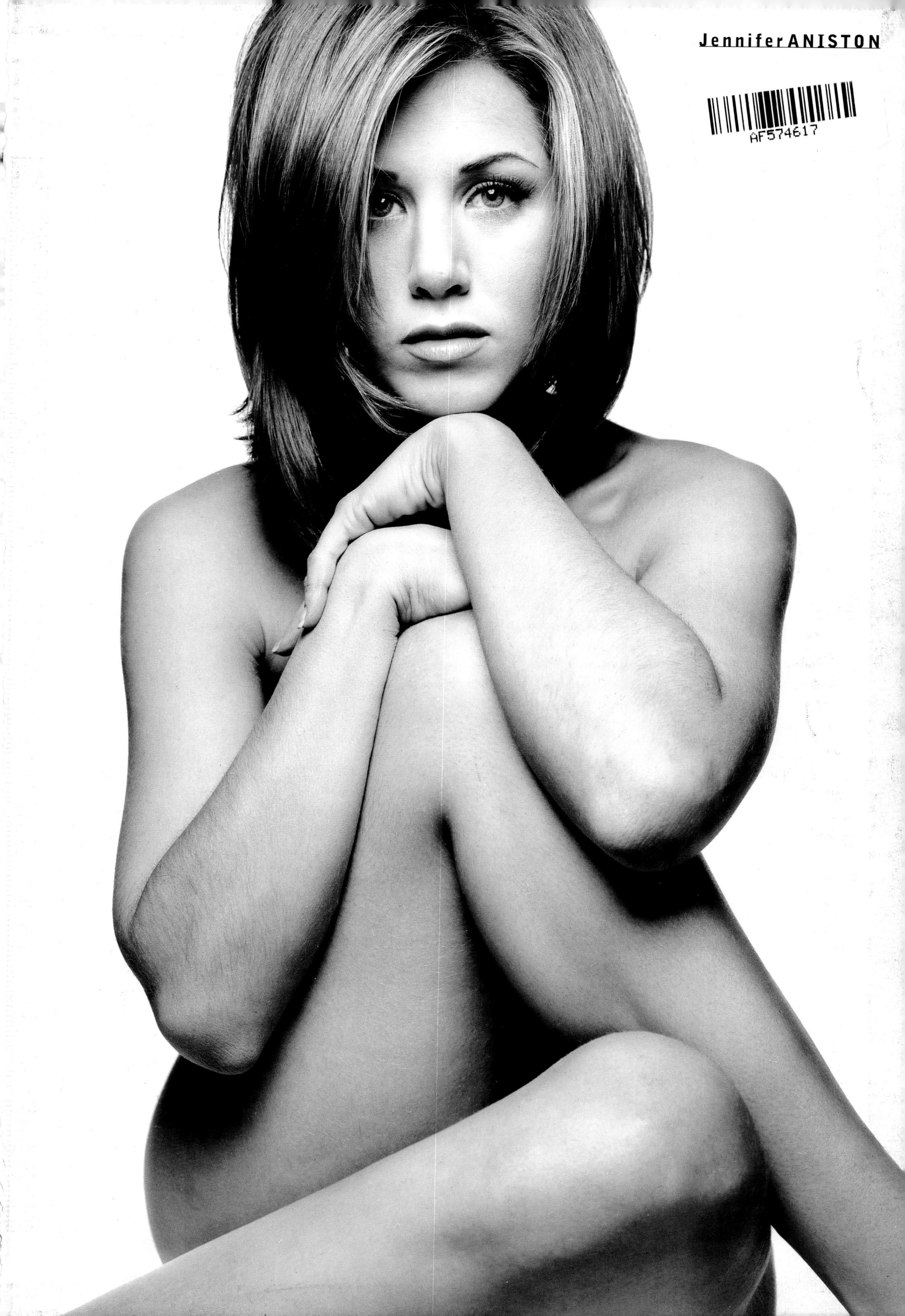
JenniferANISTON

OUTRAGEOUS

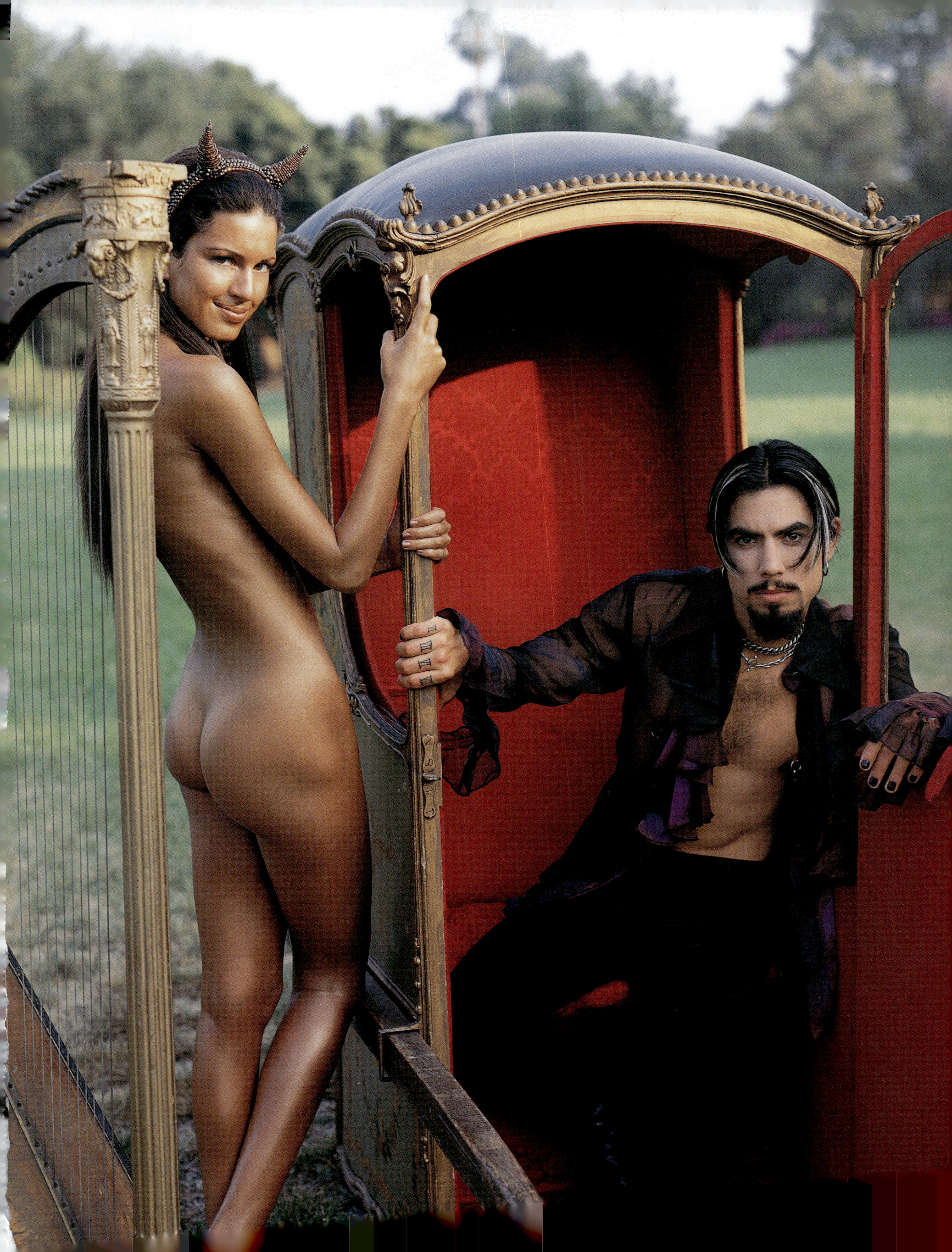

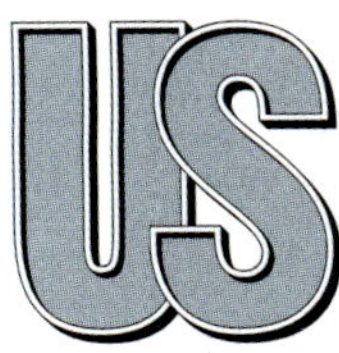

OUTRAGEOUS

A Rolling Stone Press Book

EDITOR Holly George-Warren
SENIOR EDITOR Shawn Dahl
EDITORIAL ASSISTANT Ann Abel

DESIGNER Richard Baker
PHOTO EDITOR Jennifer Crandall
DESIGN ASSOCIATE Rina Migliaccio
DESIGN ASSISTANT Bess Wong

For information, address
St. Martin's Press,
175 Fifth Avenue,
New York, N.Y. 10010.

ISBN 0-312-19284-3

First Edition
November 1998
10 9 8 7 6 5 4 3 2 1

COVER
Heather Graham by Bettina Rheims
BACK COVER
Mark Wahlberg by Mark Seliger

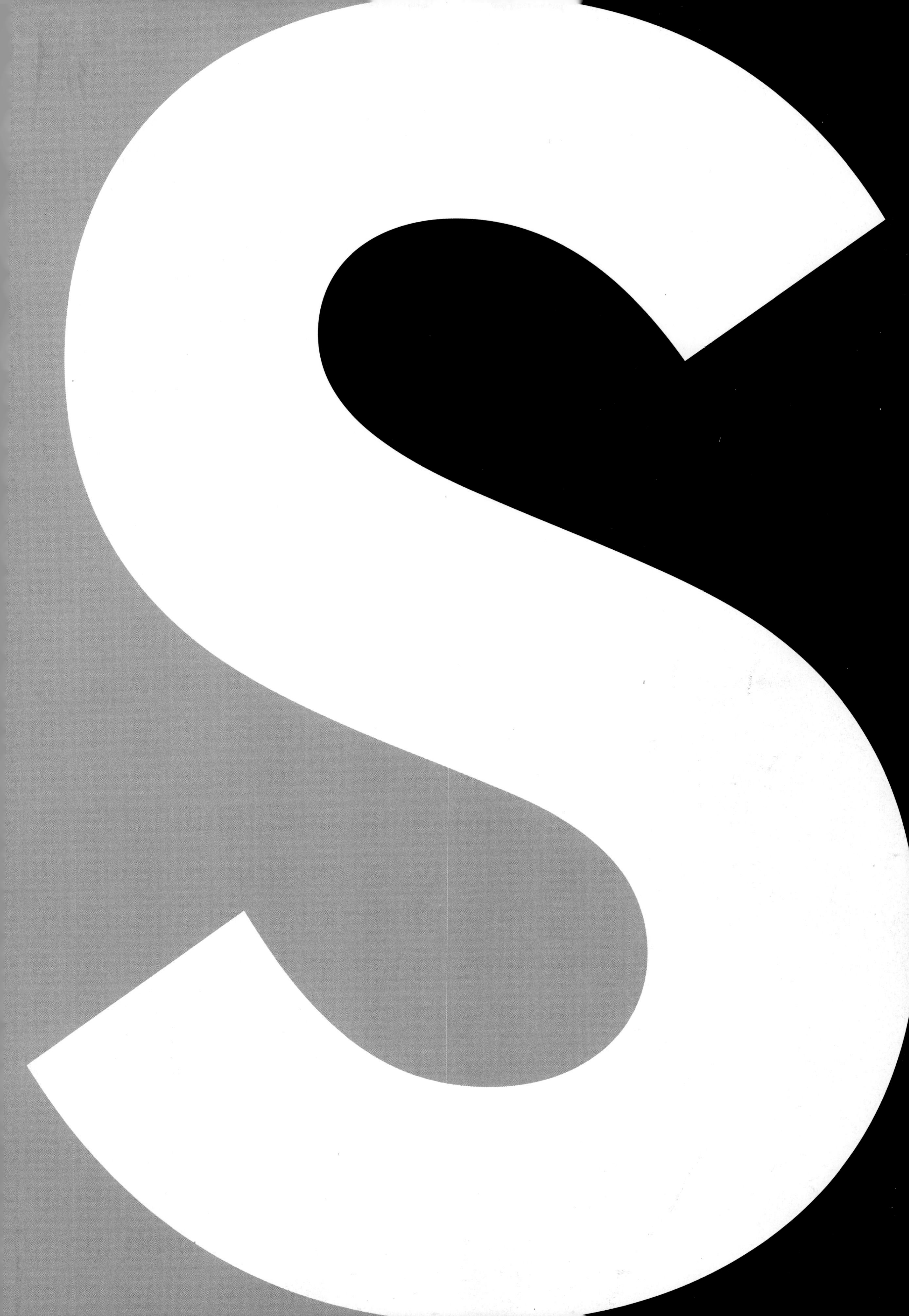

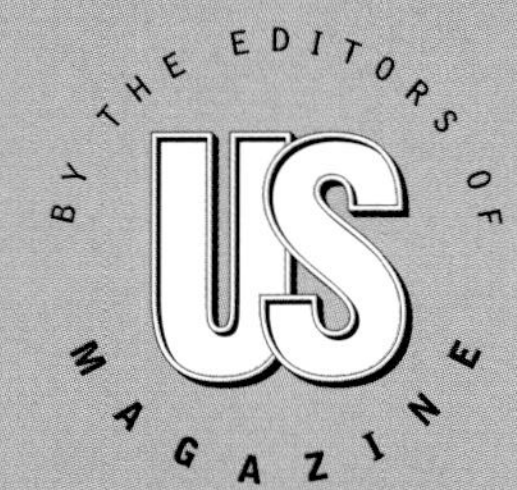

OUTRA

GEOUS

THE PHOTOGRAPHS

DESIGNED BY RICHARD BAKER & RINA MIGLIACCIO

ST. MARTIN'S PRESS

NEW YORK CITY

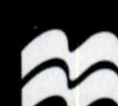

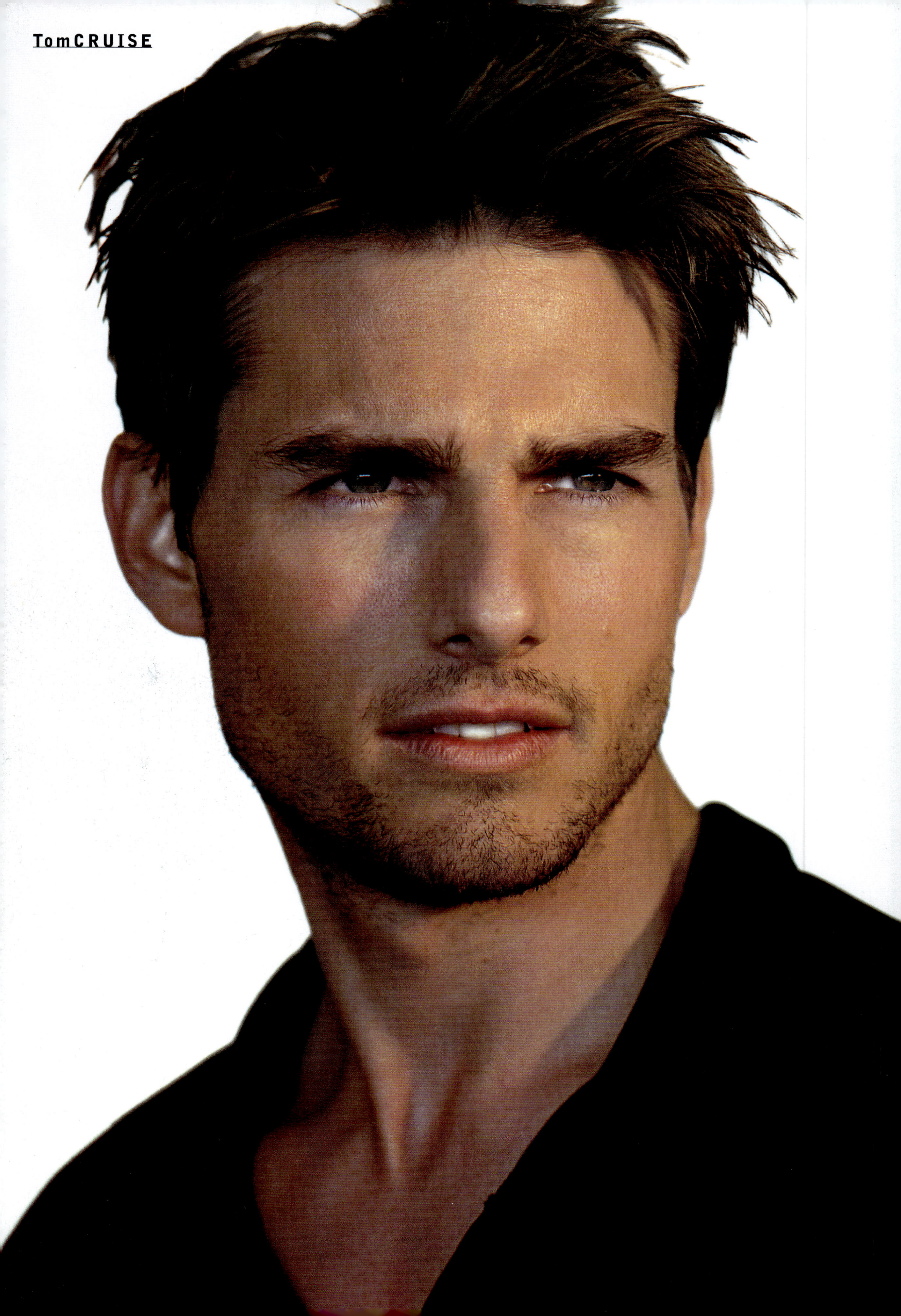

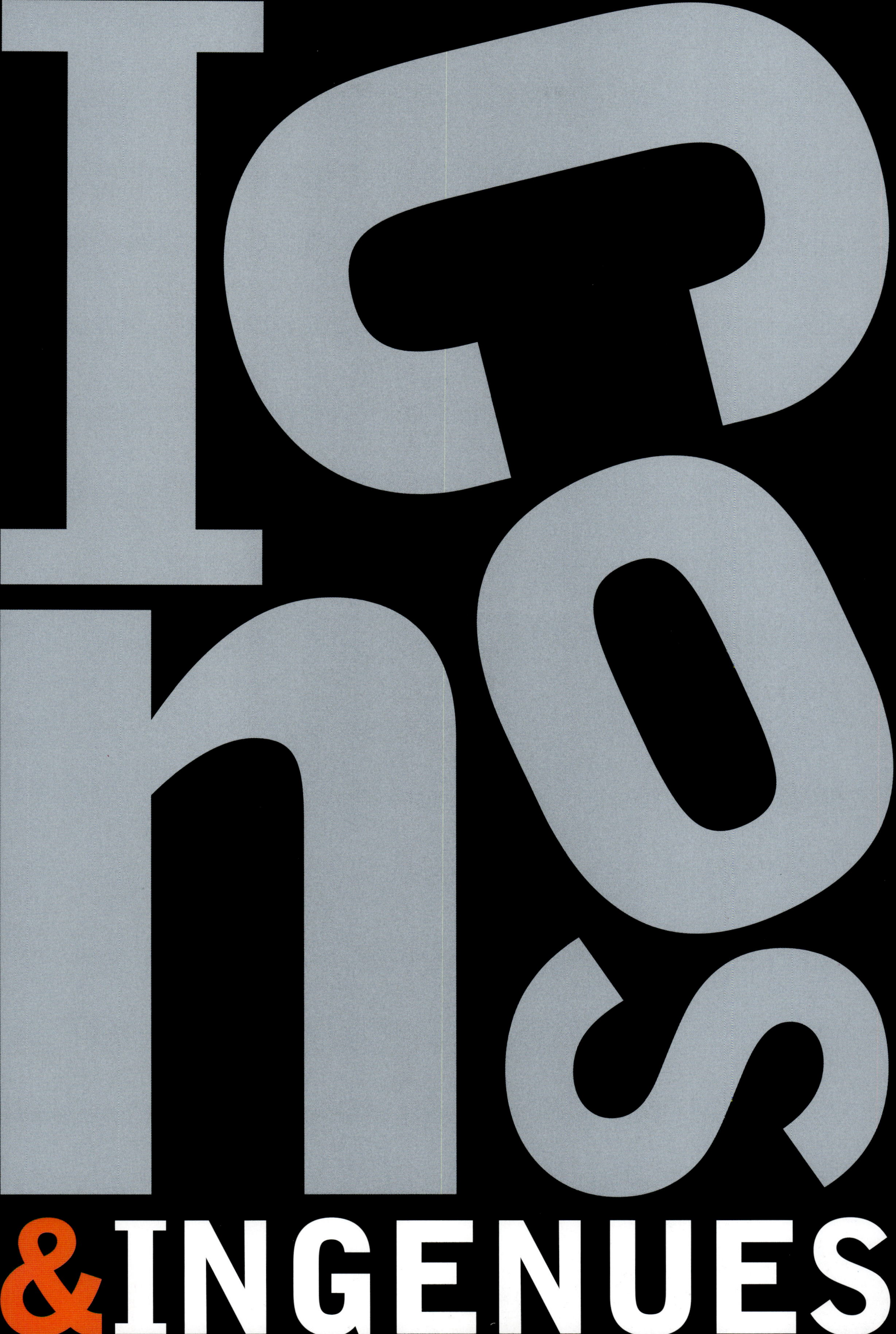
Icons
&INGENUES

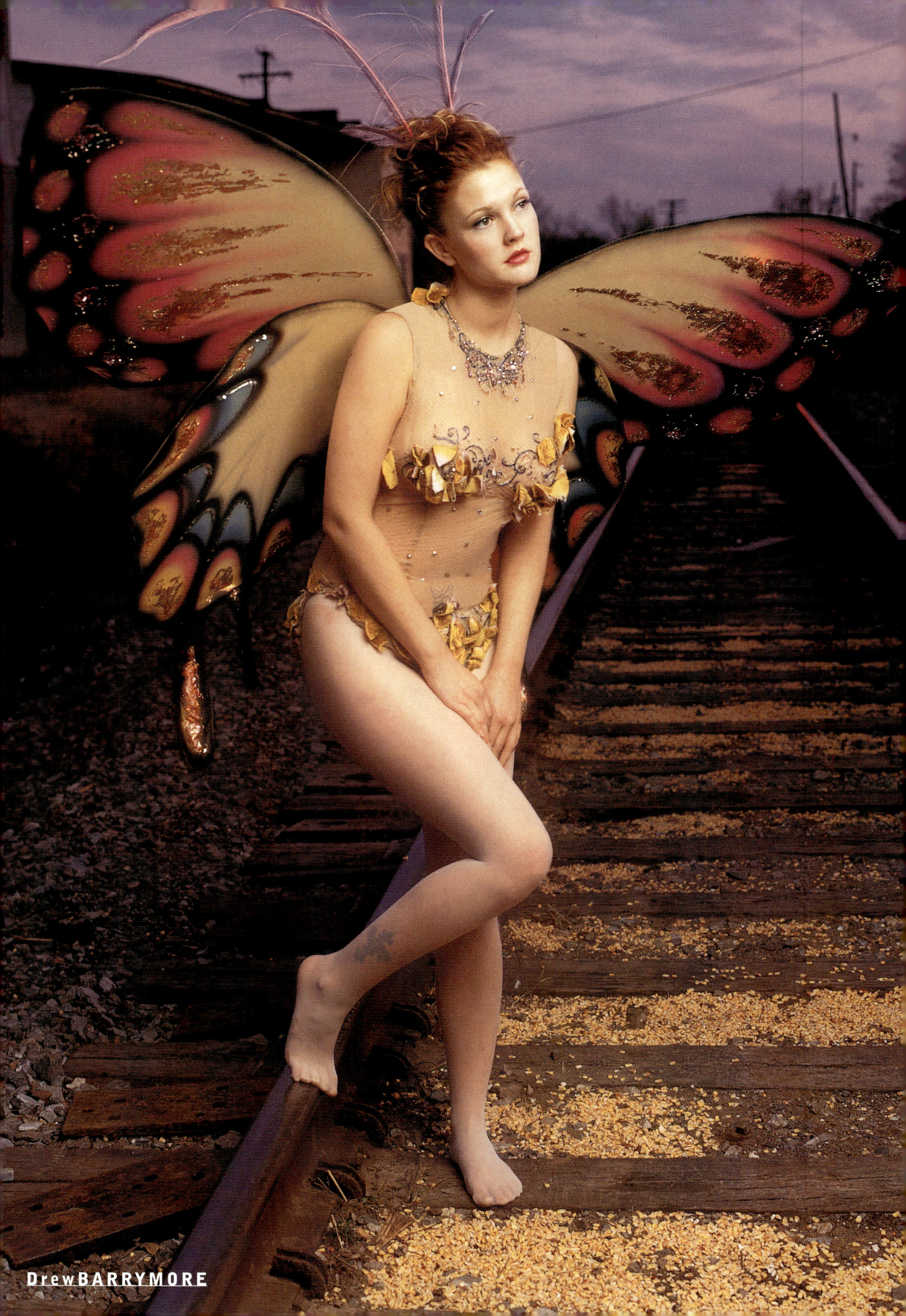

DrewBARRYMORE

What's outrageous?

Behold Drew Carey's absurdist impersonation of a lion poised next to Brendan Fraser's tamer role. Try Kirstie Alley's pink balloons and watch what Jennifer Aniston does with them on the adjacent page. Or director Tim Burton and actress Lisa Marie, whose intense connection is illustrated in the most artificial yet deeply personal way. Then there's Andie MacDowell, her graceful beauty suited up in male drag and seated next to a gigantic, surreal bunny. DO PICTURES LIE? Well, yes and no. They tell stories, for sure. Sometimes they reveal the truth in ways that words can hardly approximate. And sometimes they lie exquisitely, or reprehensibly. Photographs also provide solace, respite and cheap and vicarious thrills. To charge a picture with changing your life is both a really amazing act and highly suspect. Because what you bring to the scene is at least half the party. PHOTOS CAN ALSO represent ideals. For instance, in *US*, the stars we shoot live in rarefied worlds of wealth and beauty. Most of them were not born into it, and most of them came into it at a rather young age. SO WHAT IS IT that these photographs here give us that's real? If we take for granted that our world is saturated with glamorous images of celebrities, what makes this particular group – which accurately represents *US*'s monthly fare – special, unusual, original or otherwise engaging? Beyond the argument that these images are good because they give us something to which to aspire, or that they're evil because they remind us of what most of us will never have, there's another idea: that these images and their subjects describe another aspect of being human. Rather than illustrating the lavish lifestyles of the stars, this collection of photographs depicts that human component which particularly comes in handy when taking pictures – *play*. FROM MARTIN LANDAU prancing in tails in a public restroom to Fiona Apple peering from the middle of a bamboo forest, *Outrageous* is actively fantastical. You might not expect to see a button-down guy like Chris O'Donnell cavorting in the fountain at Trafalgar Square in London. By the same token, you may expect former bad boy turned Buddhist Richard Gere in contemplative mode, but here he's so sensitively rendered – his hands in mid-prayer position – that his image is given a whole new depth. Every picture, no matter how contrived or collaborative, reveals personality, a willingness to amuse. As they should. Let them entertain us. IMAGE REQUIRES COLLABORATION. The late Gianni Versace made fashion history by understanding that principle. One of his more ambitious and interesting projects, Courtney Love, credits the designer as the only style maven who really understood her. She told *US* that she has suggested to other designers, "If we're going to play a game, let's play together." Love, whose work and life have always borne an uneasy and rich relationship with beauty and fame, is perhaps the most startling but hardly the only example in *Outrageous* of the power of image in both its two and three dimensions. FOR ALL THAT STARS attempt to manipulate their images, however, the truth usually emerges. You can hide sadness, or madness, or badness, for only so long. A quick shot of Leonardo DiCaprio captures the young actor's reaction to the overwhelming fame that threatens to engulf him. On the other hand, you have Sir Anthony Hopkins, portrayed close up in black and white as the esteemed and formidable British thespian he is, who outright says, "I just wanted to get famous. All the rest is hogwash." OR "X-FILES" STARS David Duchovny and Gillian Anderson. Reports of their cordial-at-best relationship on set and off might be dismissed as nasty rumor, or not. But see them gender-swap and role-play for photographer Mark Seliger and you wonder who's zooming whom – or at least marvel that they can have such good humor to spoof themselves. NOT ONLY DO IMAGES easily play against type, creating, in effect, a fuller picture, but they bolster words as well. Take Nicole Kidman, for instance. How many times have you heard the contention that Kidman, for all her lovely charms, is a wee bit chilly? She can protest in her interview that she's misunderstood and regale us with tales of her bawdy behavior, but the pictures of her loosening up at a party of one bring home her contention. Not to say that images, like words, can't nudge us toward what we might not have believed before. But why would she bother to go to so much trouble? She looks like she's having a good time, and I think we can trust her. WHAT IS TO BE LEARNED? If photographs that are not candid automatically seem opaque, less than true, think again. For all the engineering of photo scenarios, they can also reveal what the stars think of themselves by what they show to the world. And if the power of the image mystifies you, consider the simple strength in the confession of Drew Barrymore, who told *US*, "I used to look in the mirror and feel shame; I look in the mirror now and I absolutely love myself." In *Outrageous*, if you are willing to look beneath the surface sheen, you will glean some intriguing material about your favorite entertainers.

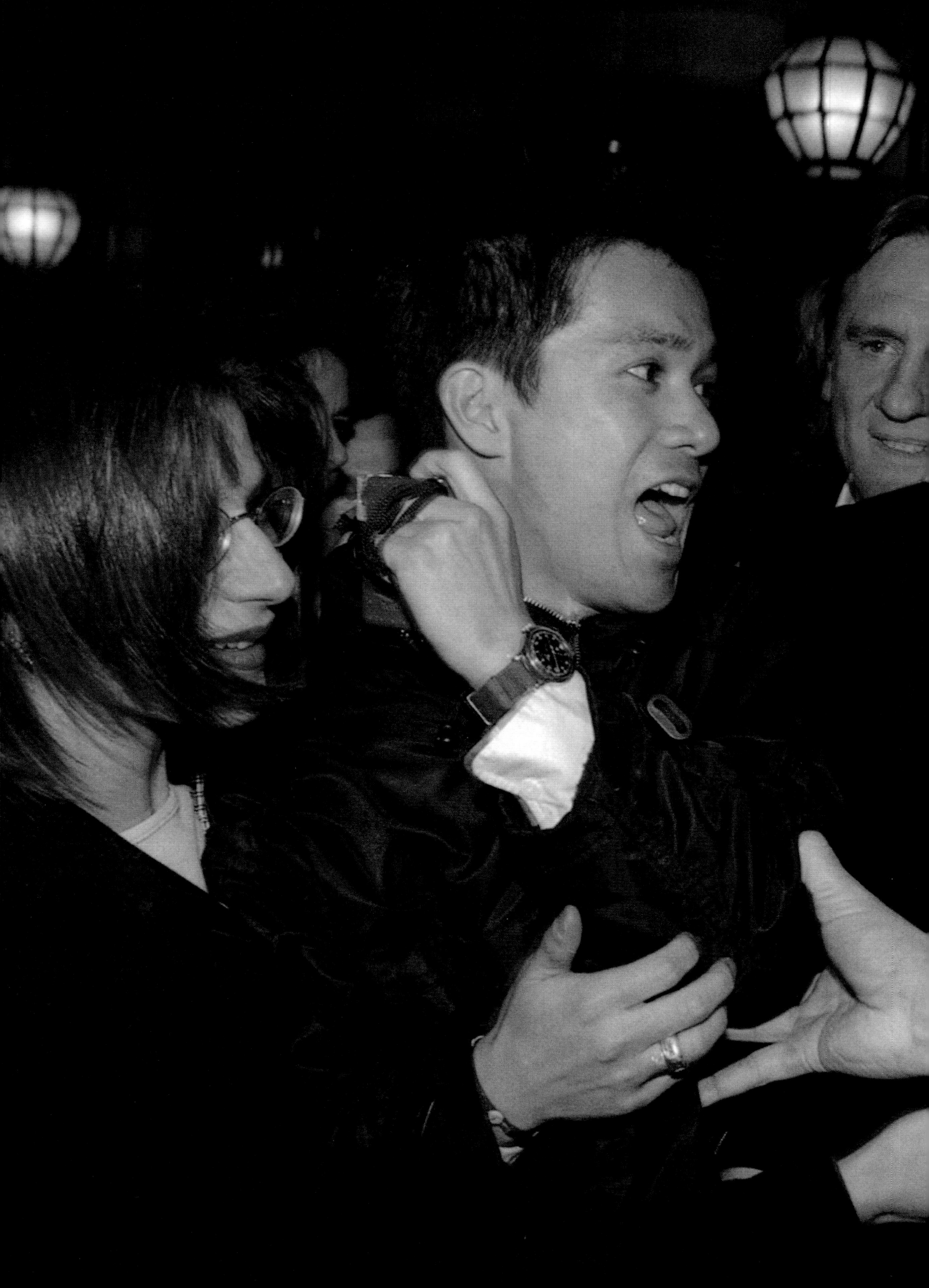

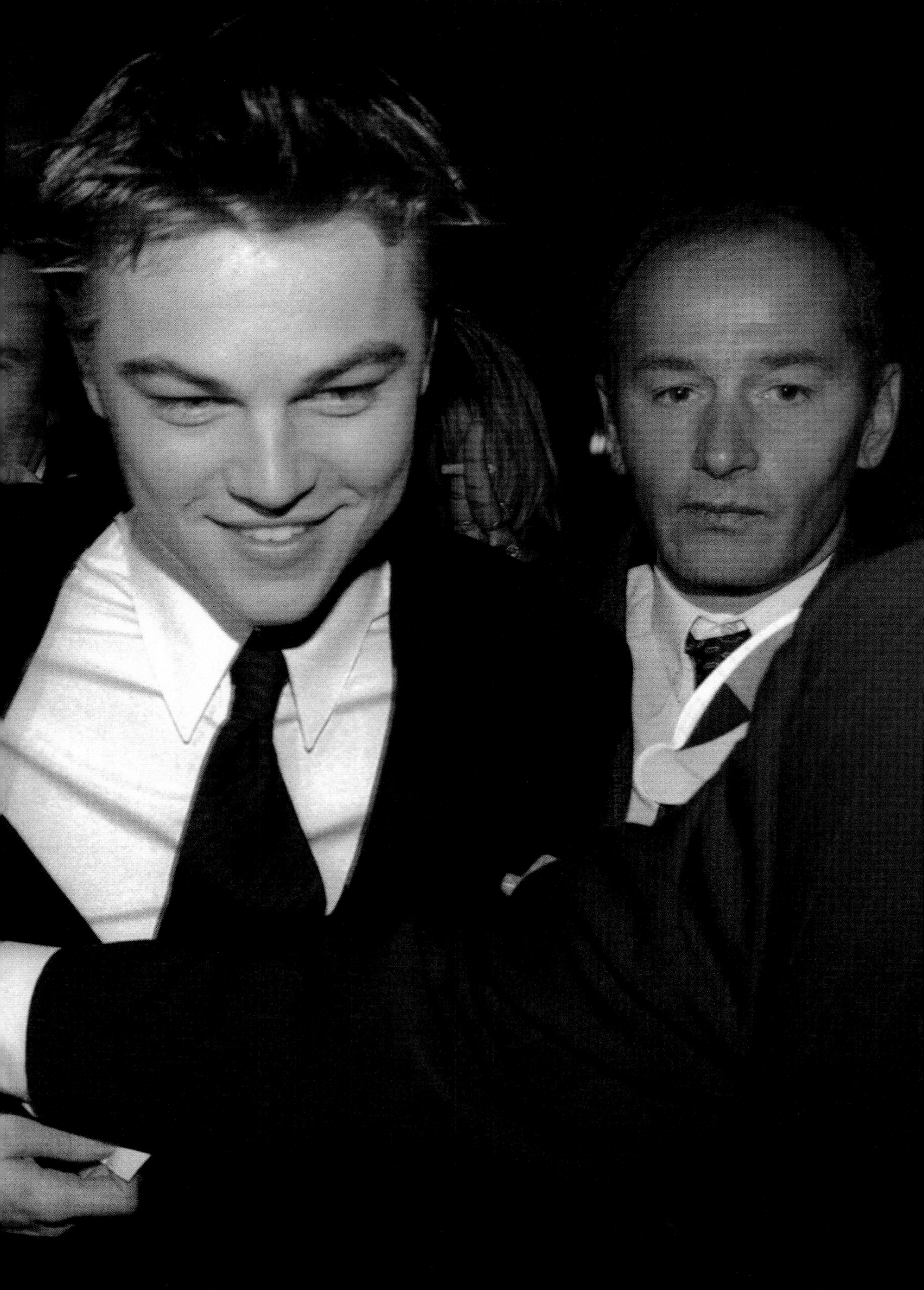

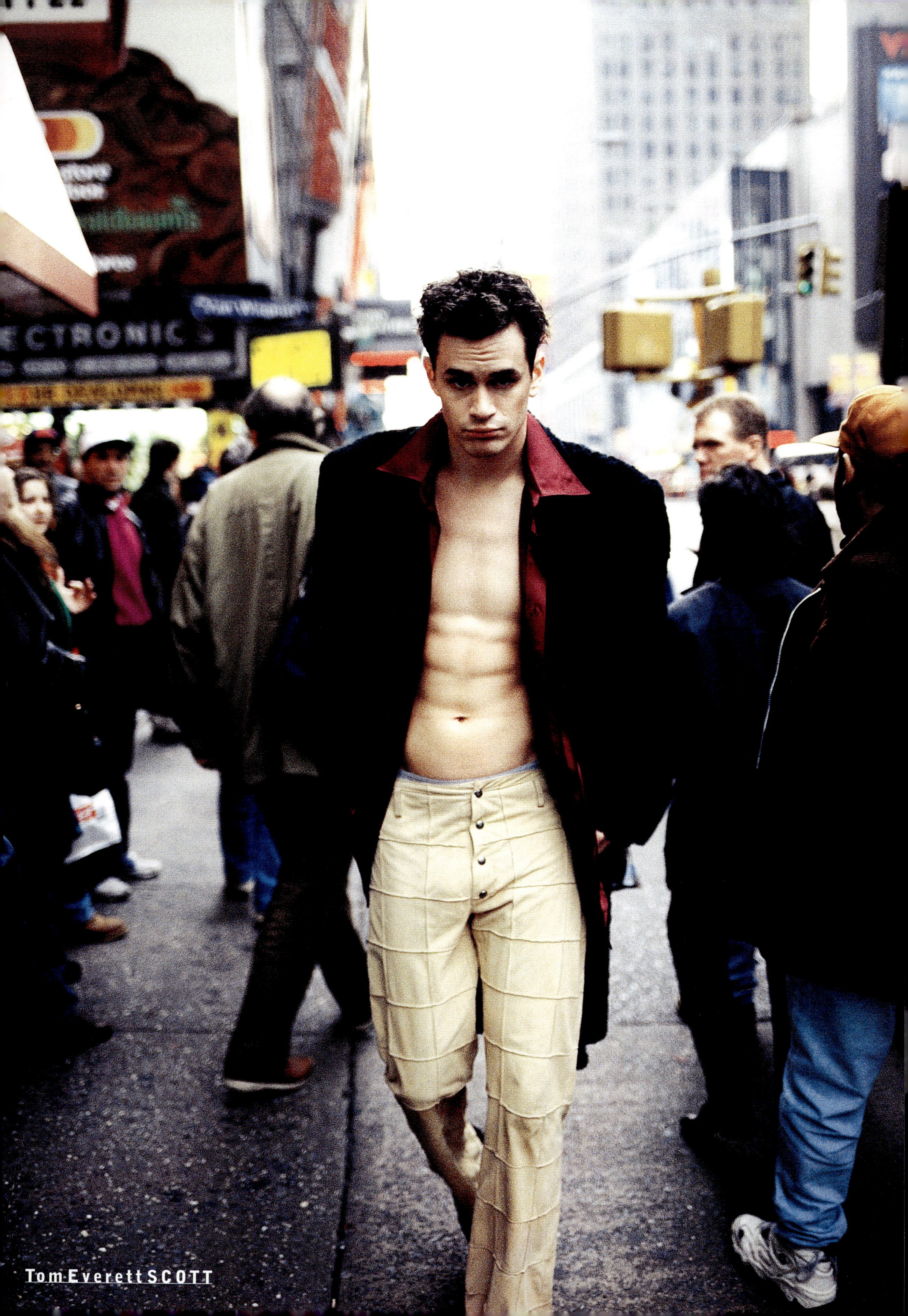

Tom Everett SCOTT

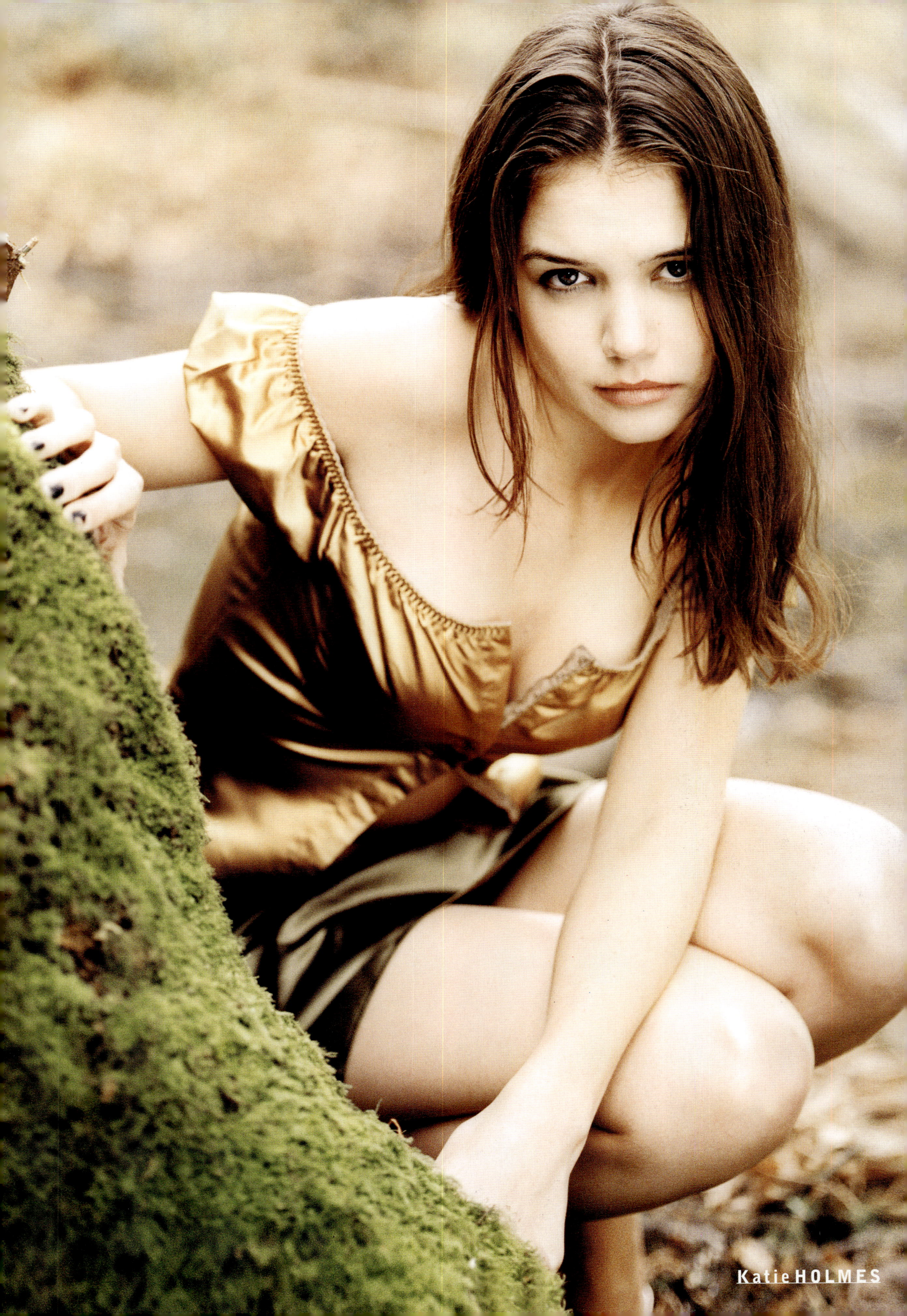

Katie HOLMES

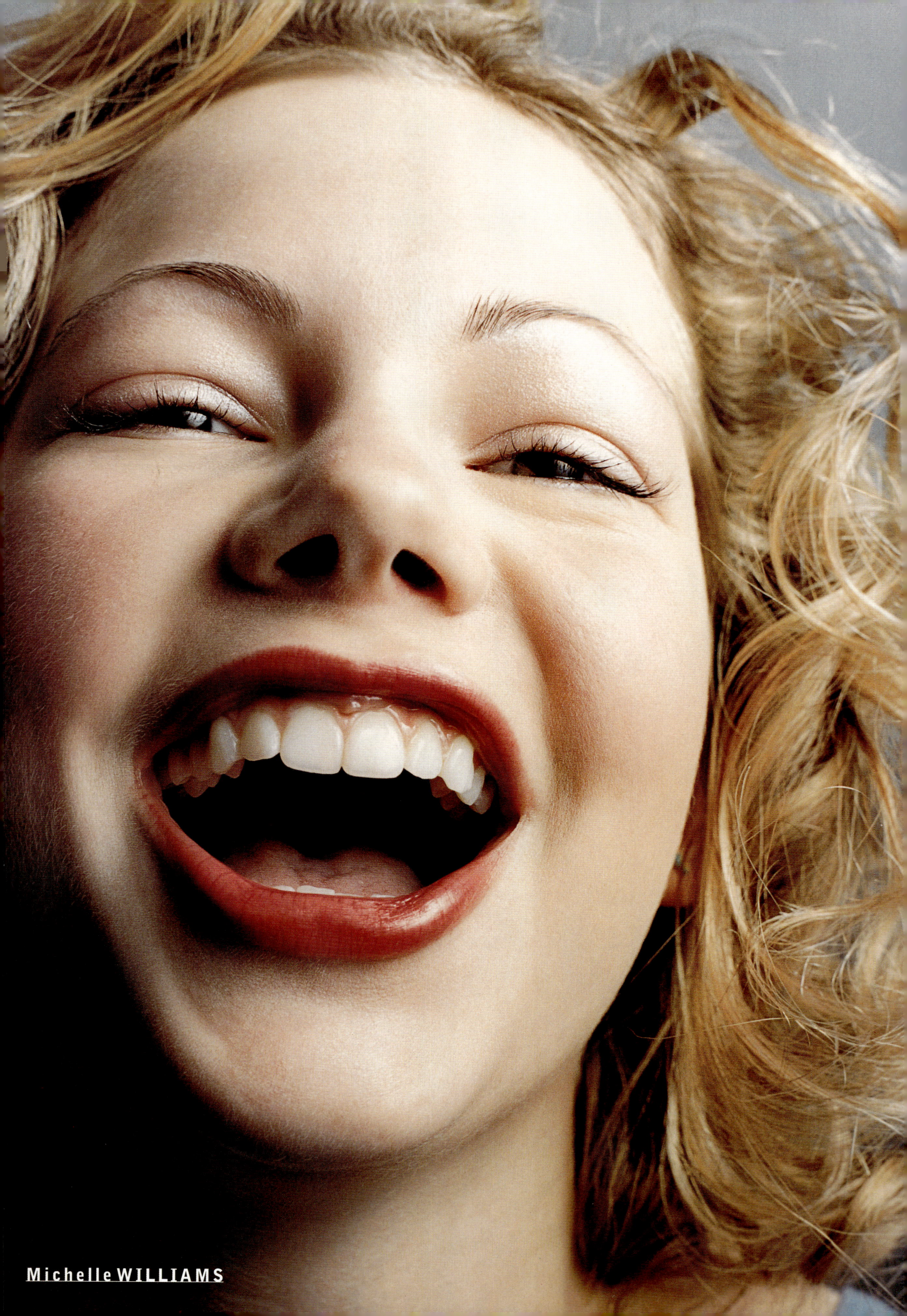

Michelle WILLIAMS

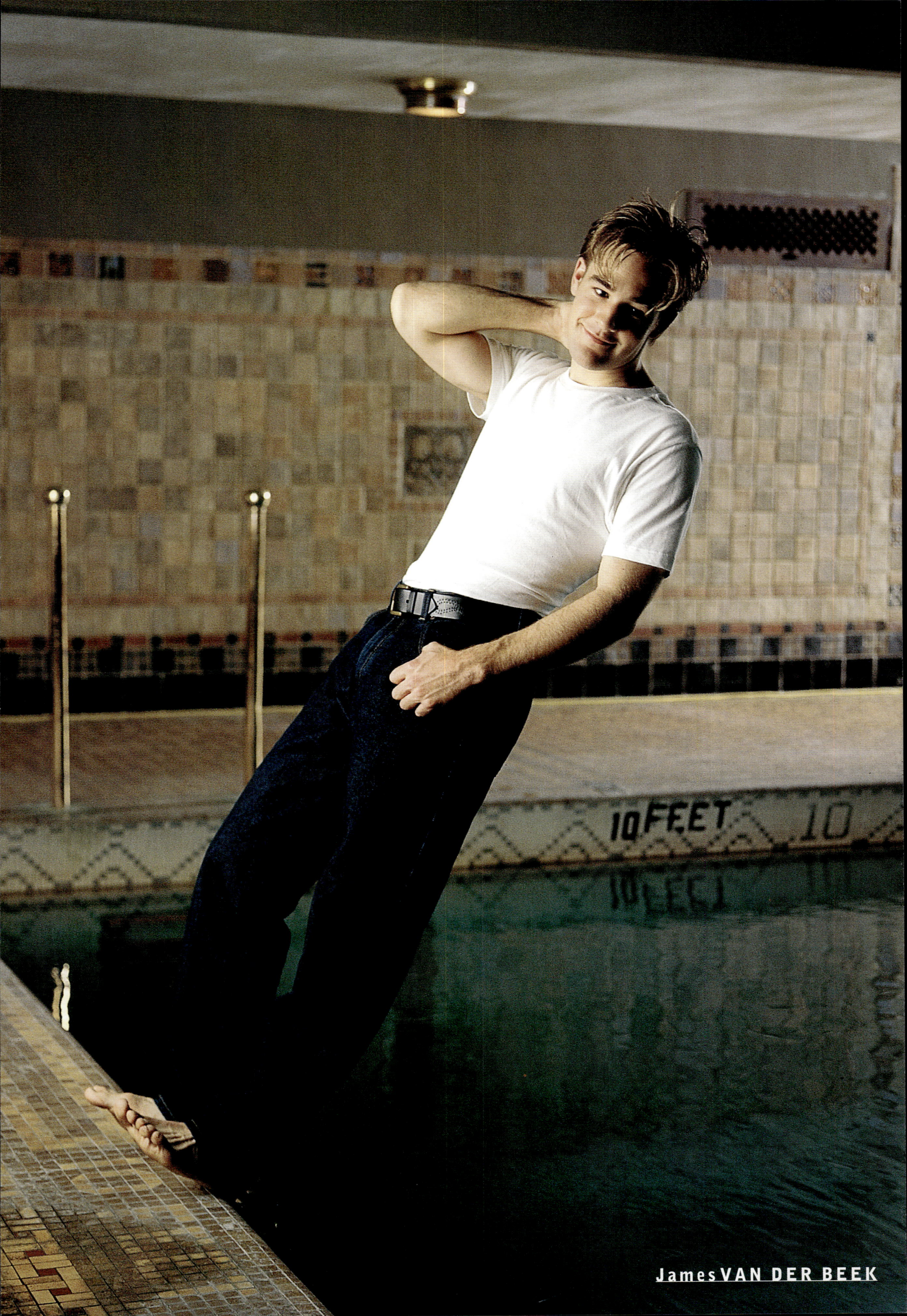

James VAN DER BEEK

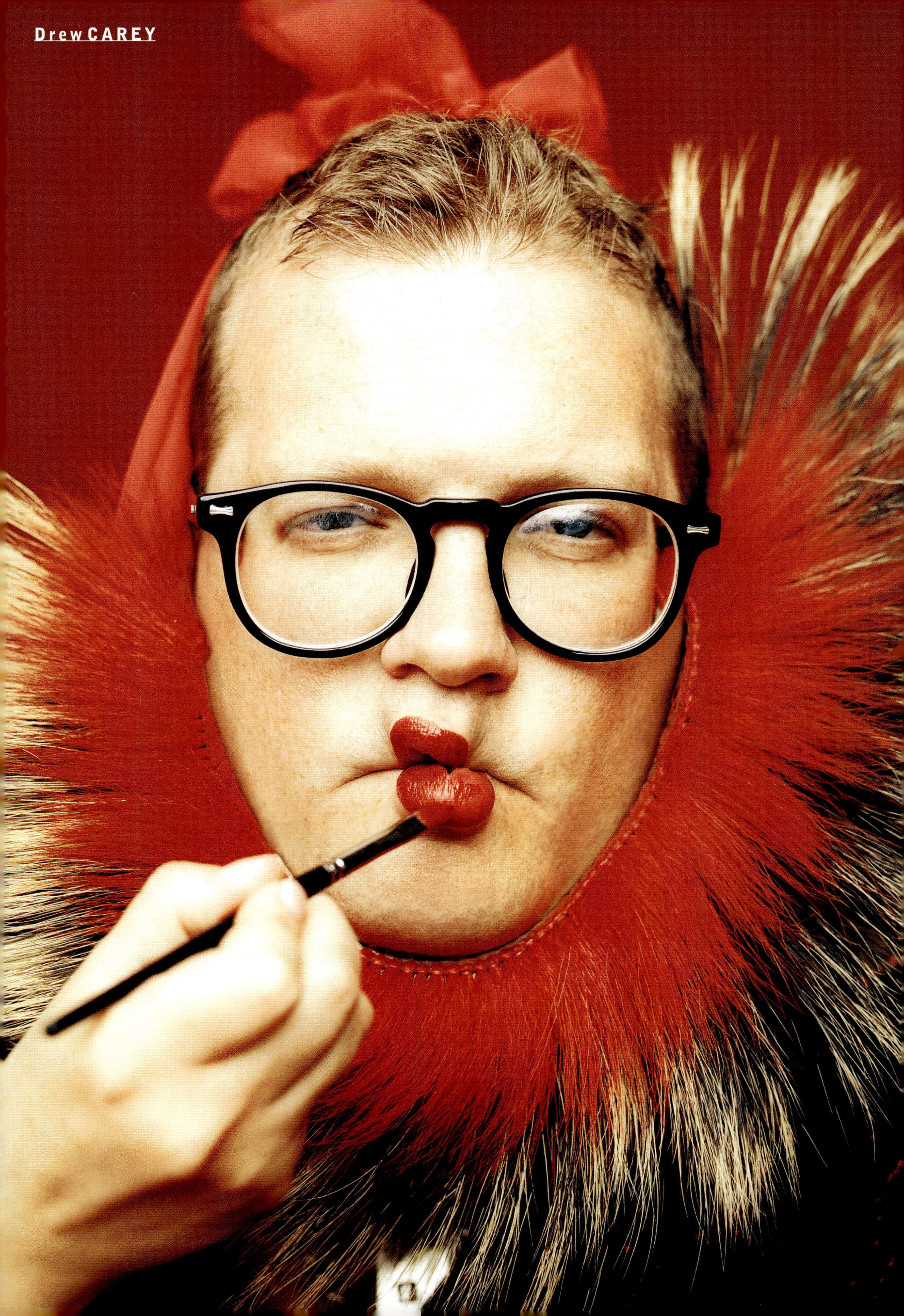

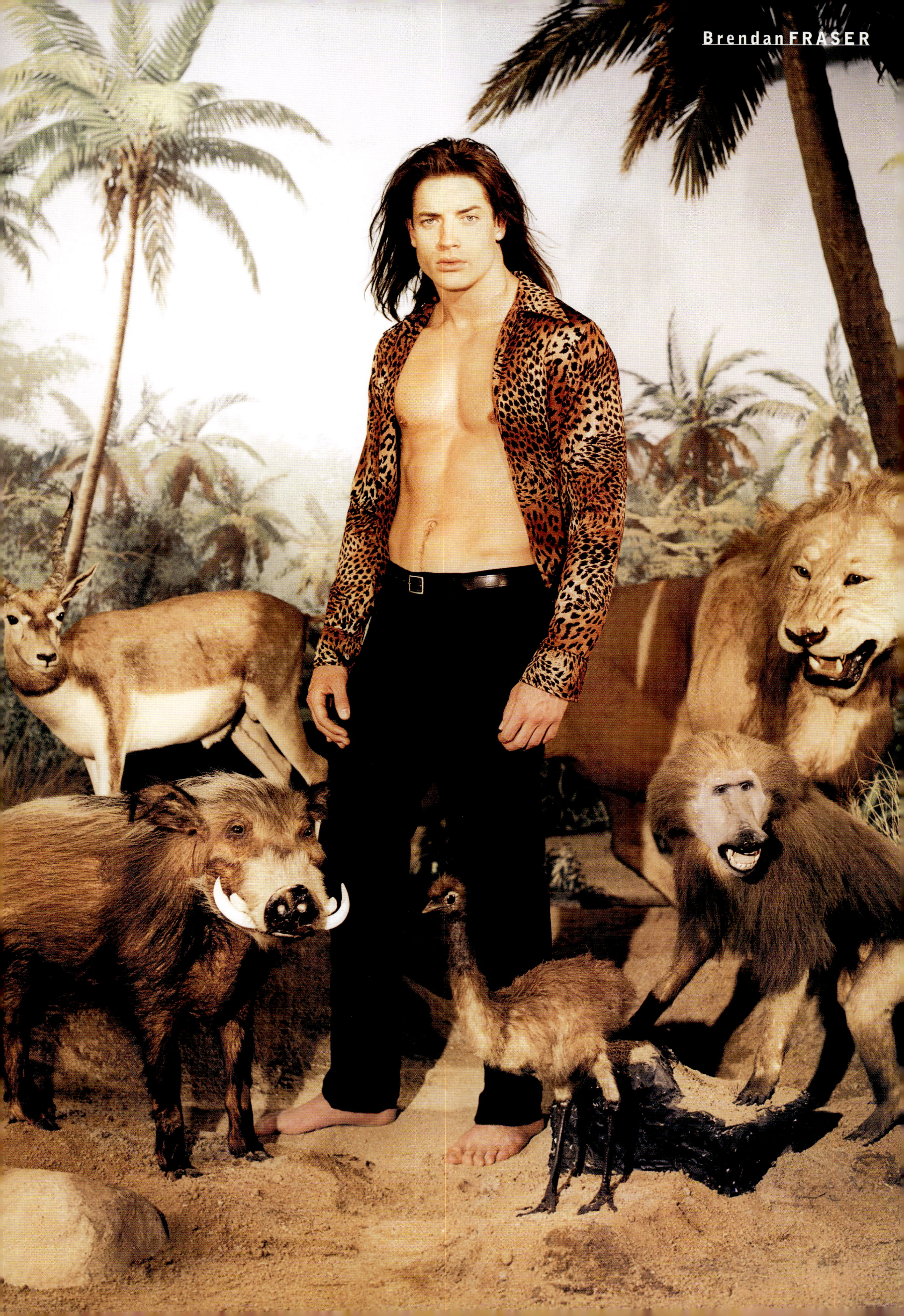

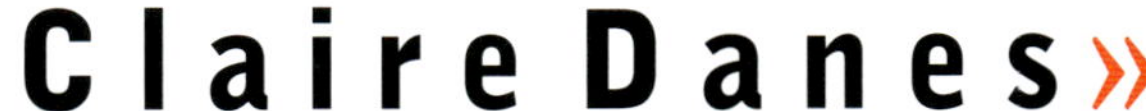

What's the downside of acting?

Being swept away from your friends and family all the time. It's really impossible to have any sort of relationship. I no longer have a group of friends to hang out with regularly. I can't belong to any class or study group. There's no way I could be on a sports team or anything like that. It's hard. The things that are good are often the same things that are bad. But it's really fun to go to these different countries and meet all these different people. And I love the work. I think actors share a lot of the same traits, so I think you know what they're all about and they know what you're all about. There's a feeling of belonging, which I really appreciate.

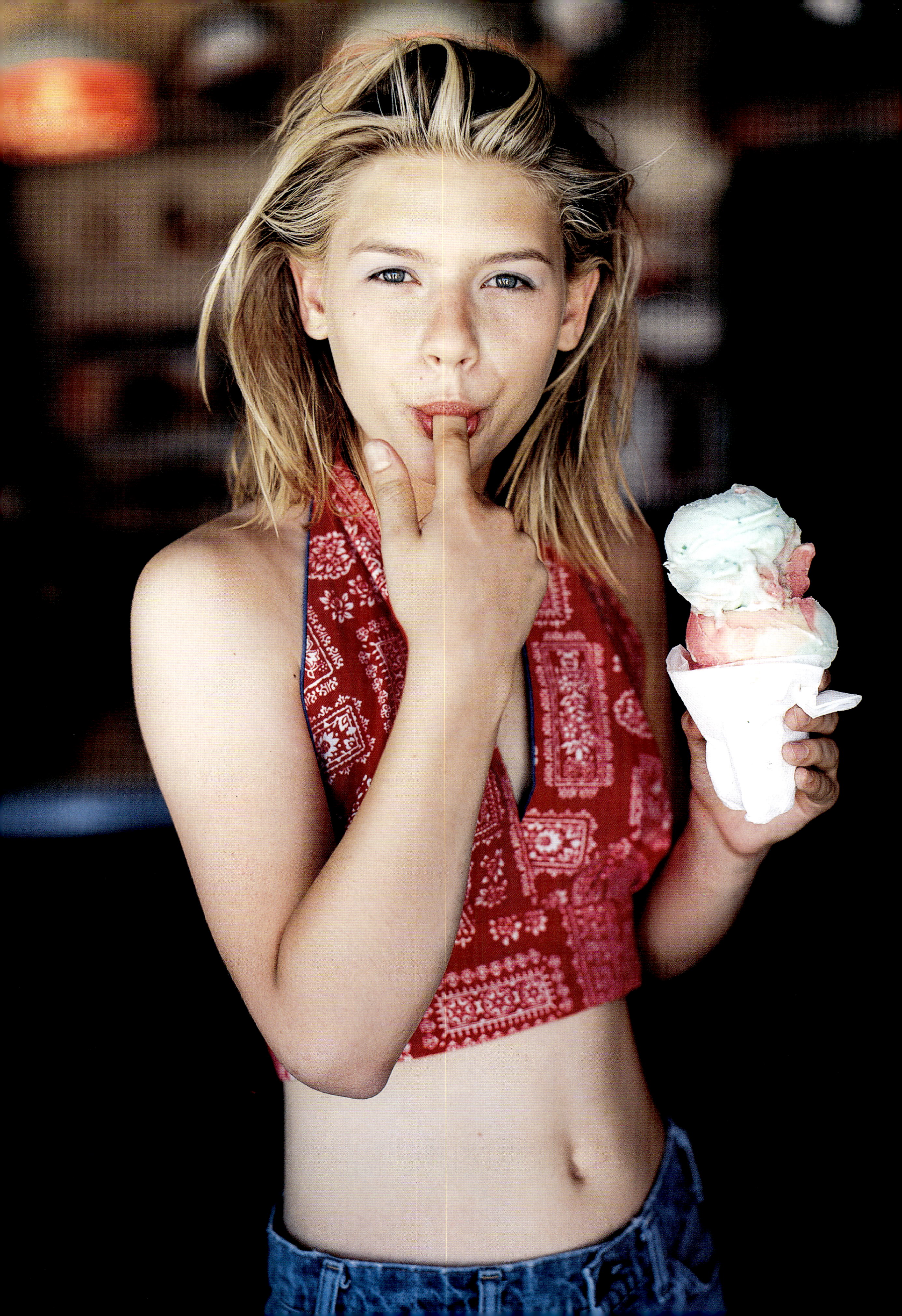

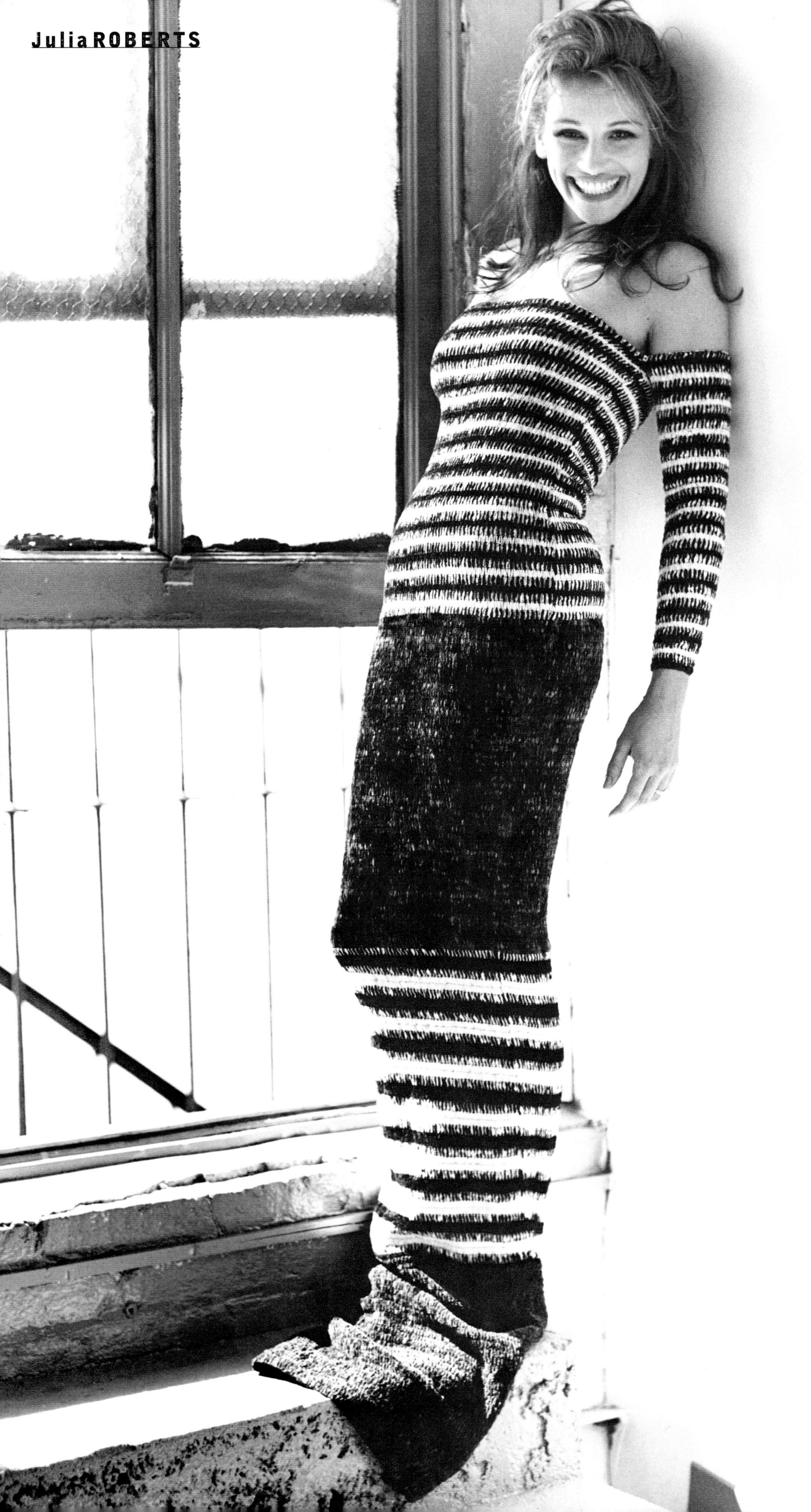

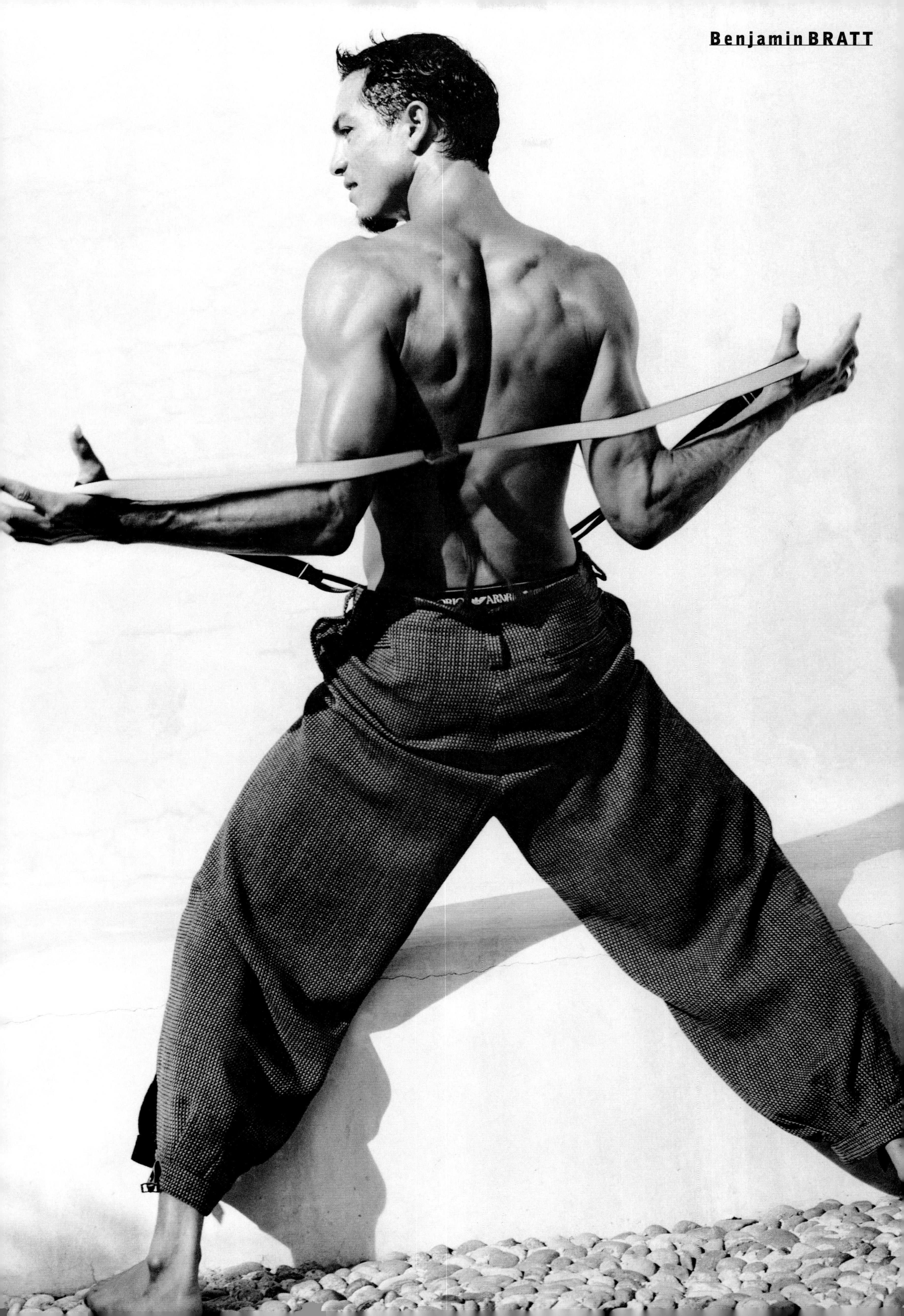

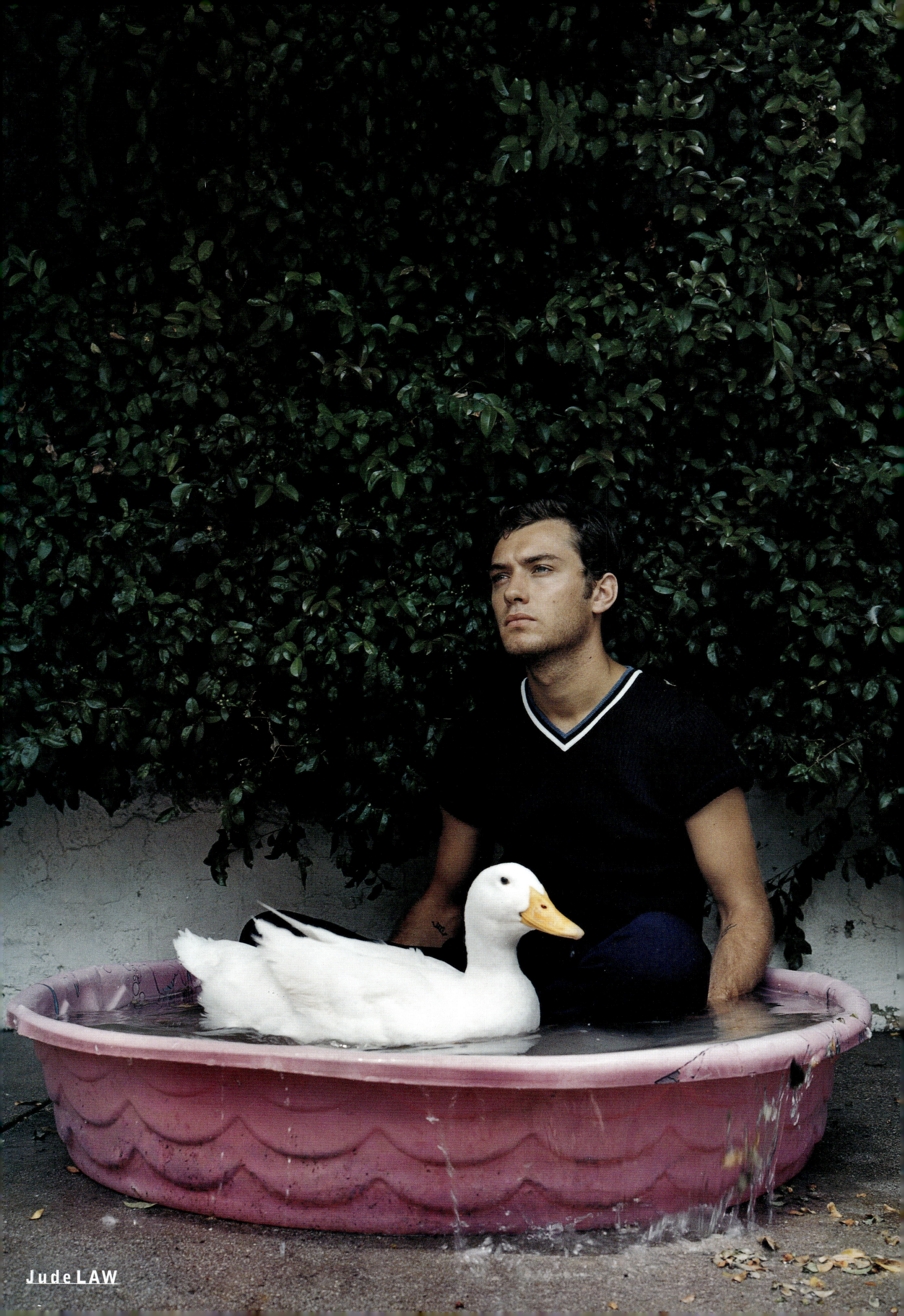

Jude LAW

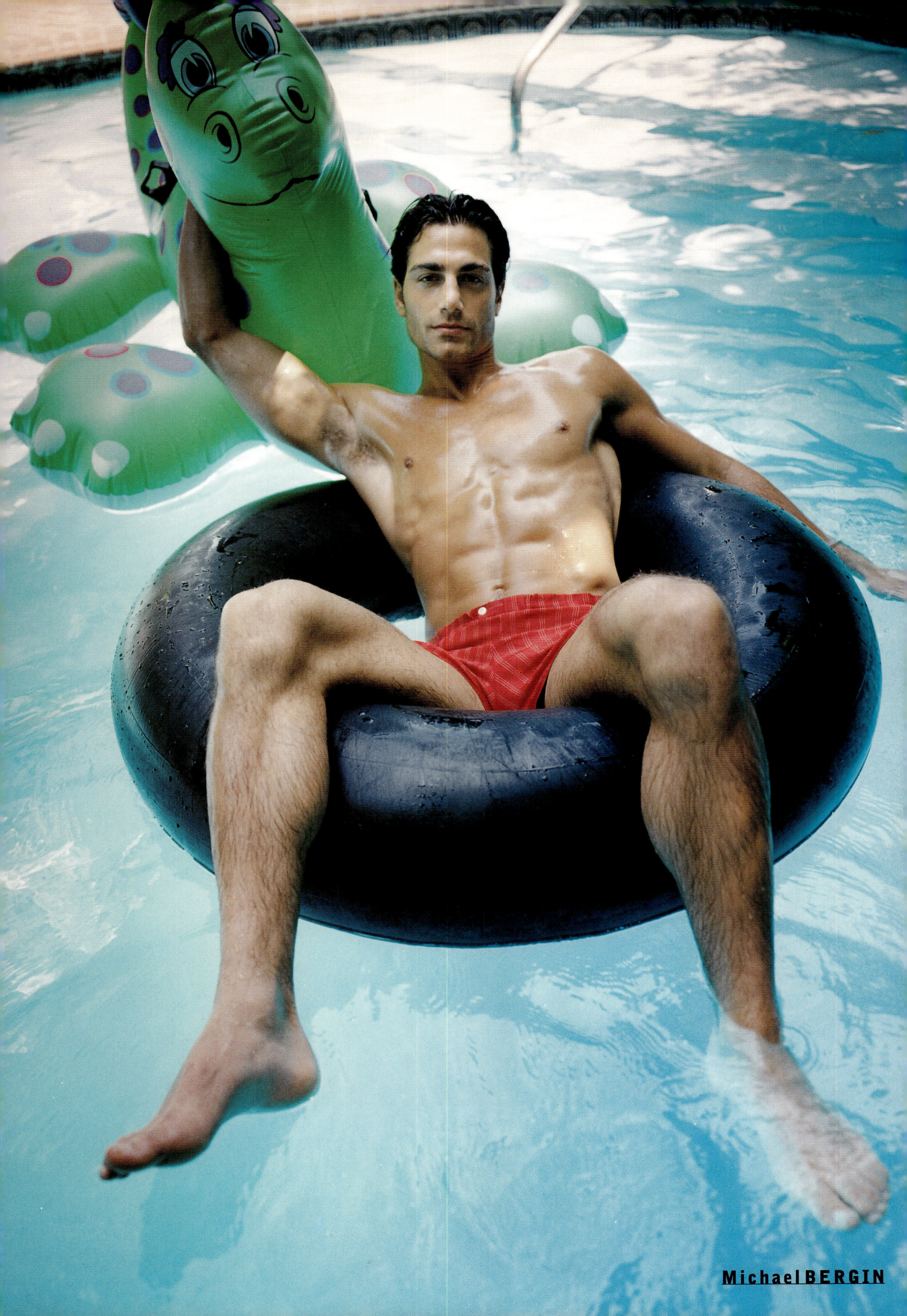

Michael BERGIN

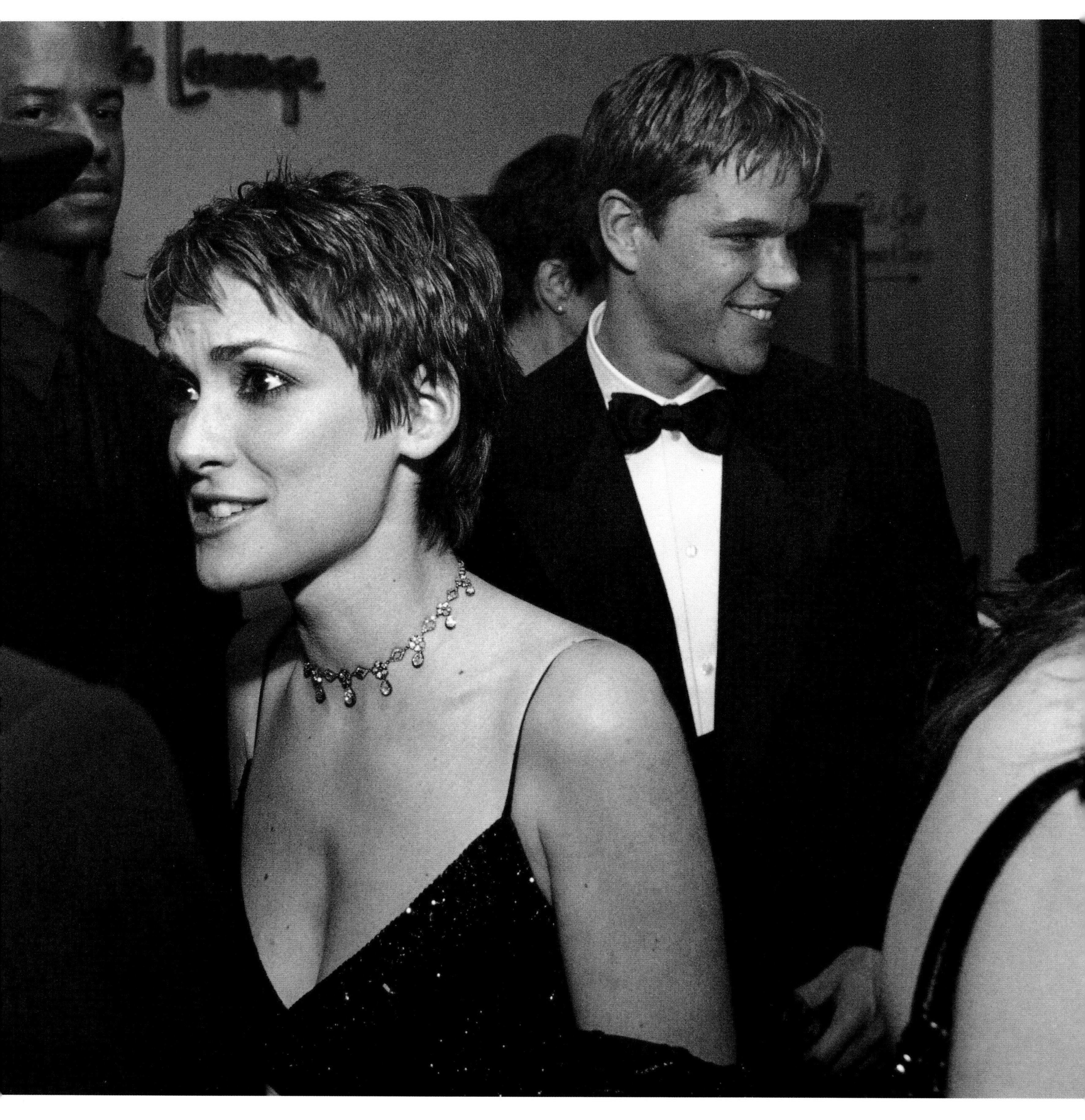

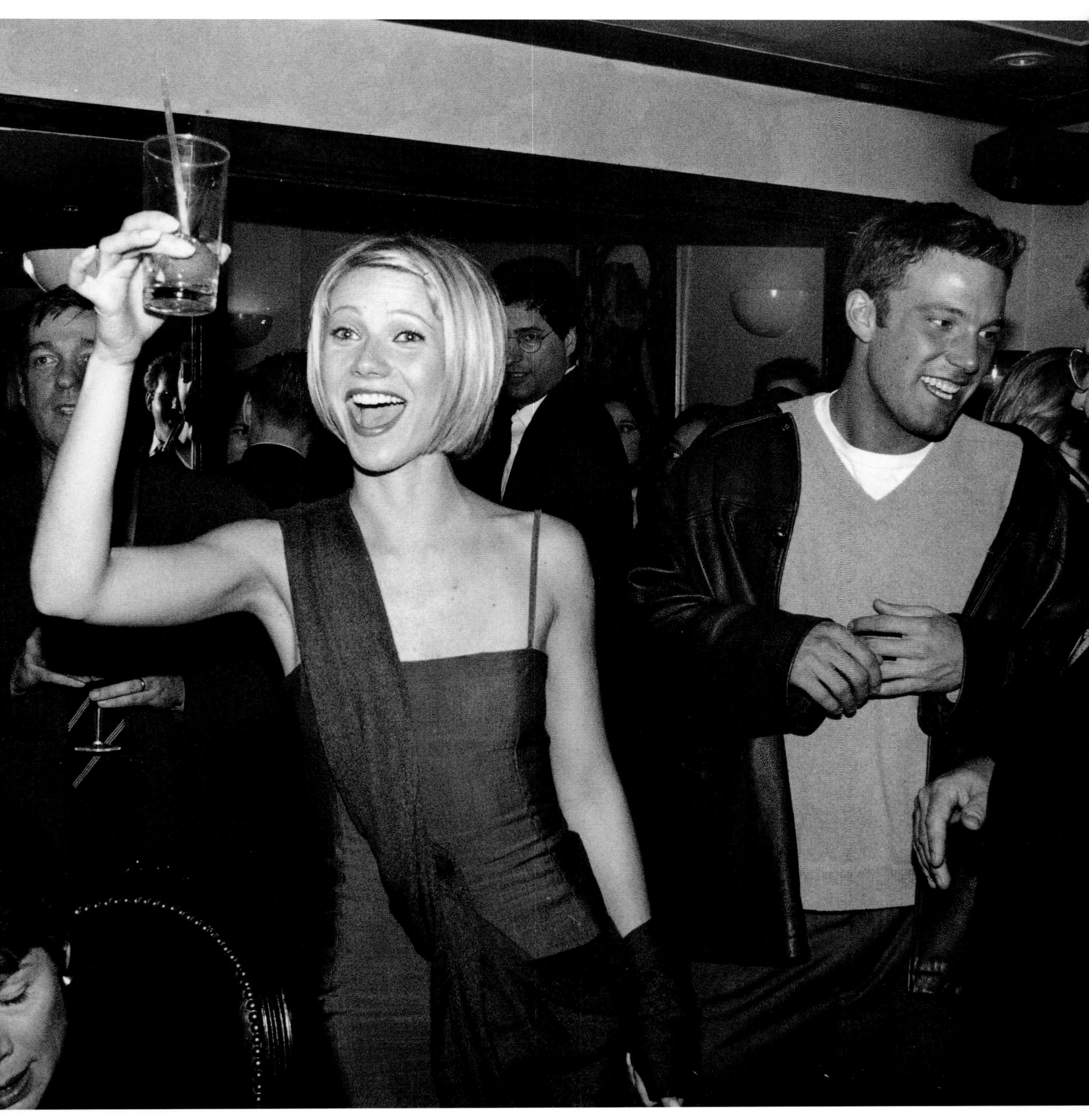

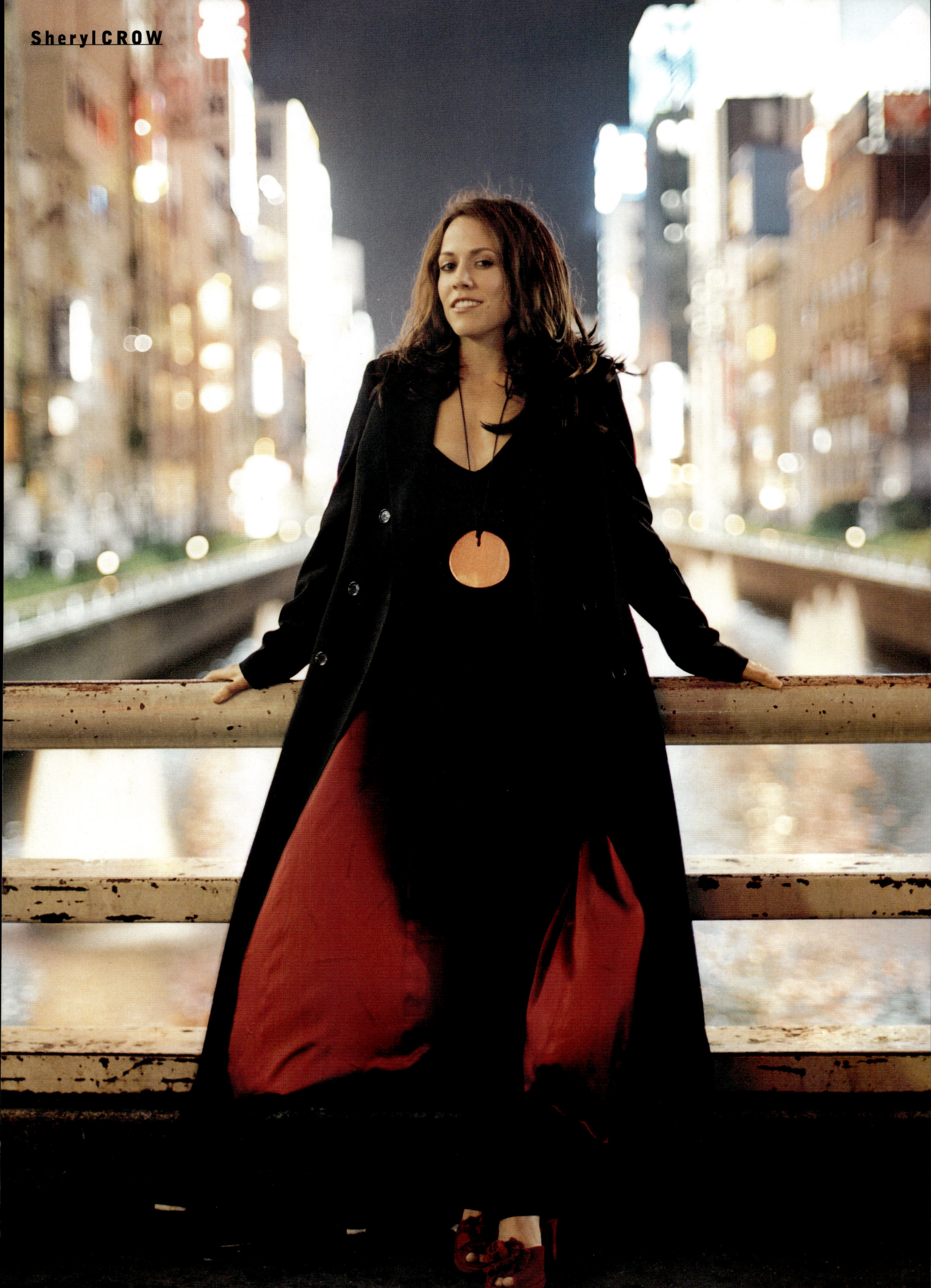

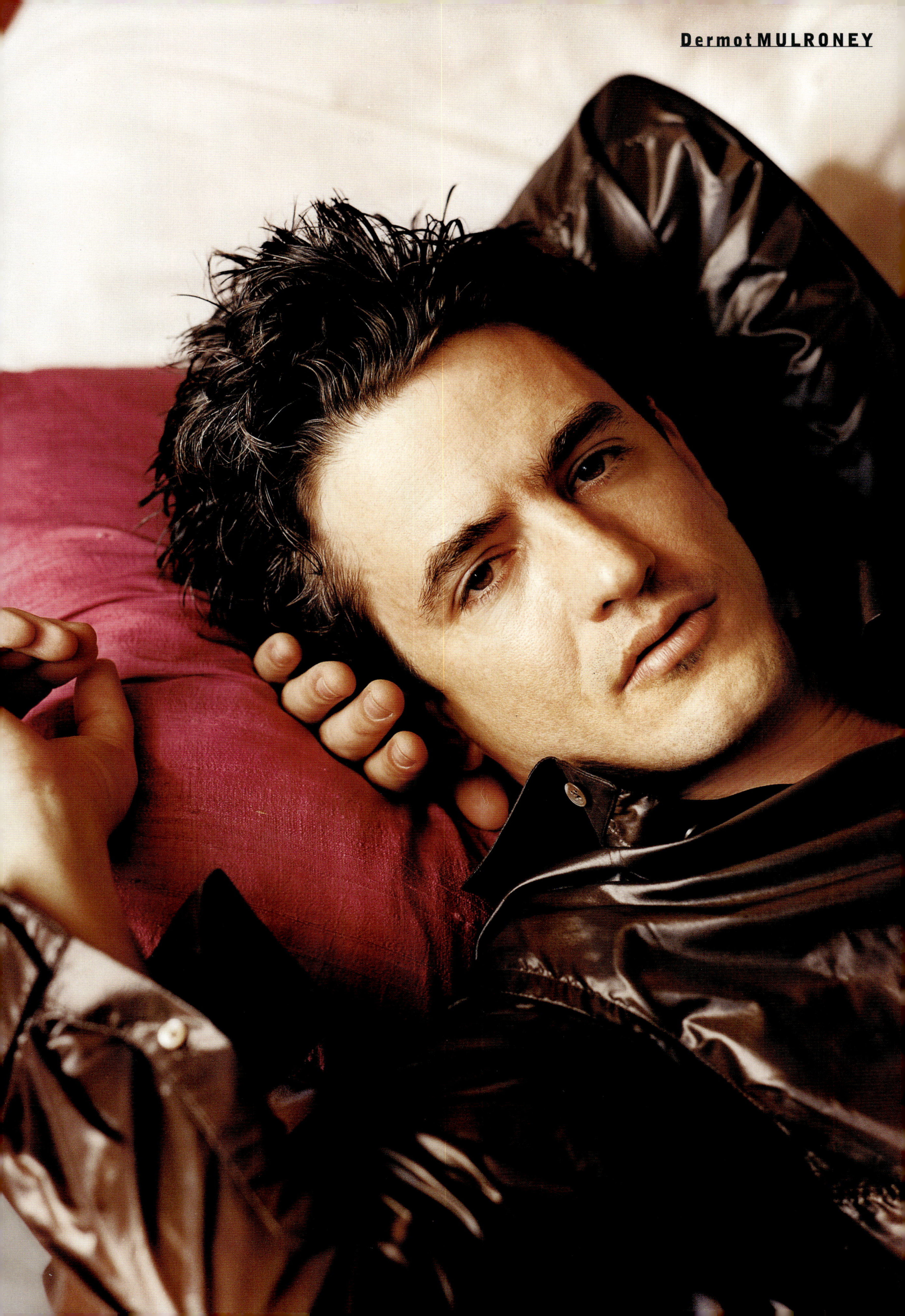

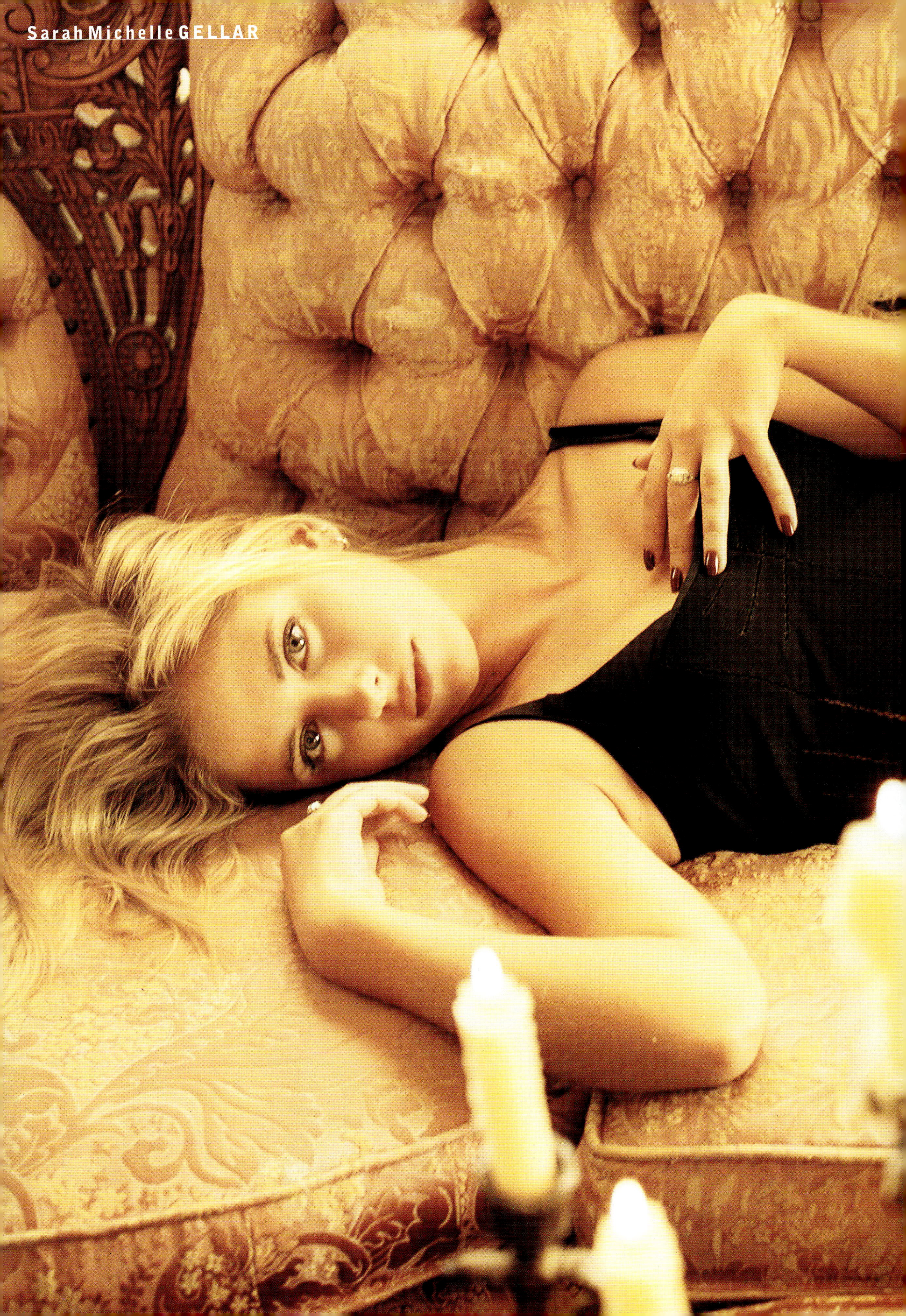

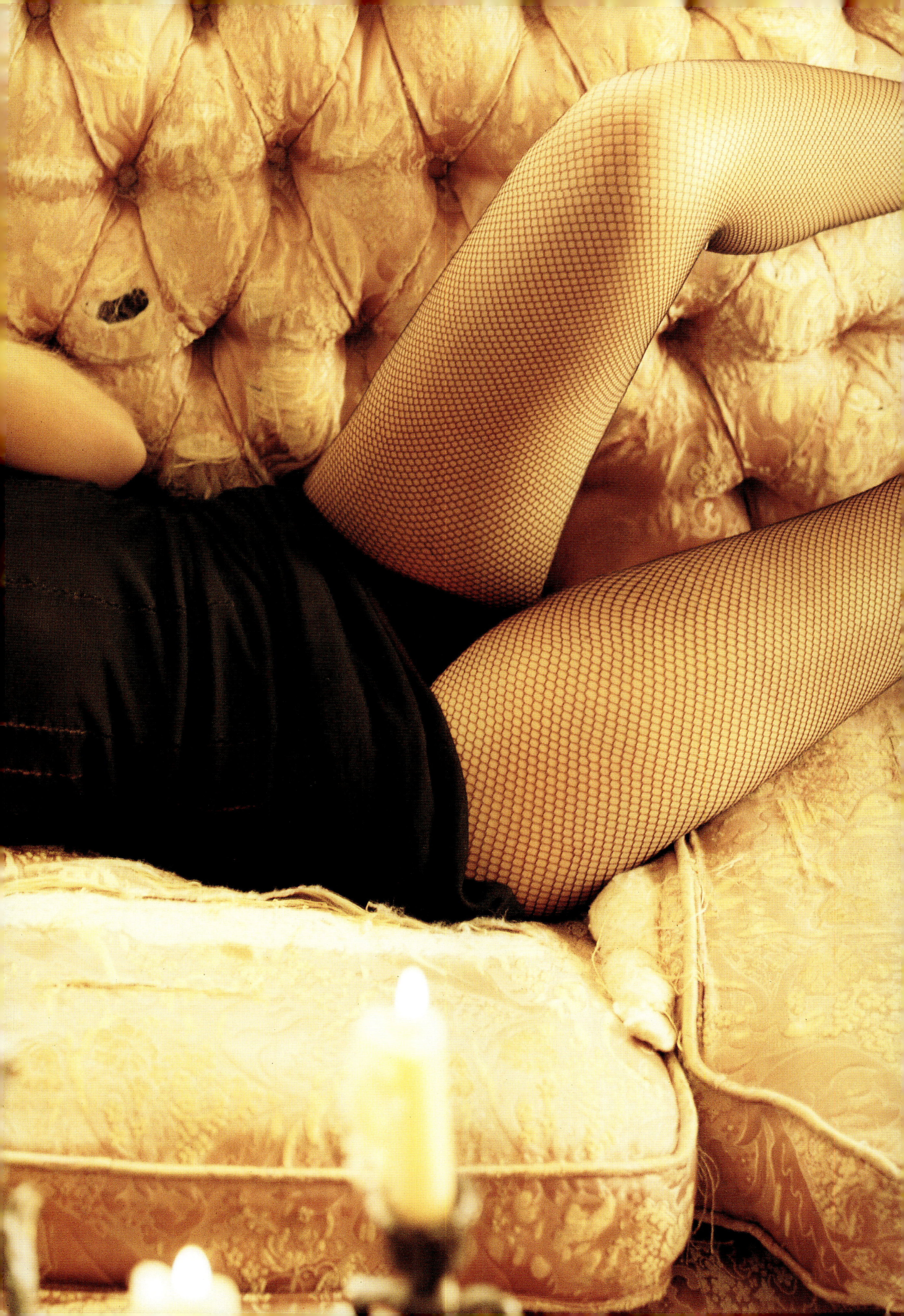

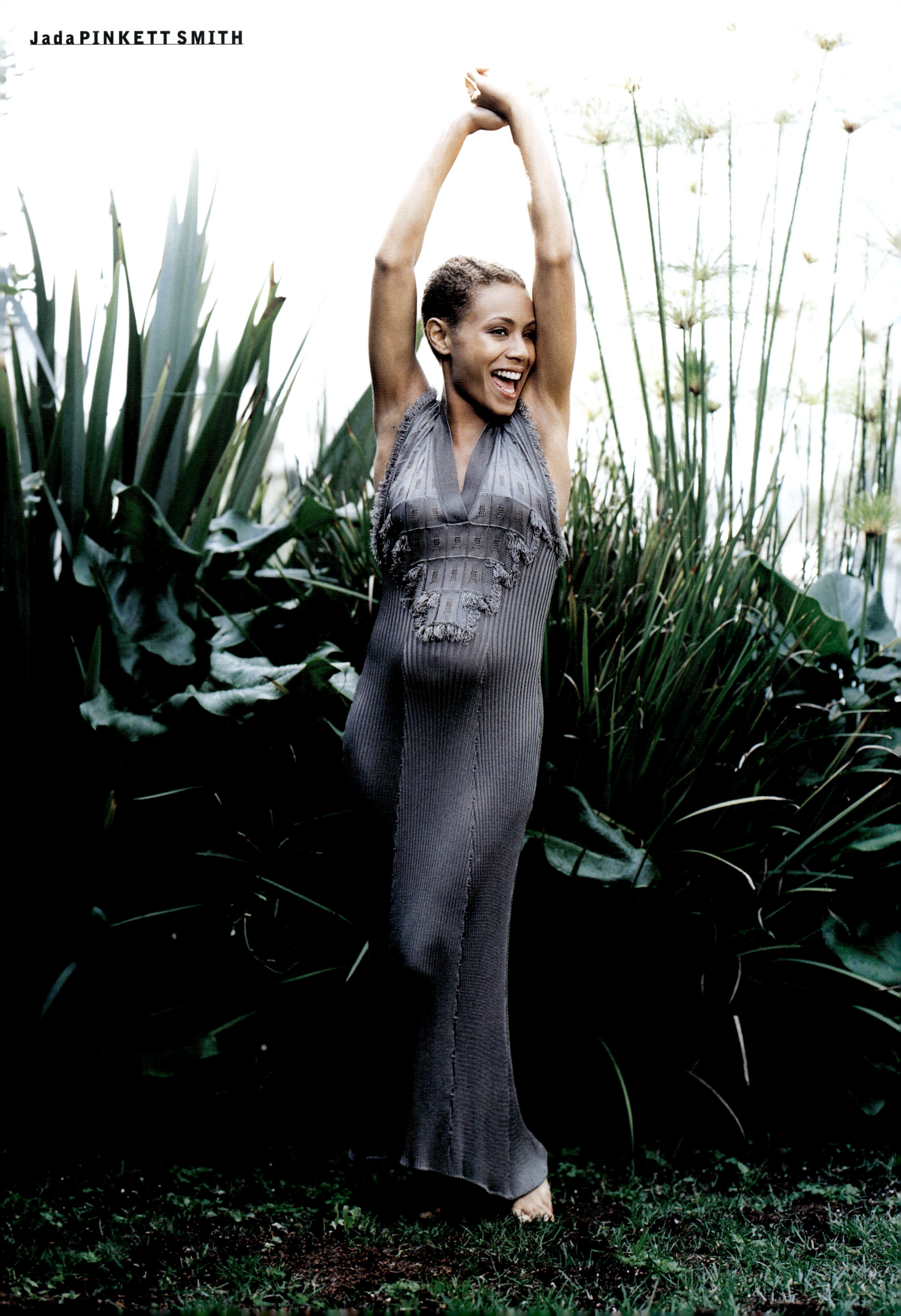

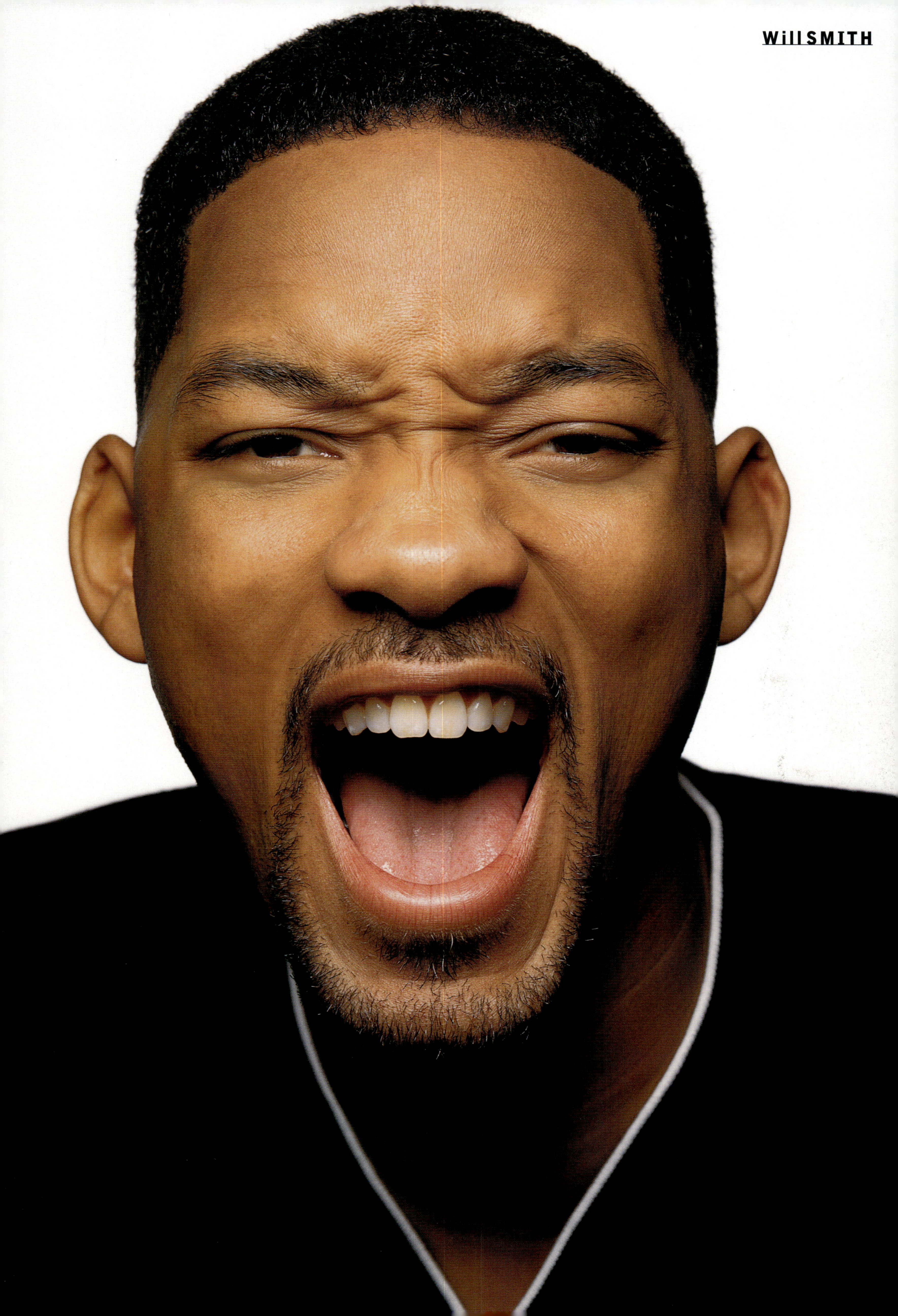

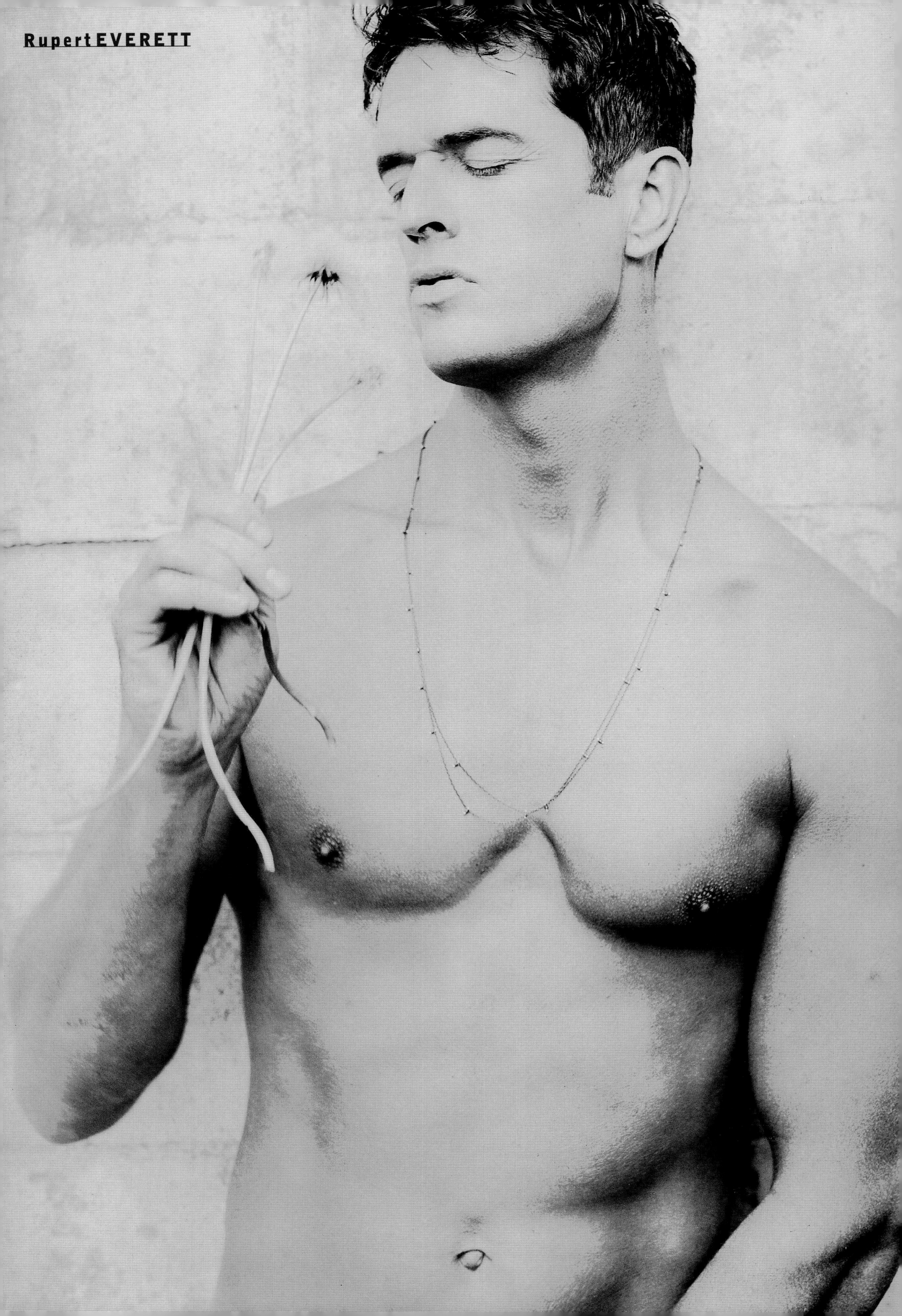

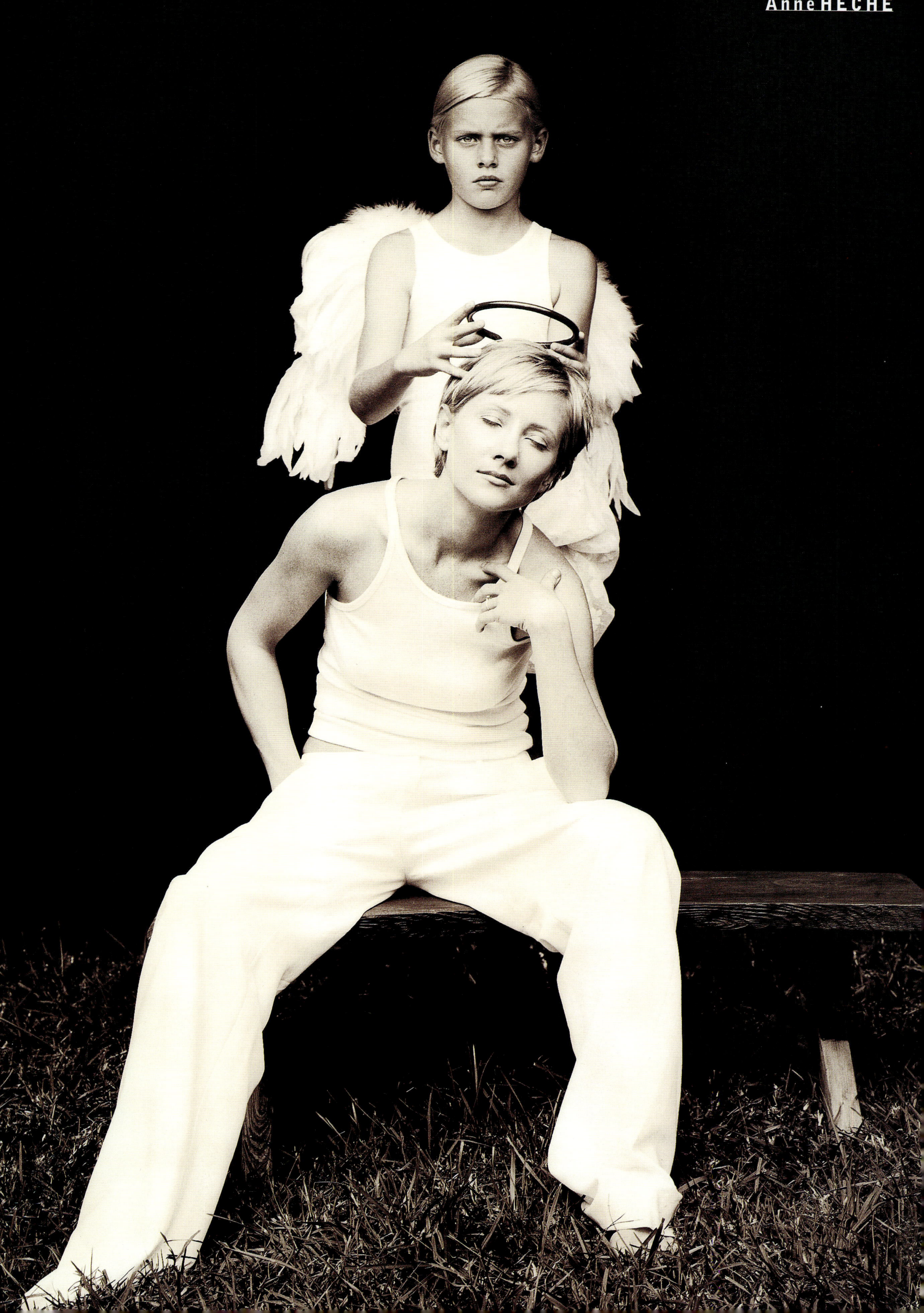

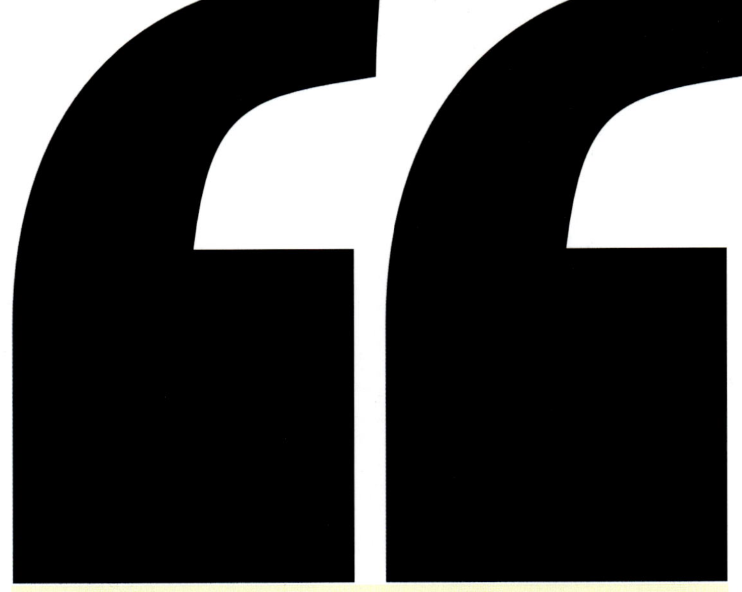

What is the biggest misperception about you? The biggest misperception about me is that I'm aloof. Really, I'm just shy. When I was at school, people used to think, 'Oh, she's aloof.' I'm not. I'm the kind of person who can't walk into a party by myself. I'll drive to a party, and if I'm outside in the front, I have been known to turn around and drive home. That's one of the most horrible things: to walk into a party by yourself. **In Hollywood, actresses typically seem to be pitted against one another. Given that, do you find it difficult to forge friendships with other women?** I'm a great female friend. I'm a woman's woman. I have a lot of friends, ones that I grew up with. Girlfriends. It's a lot of work. You've got to always call, write letters. They're like my roots. I cling to that. I have ten girlfriends that I went to school with when I was eight years old. I mean, girlfriends that I know back-to-front and inside-out. One of them is married, with a kid. One is a hotel manager. Two of them are actresses. Another one works for a television station. Another is a hairdresser. All things, from all walks of life. Every time I go to Australia, it's a huge party. It's great. They've known me for so long that it's like, 'Nicole! Can you believe what's happening?' Pinch, pinch. **Define 'woman's woman.'** With some women, if a guy walks into the room, then he's the focus of their attention. I'm not that kind of woman. I'm more interested in the women in the room than the men in the room. I love, you know, men. They're great. But I feel more comfortable with other women – except with Tom, who is my best friend. Maybe it's because I didn't have any brothers – I had a sister. My cousins are girls. My mother is a really, really strong woman. Maybe that has something to do with it. **The public perception of you and your husband Tom Cruise is of a very insular couple – just you two together. Why?** You're kidding me! We just went to Paris with six friends and went wild. I suppose it's because we don't go out to a lot of Hollywood things. We have a lot of friends who just come over, play pool. We're not really out and about being photographed. **What's your agreement when it comes to filming? Do you and your husband accompany each other on location?** It kinda works itself out. Meaning that if it's a great film, I'm not going to tell him that he can't work. And

Nicole Kidman»

vice-versa. We're not in a situation where we can do that. If it's a mediocre film, then, hey, we'll take it or leave it. **Who makes friends first – you or Tom?** It's different. Tom makes male friends faster. I make female friends faster. Tom's a real kind of guy-guy. Sensitive. But a guy-guy. Right now he's training for a triathalon. That kind of guy. I have to go to the race tomorrow and start him off. We only got back from Paris two days ago, so I said, 'You're going to be jet-lagged.' He was, [low masculine voice] 'No! I can do it, I can do it.' But I'll be there at six-thirty a.m., cheering him on. I should be doing it. But I'm not that fit. **Describe the feeling of falling in love with your husband.** I think when you fall in love with someone that you're going to marry, that you're going to be with for the rest of your life, there's something so different about that. I can't describe it. But I'd never felt that before. I didn't think I was going to get married. **It's been said that you lighten Tom up. What would your old friends say that he does for you?** Um ... I don't know. What does he do for me? I suppose he gives me more confidence. Whenever you're in a relationship with someone that really supports you, that really loves you, you feel more confident as a person. And I was a lot more insecure before I met him. It comes from being a five-foot-ten redheaded, freckle-faced, gawky teenager that nobody ever wanted to dance with. **Oh c'mon.** No, I would have *loved* to have the beauty. I didn't have the beauty – that was the problem. I was the one who would sit at the side of the dance hall. I would literally have that horrible, sinking feeling in my stomach: 'I'm not going to be asked, I'm not going to be asked.' Out of, you know, sixty, seventy kids, I'm going to be the one left. **What's your idea of fun?** I love Italy. I love the whole lifestyle. I love siestas. I love an afternoon siesta and then get up and have dinner at ten o'clock. Stay up till four. I love that hedonistic lifestyle. I mean you eat well, drink well. You really live for fun. I love red wine. I suppose that's not sounding like a good role model. *Ummm.* Love red wine. I drink beer. Where I come from, you have to drink beer.

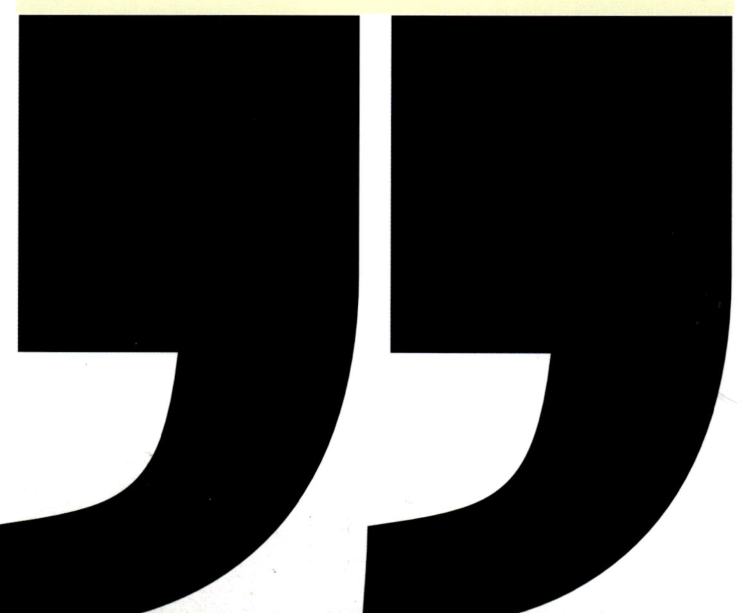

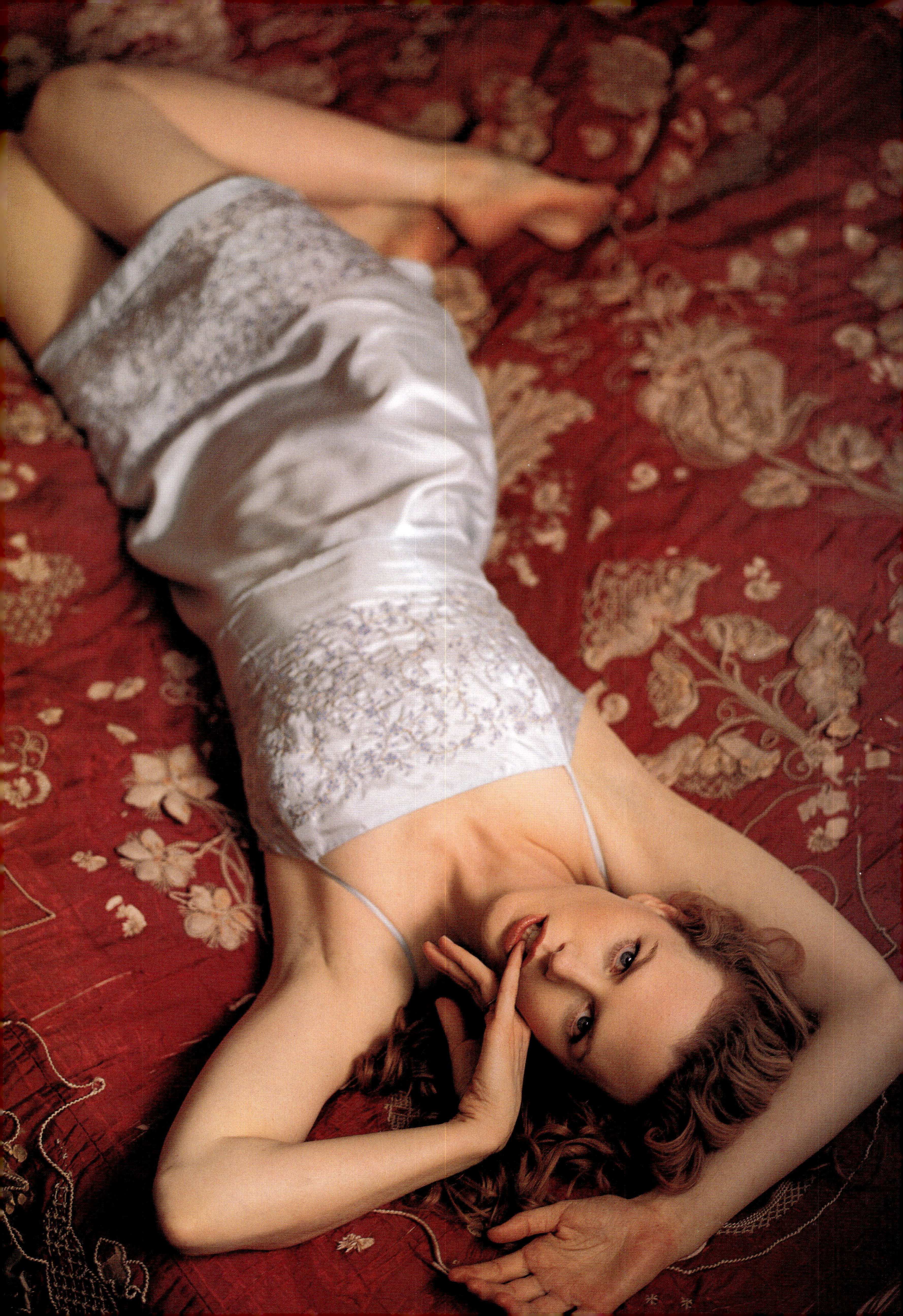

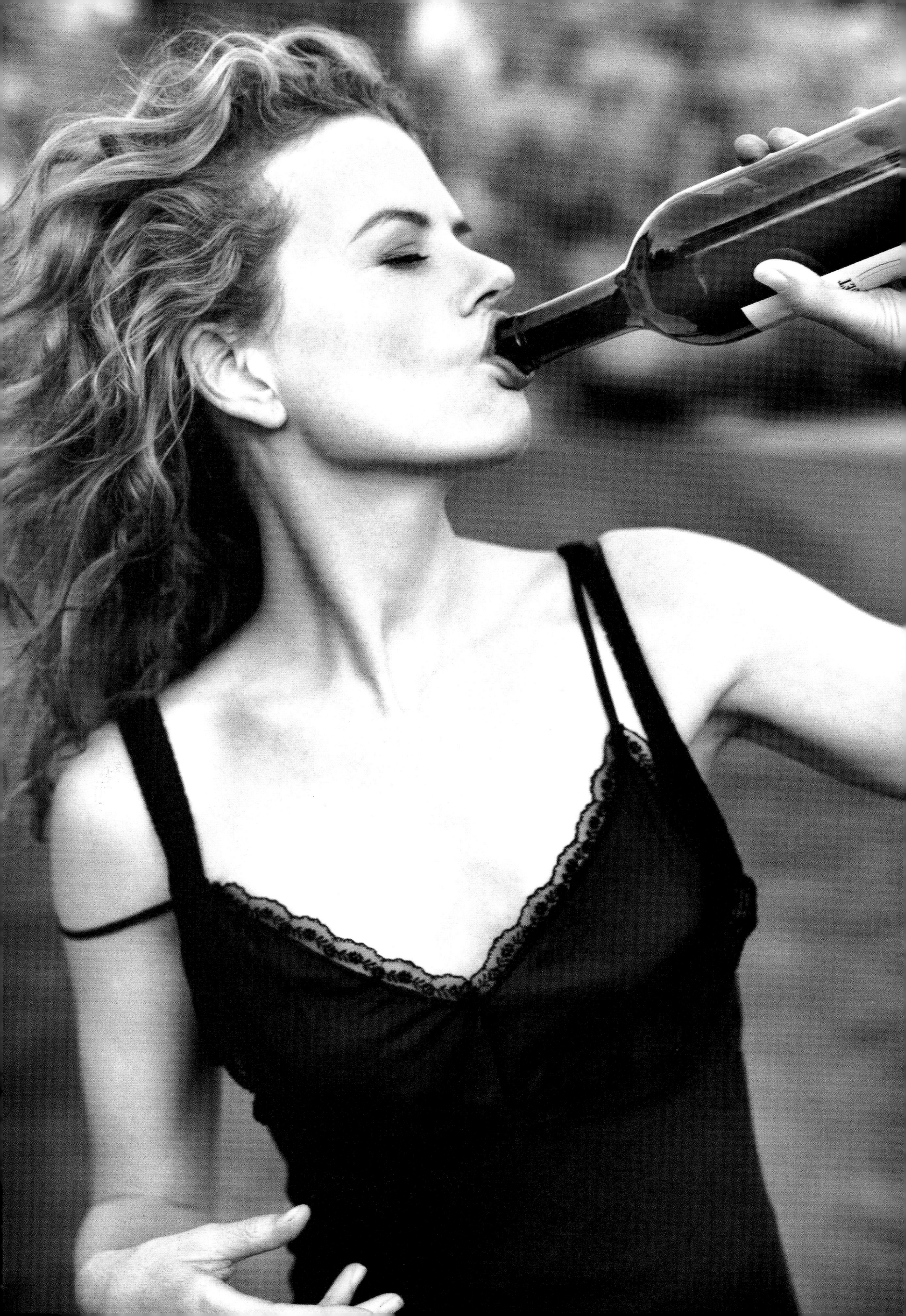

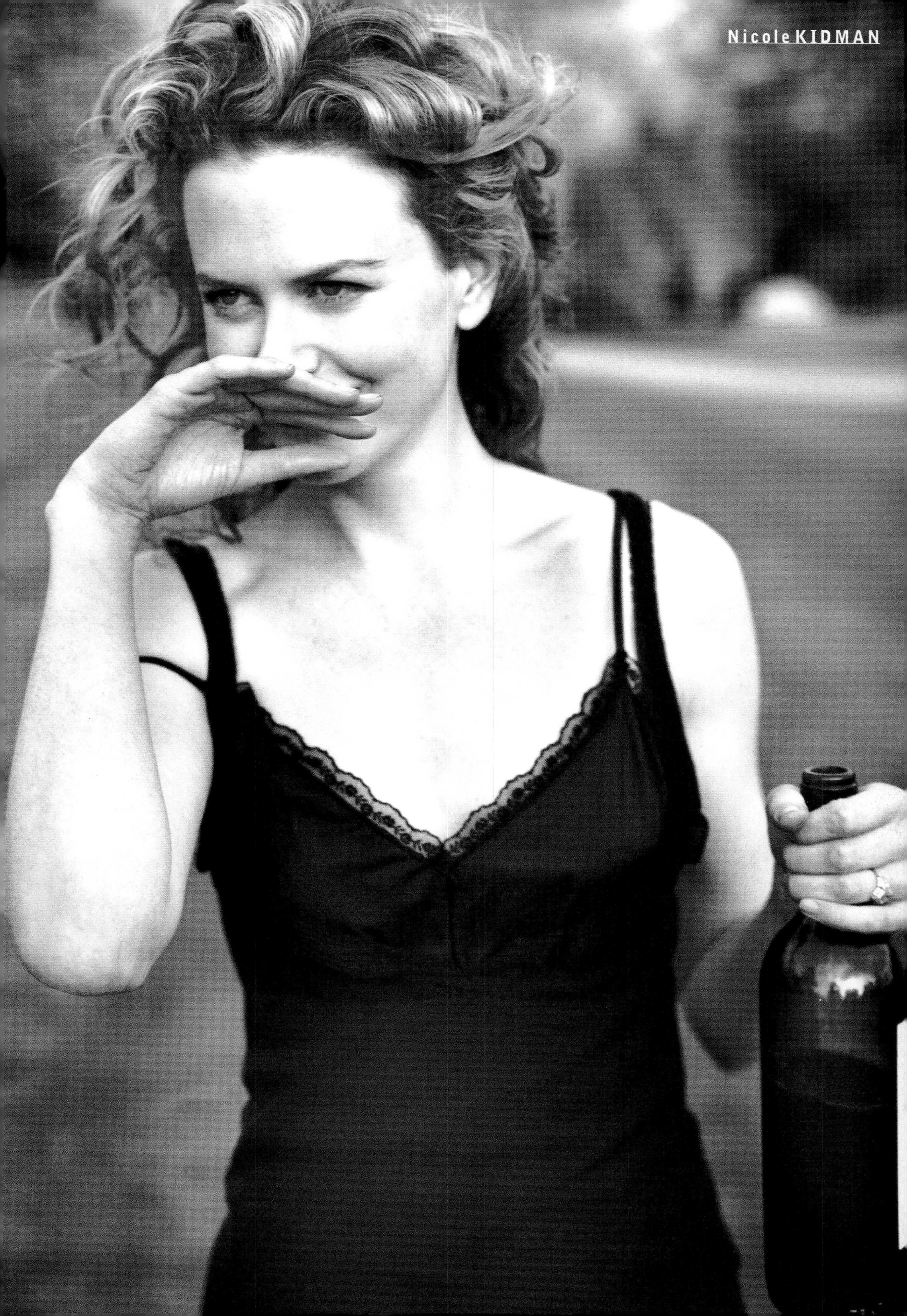

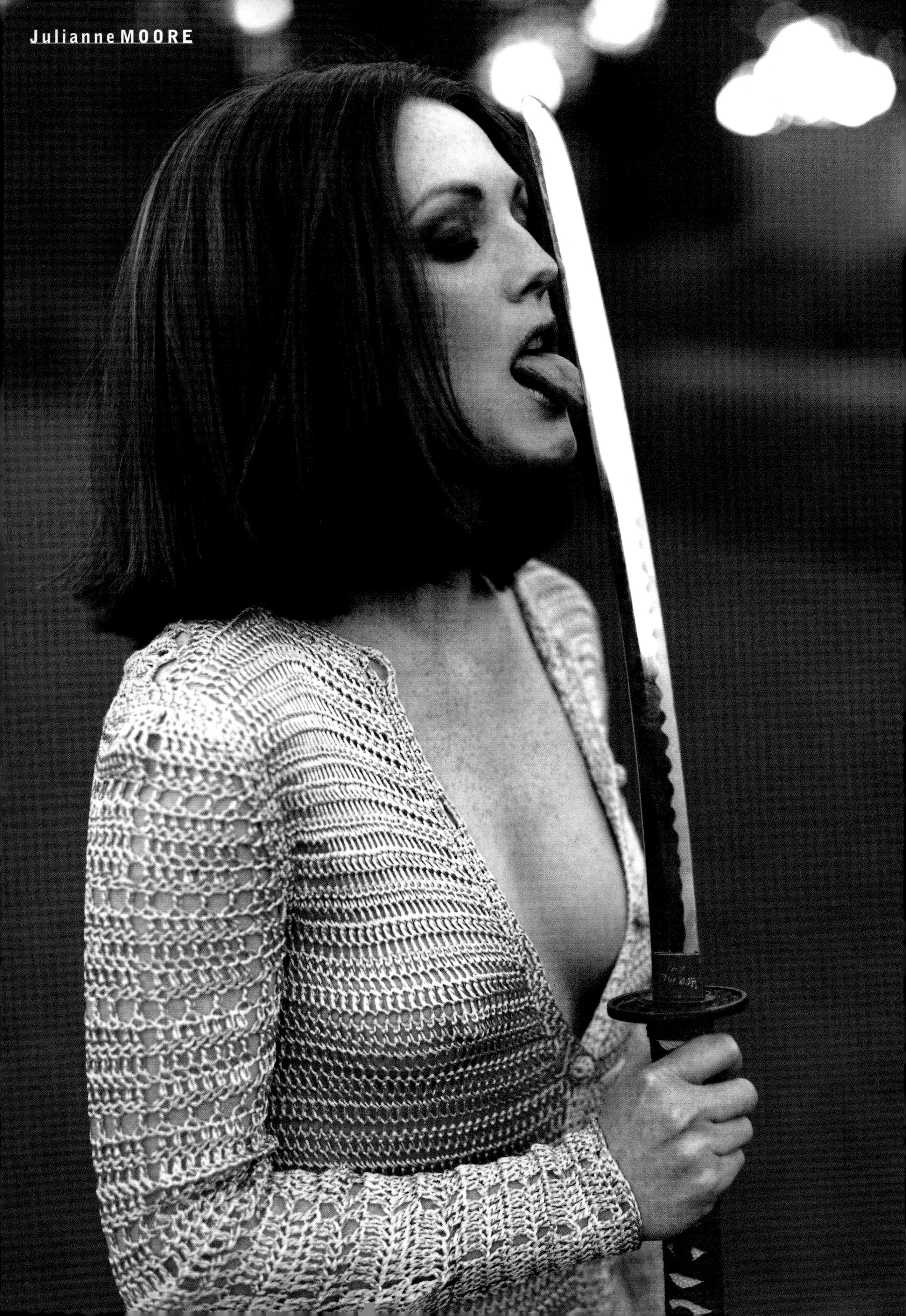

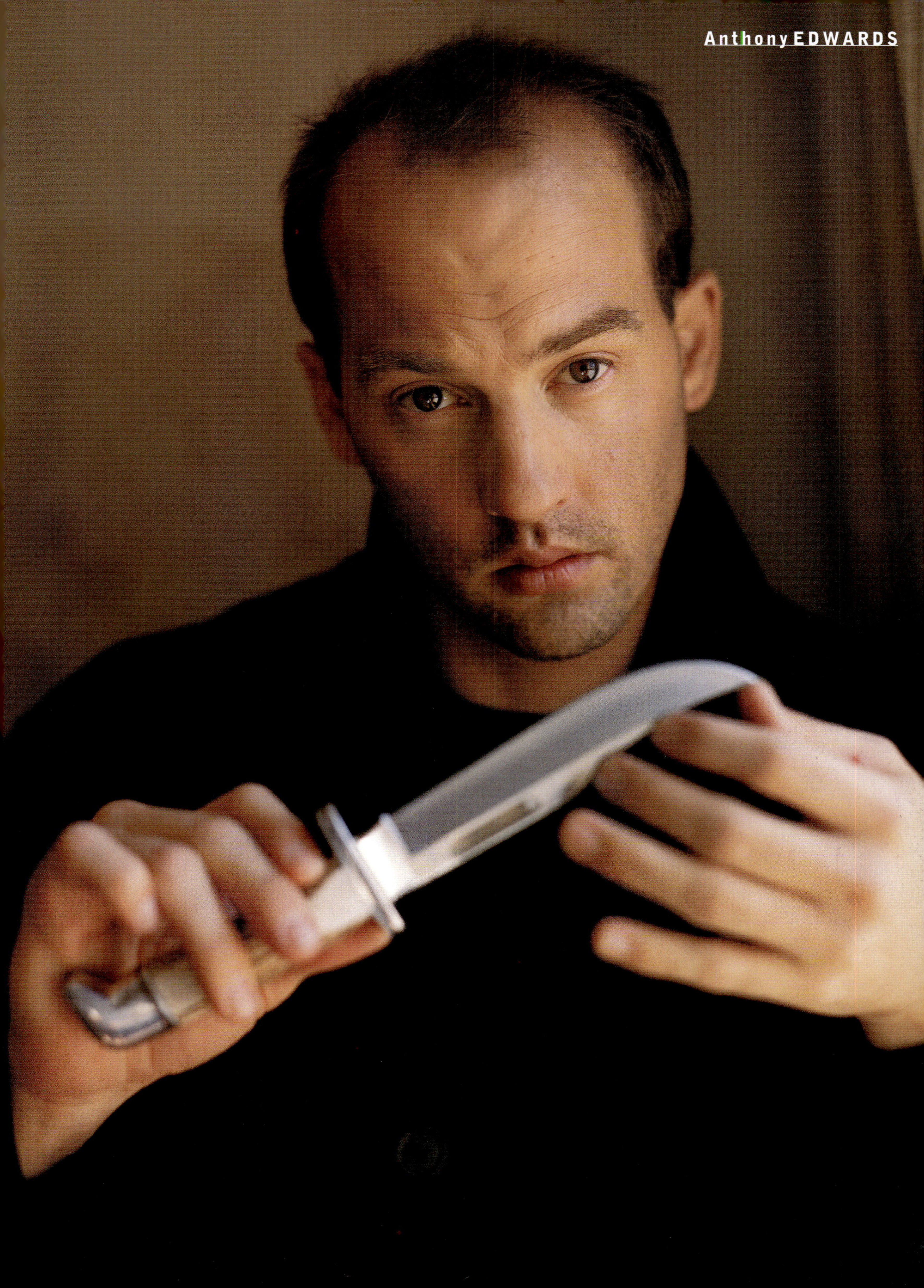

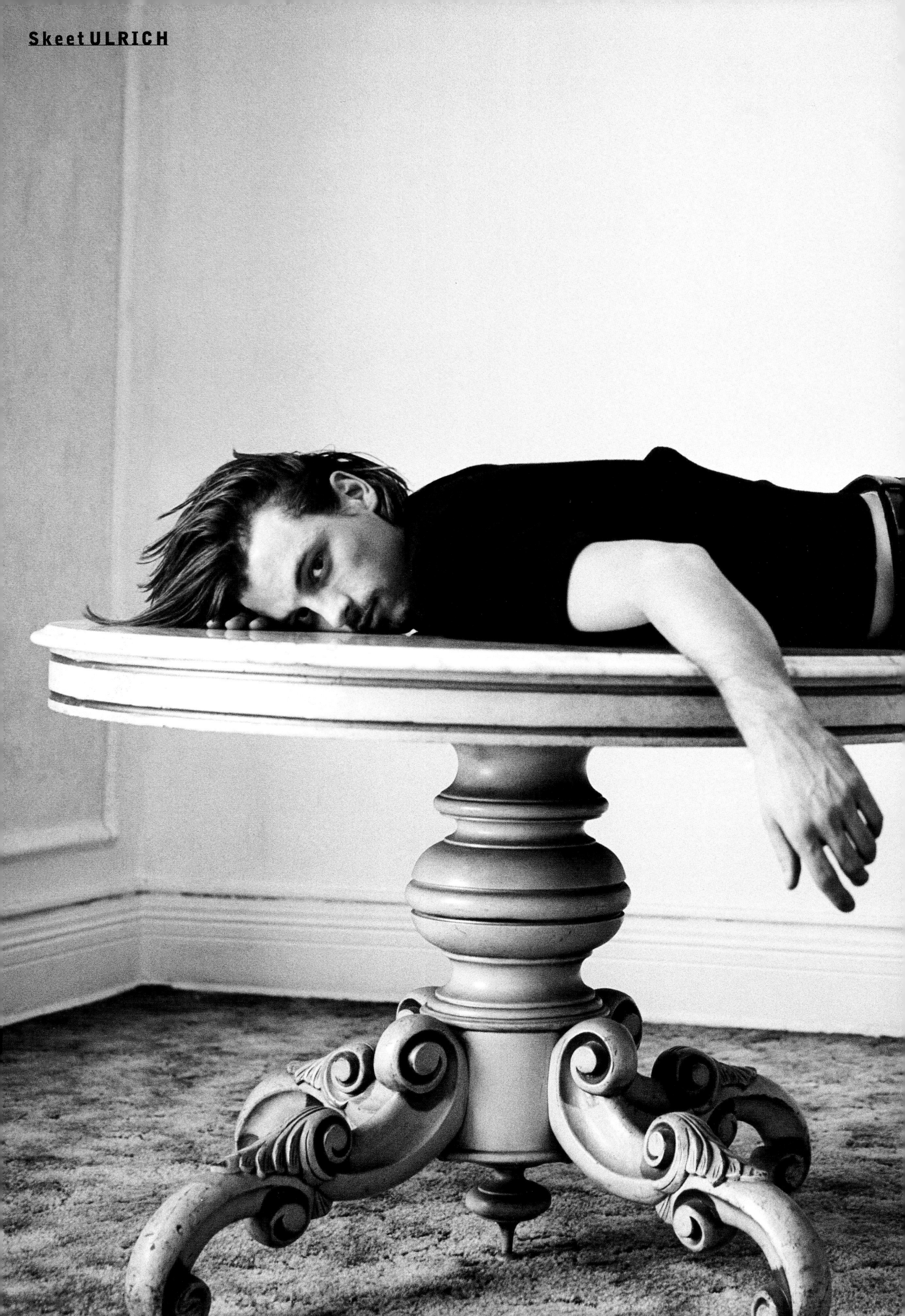

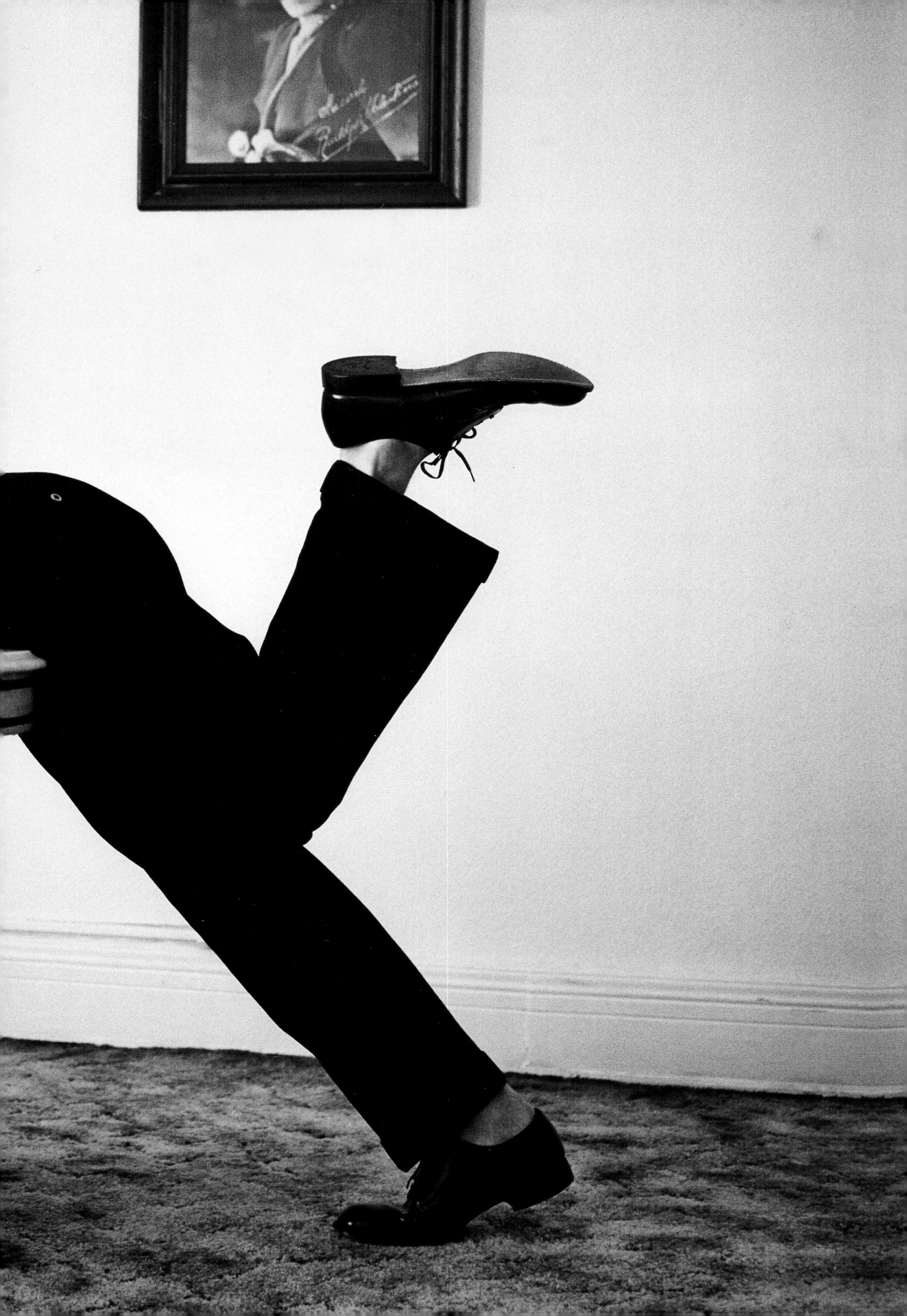

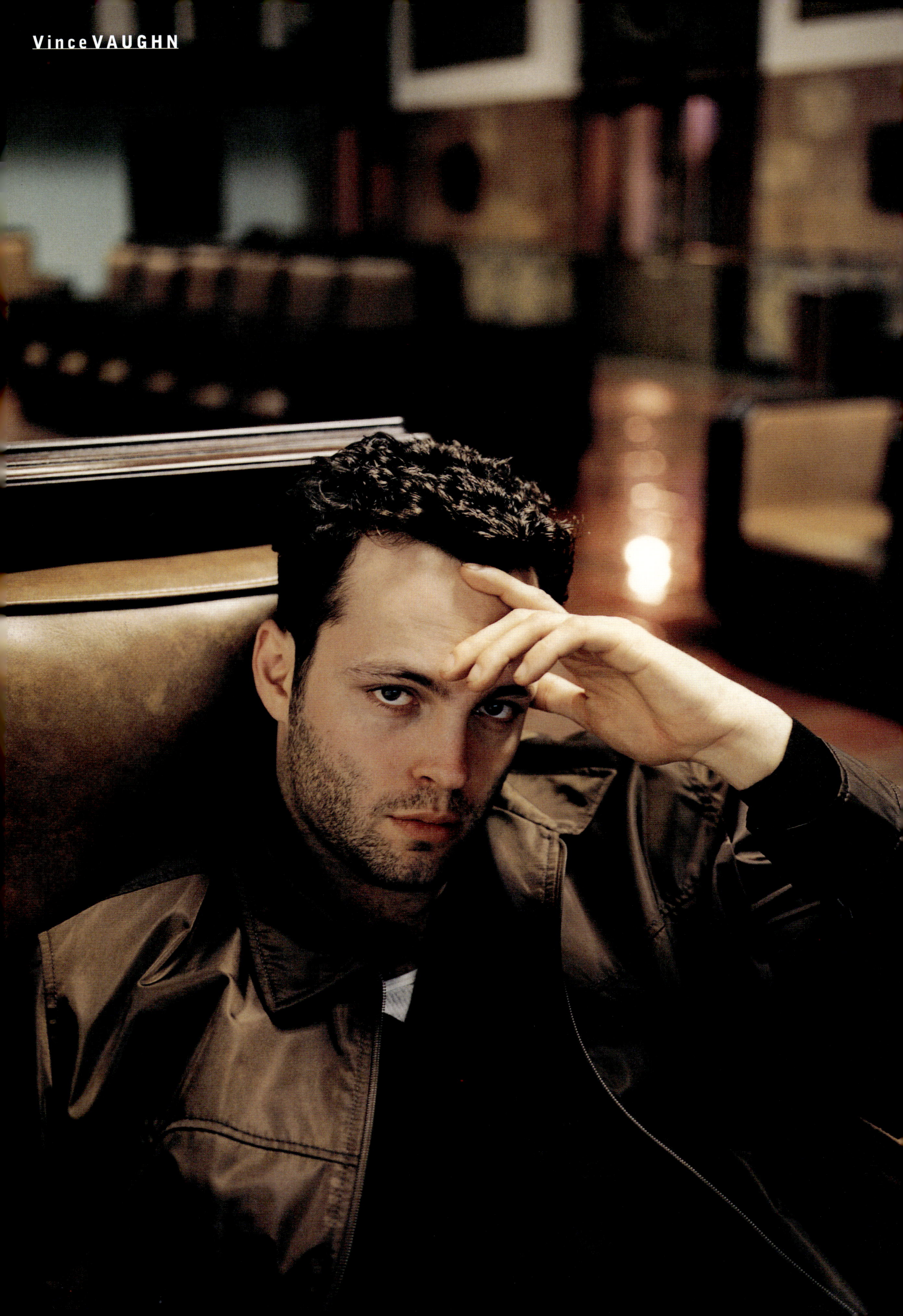

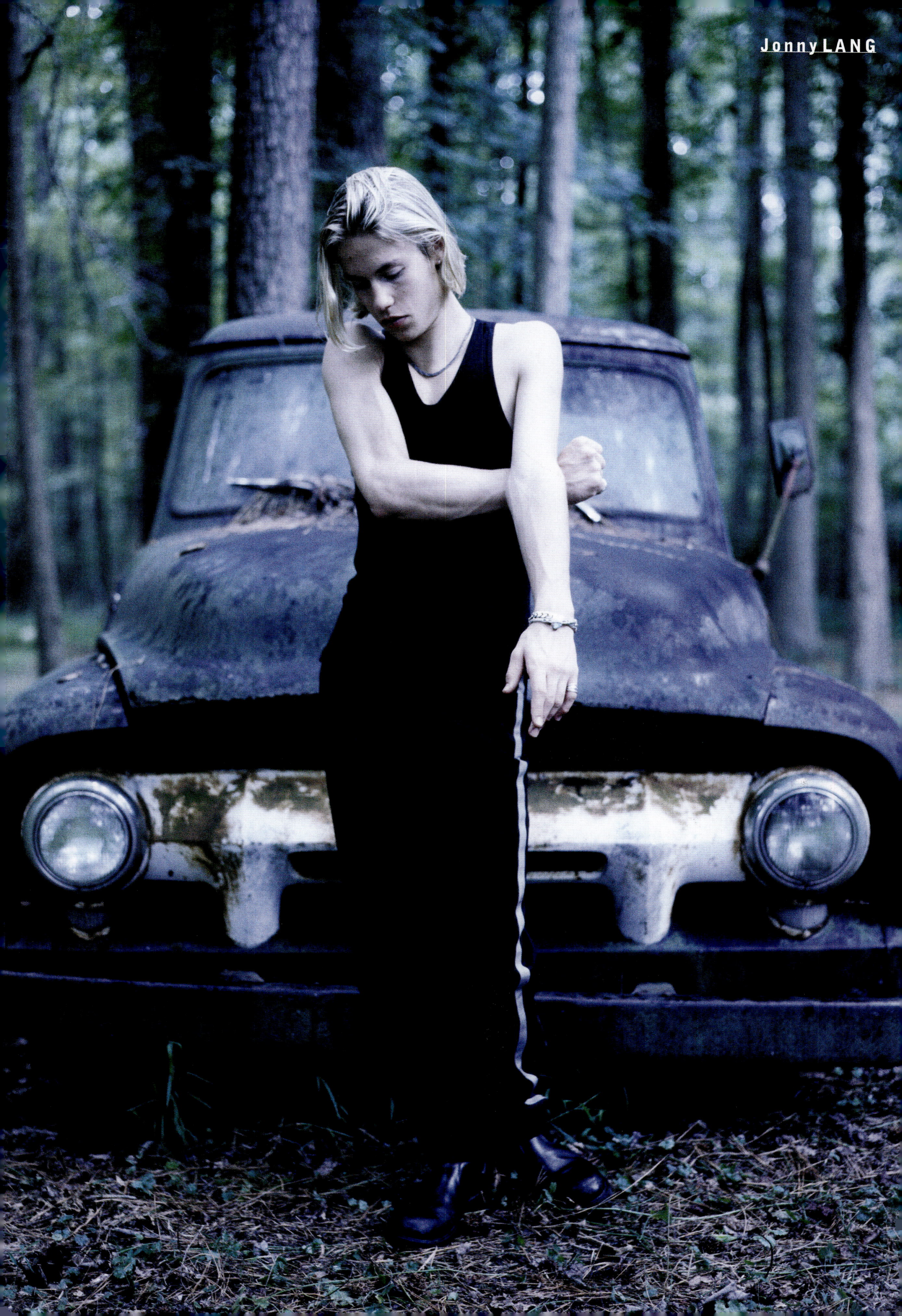

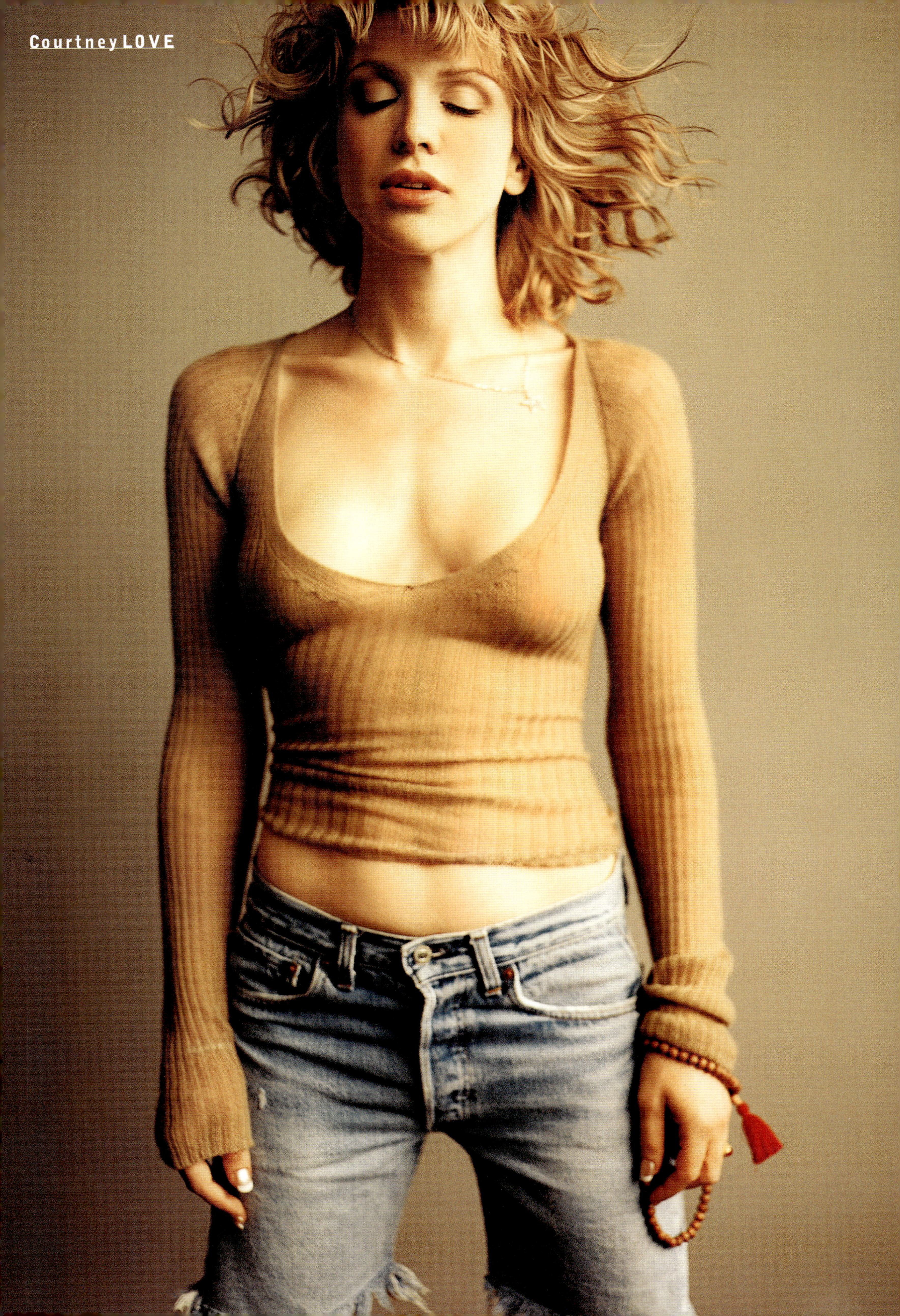

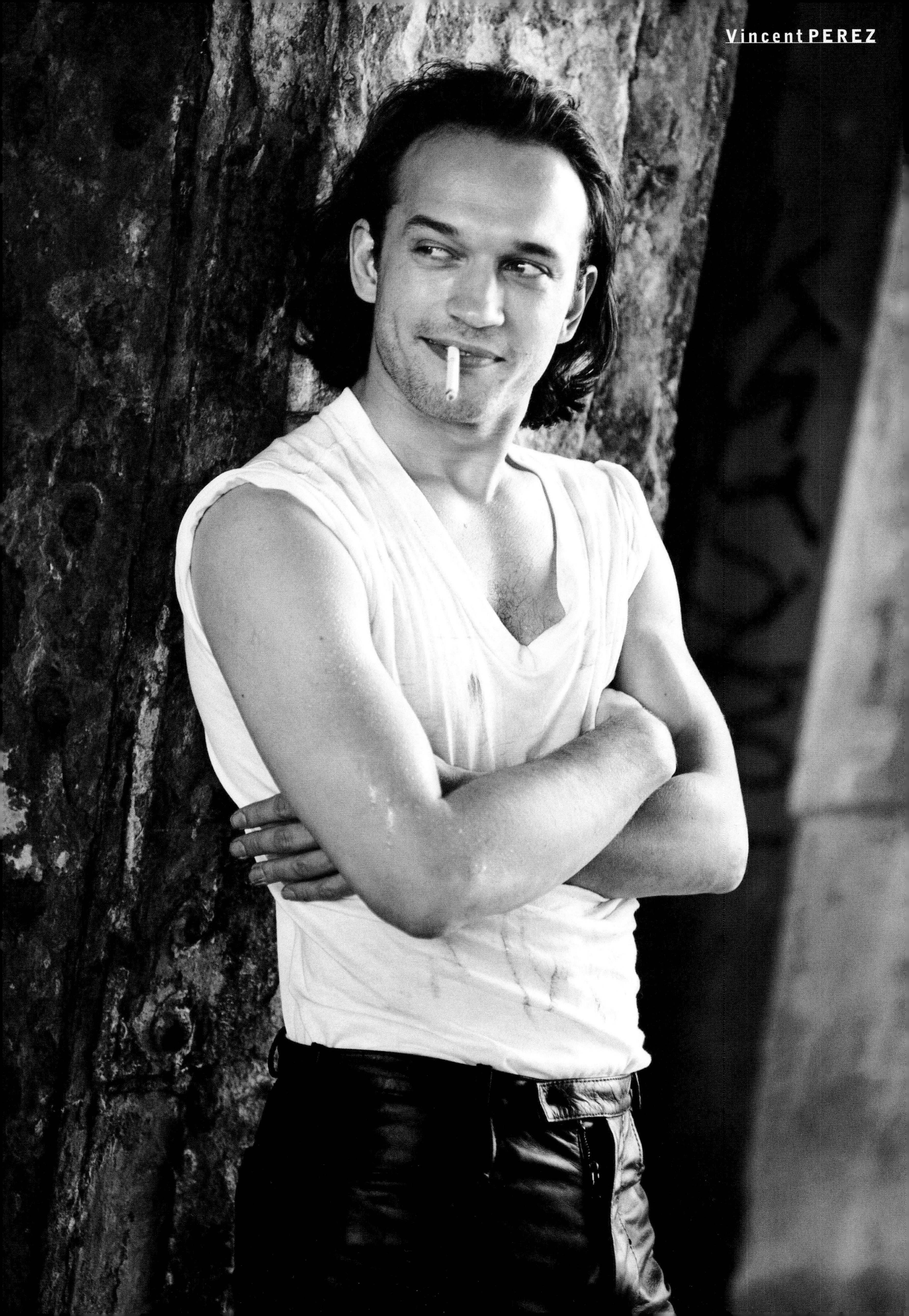

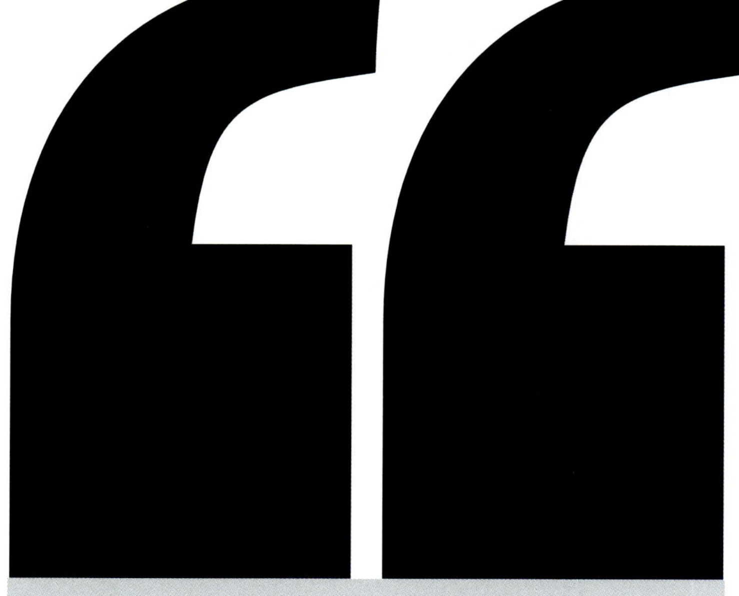

You like road-tripping across America. What's the appeal? I love traveling. I like to keep moving. I love the big open spaces in America, and when I finish ['Meet Joe Black'], I'm going to drive to California from New York. I'm going to get a Budget rental car, go up through Chicago, down to Route 80. I've got my map right here – the Rand McNally. It's my bible. **Assuming you don't wear disguises when you're driving, what kind of reactions do you get along the way?** Earlier this year I got in the car one day and thought, I'll go to Texas. I did the whole of Texas in one day and thought, God, this is pretty flat and monotonous, I think I'll go up to Seattle. So I turned left somewhere and drove up. I stayed in Vail one night, Salt Lake City another and then in this tiny city just over the Washington border: Yakima. I stayed in this little motel and was having the buffet breakfast the next morning and there was a couple there, a husband and wife in their sixties, and I was drinking my coffee, reading my book and I'd look up and she was [he pantomimes staring, then looking away]. She went out to the lobby and then came back and said [in a flat, Midwestern accent], 'You are who I think you are. What are you doing in Yakima?' I said, 'I'm on my way to Seattle.' And she said, 'Oh, we're on our way to Seattle to see an opera! Would you like to come and have some coffee with my husband and I?' So, I went and joined them for a little while. **You grew up in the same small town in Wales as Richard Burton? Did you ever meet him?** I got his autograph when I was fifteen. He'd come from Hollywood with his wife Sybil, who has since become a close friend of mine. Everyone knew when Richard was back because he used to pass the shops in his Jaguar, and nobody had ever seen a Jaguar in the postwar years. I remember knocking at his door and being invited in by his sister and there's Richard shaving with an electric shaver. [Quietly] I'd never seen an electric razor. He said [deep, grave voice], 'What do you want?' 'Autograph,' I said. So he signed the autograph. He said, 'Do you speak Welsh?' I said, 'No.' He said, 'You're not a real Welshman then. Where you come up?' I said, 'Port Talbot, my father's a baker.' 'Oh, yes,' he said, 'I know. You're opposite the co-op. I used to work in there. The shoe department. I was terrible at it.' I thought, there's a kindred spirit – he wasn't good at what he did when he was a kid, either. [Excitedly] It's all coming back again. I can recall it in the cells of my body. Sybil was sitting at the table reading the paper; they'd just had breakfast and were about to go to the international rugby match. He said, 'Do you like rugby?' I said, 'No, not much.' He said, 'Then you're really not Welsh.' [Grins] He was taking the piss out of me. I went out of the house and I was walking down the street, slowly, looking at his autograph, and the Jaguar car came down the road and Sybil waved and I thought, I've got to get out of this place. I've got to become what he is. And I think something deep in my subconscious mind, or whatever it was, [snaps fingers] set the target. I thought, I'm going to be famous. **Have you ever considered writing your memoirs?** A publisher asked me to write an autobiography and I sat down and started but I got very self-

Anthony Hopkins »

conscious and I kept thinking, oh, this is bullshit! I can't be bothered. I'm not interested in my own life, but I remember everything. Back to the age of two or three. I'm obsessed with dates. My wife will say, 'When did we do that?' And I'll say, 'October 20th, 1974.' As long as I can remember, I've been a savant. **Are there people in England who've accused you of selling out?** Oh yeah, yeah, but I don't give a damn. **But you got the last laugh – you got away.** Yeah, and it's a good life. I feel so much like my father. My father was a down-to-earth basic man. He'd hear me playing the piano and ask, 'What's that you're playing?' I'd say, 'Beethoven.' 'No wonder he went deaf! For God's sake, get out of the house.' He was real meat and potatoes. Didn't give a shit about culture and neither do I. **So, in the end, you've become your father?** Yeah. I have no interest in Shakespeare and all that British nonsense. **But did you once?** Only through ambition. I just wanted to get famous. All the rest is hogwash.

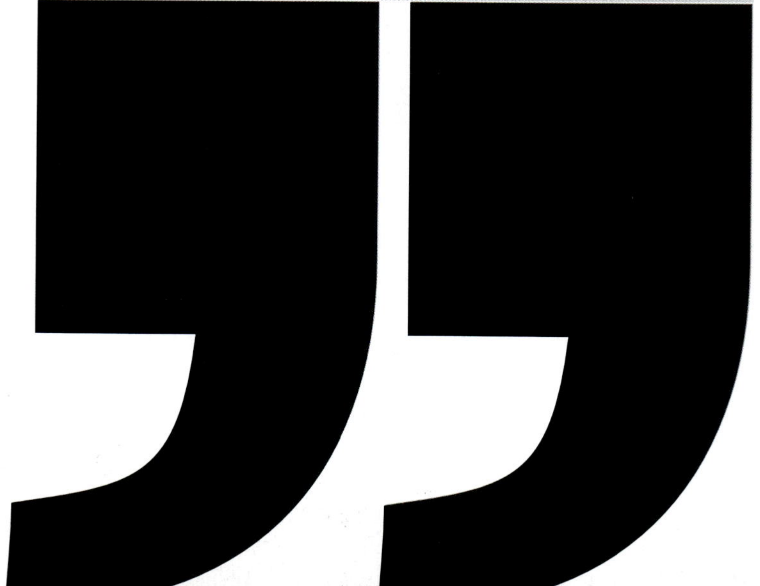

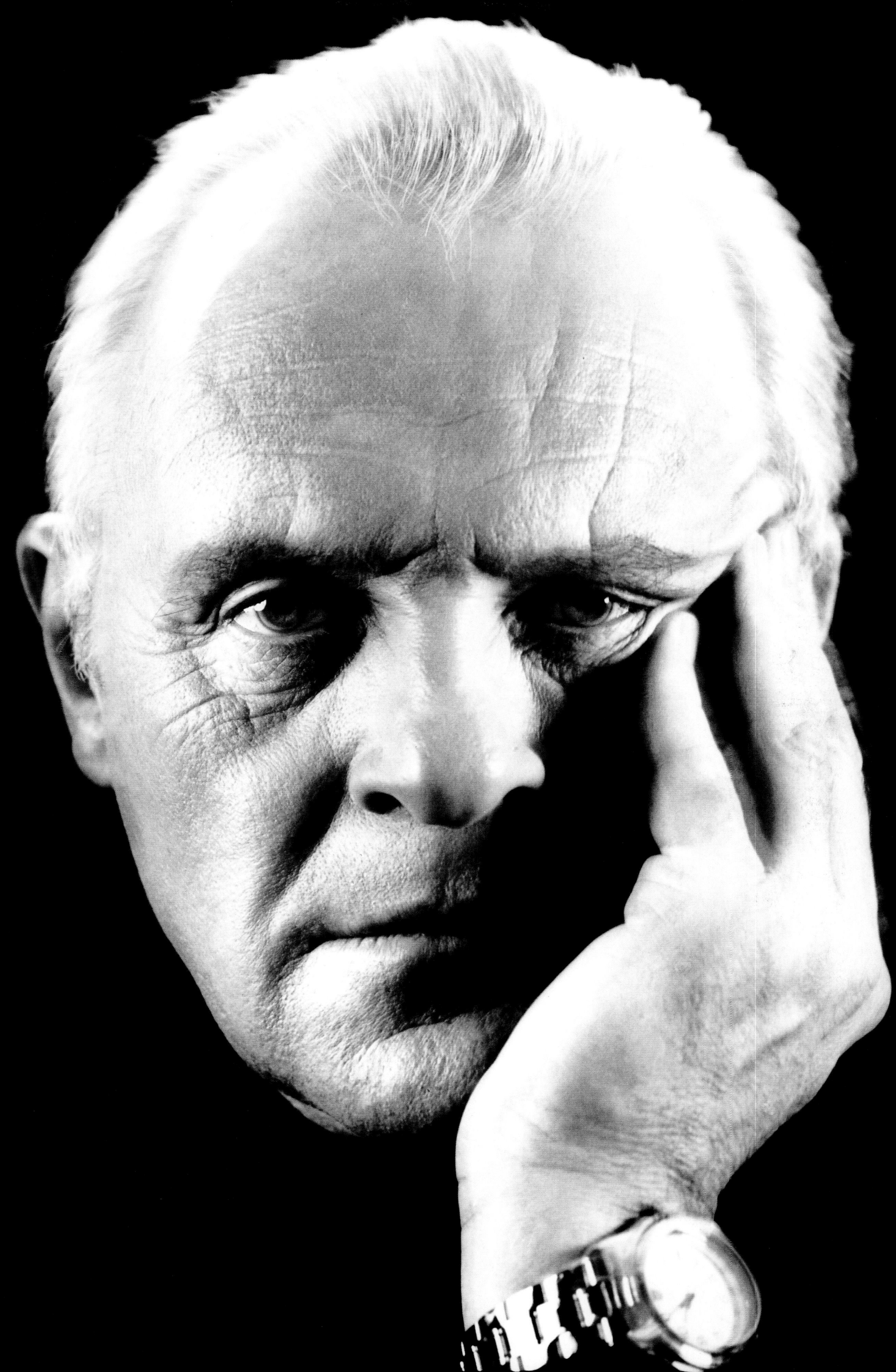

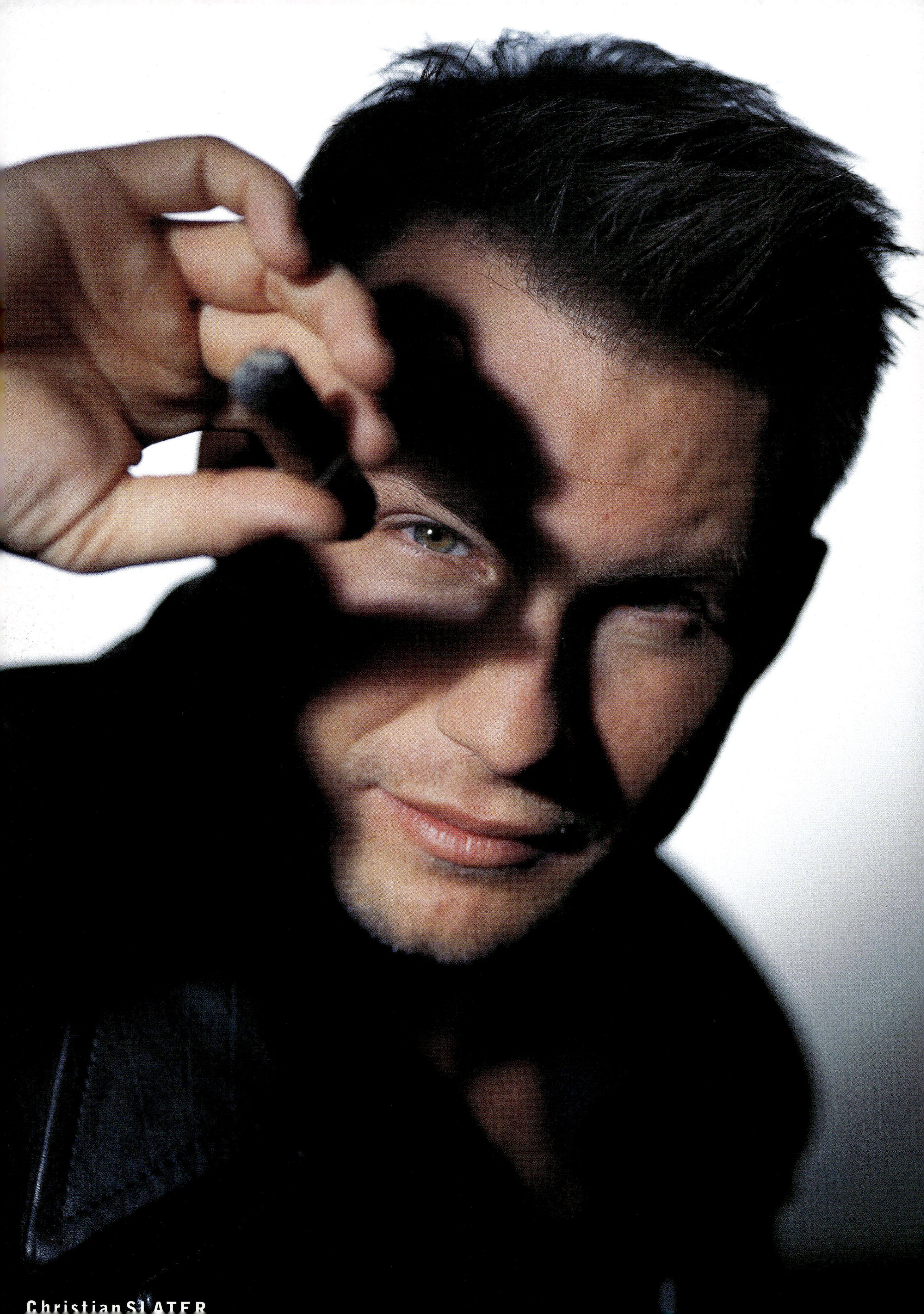

Christian SLATER

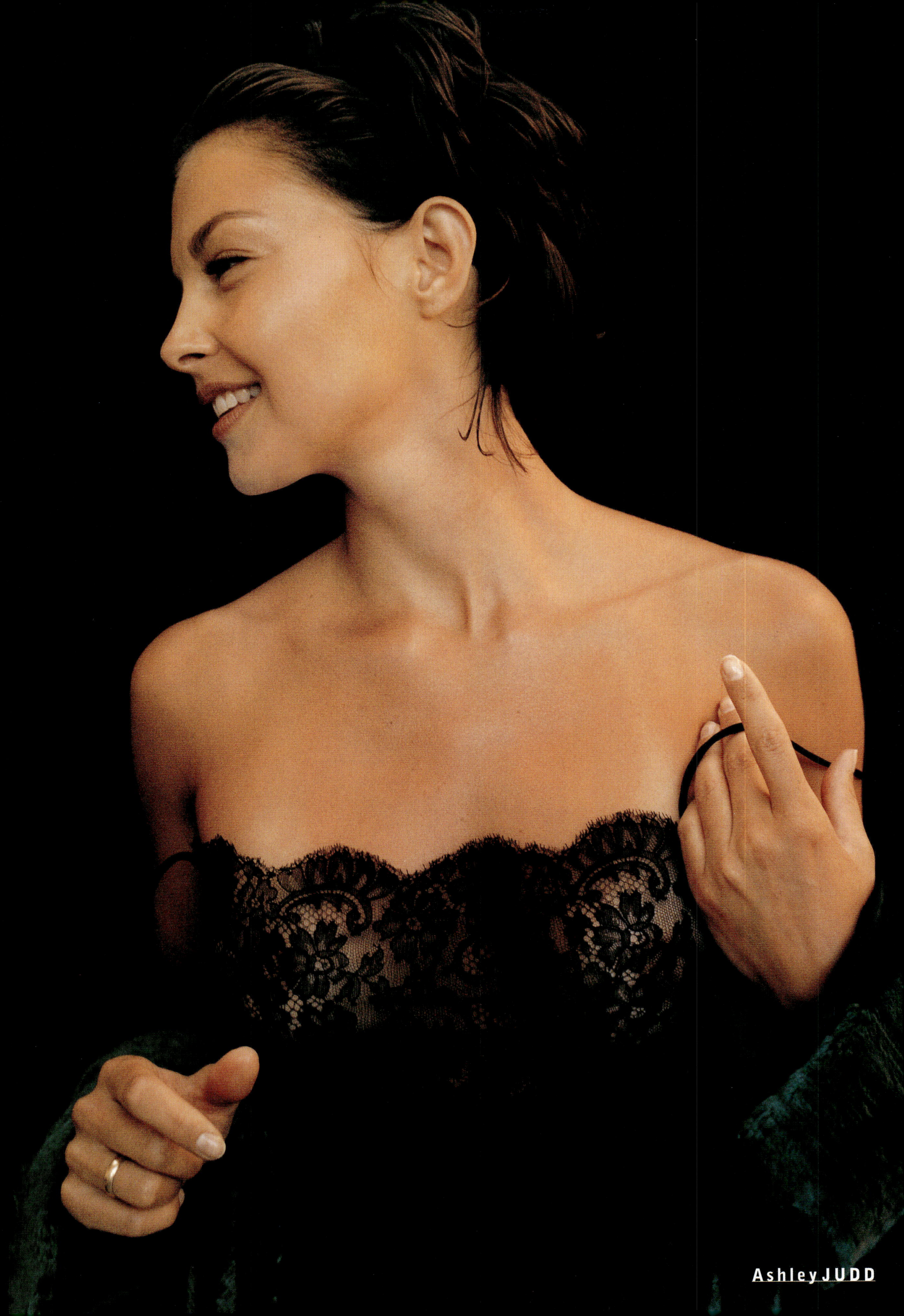

Ashley JUDD

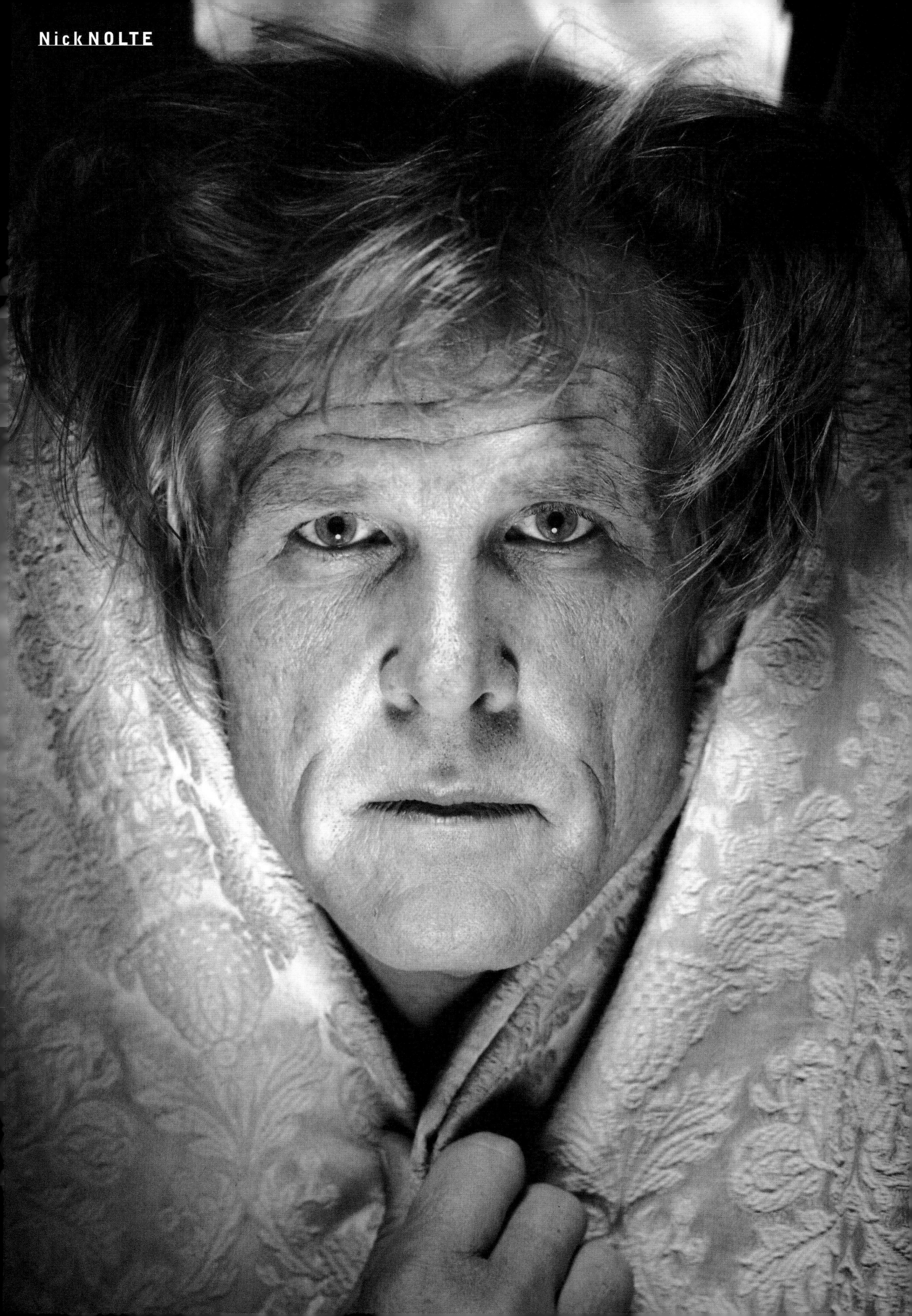

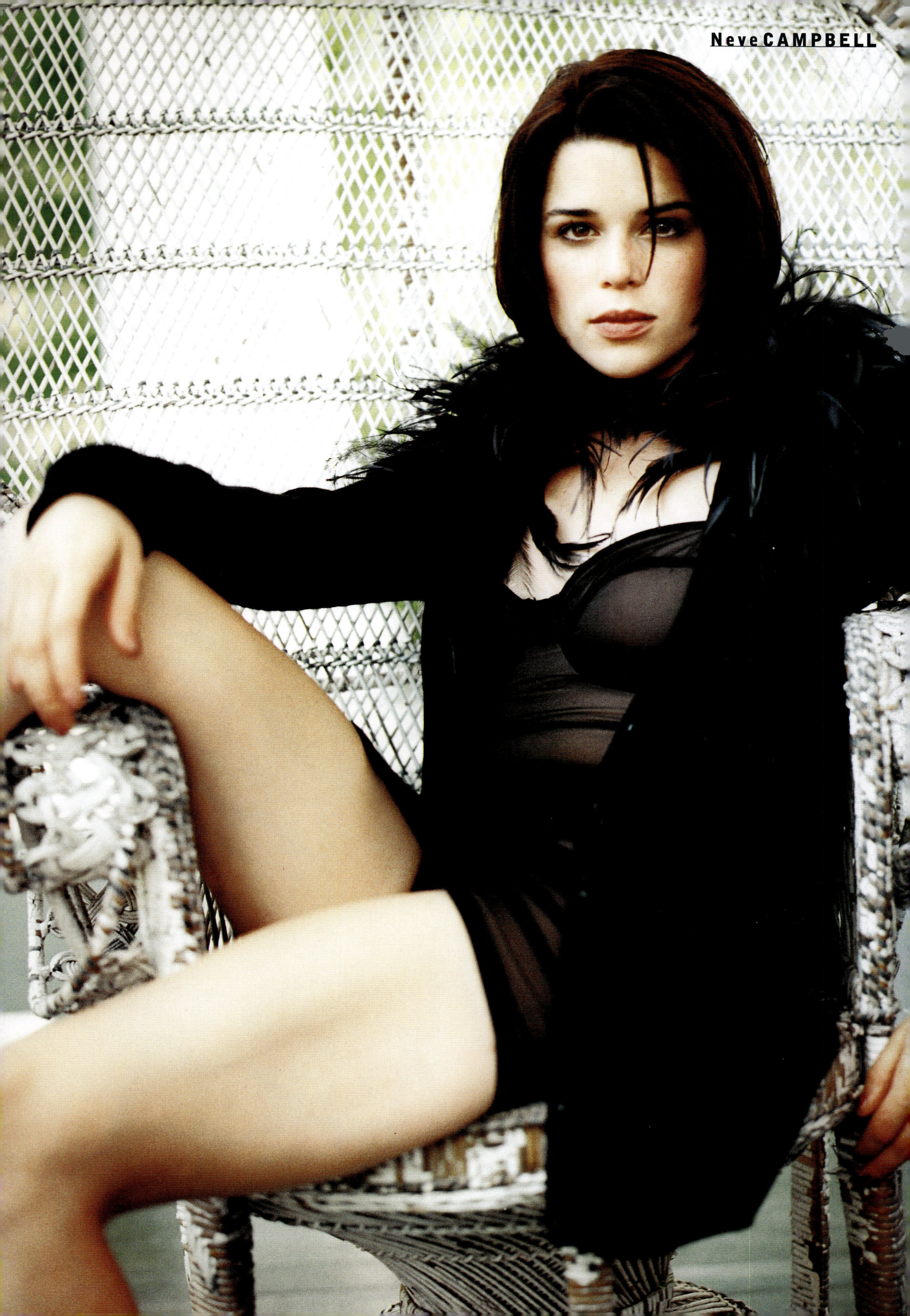

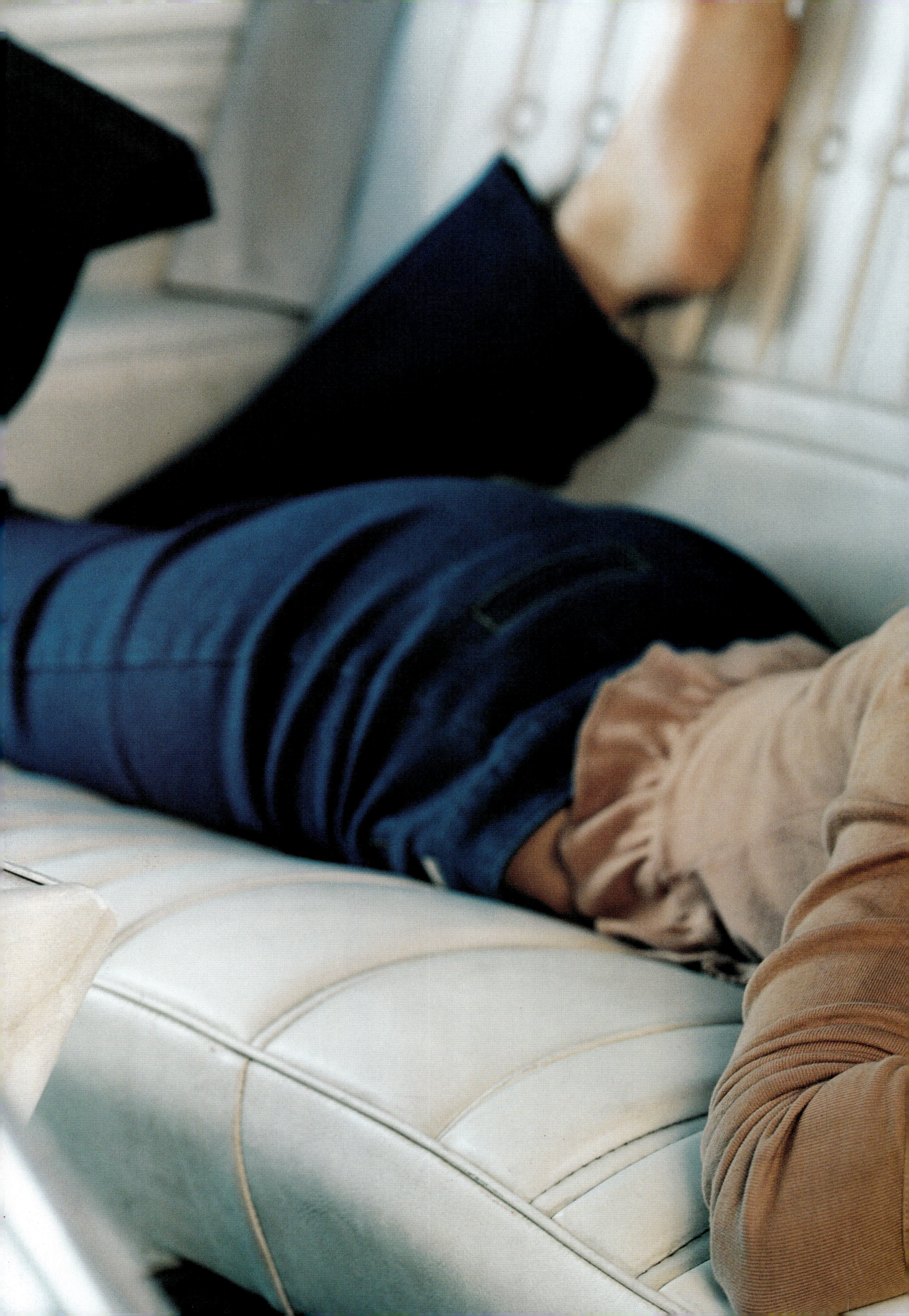

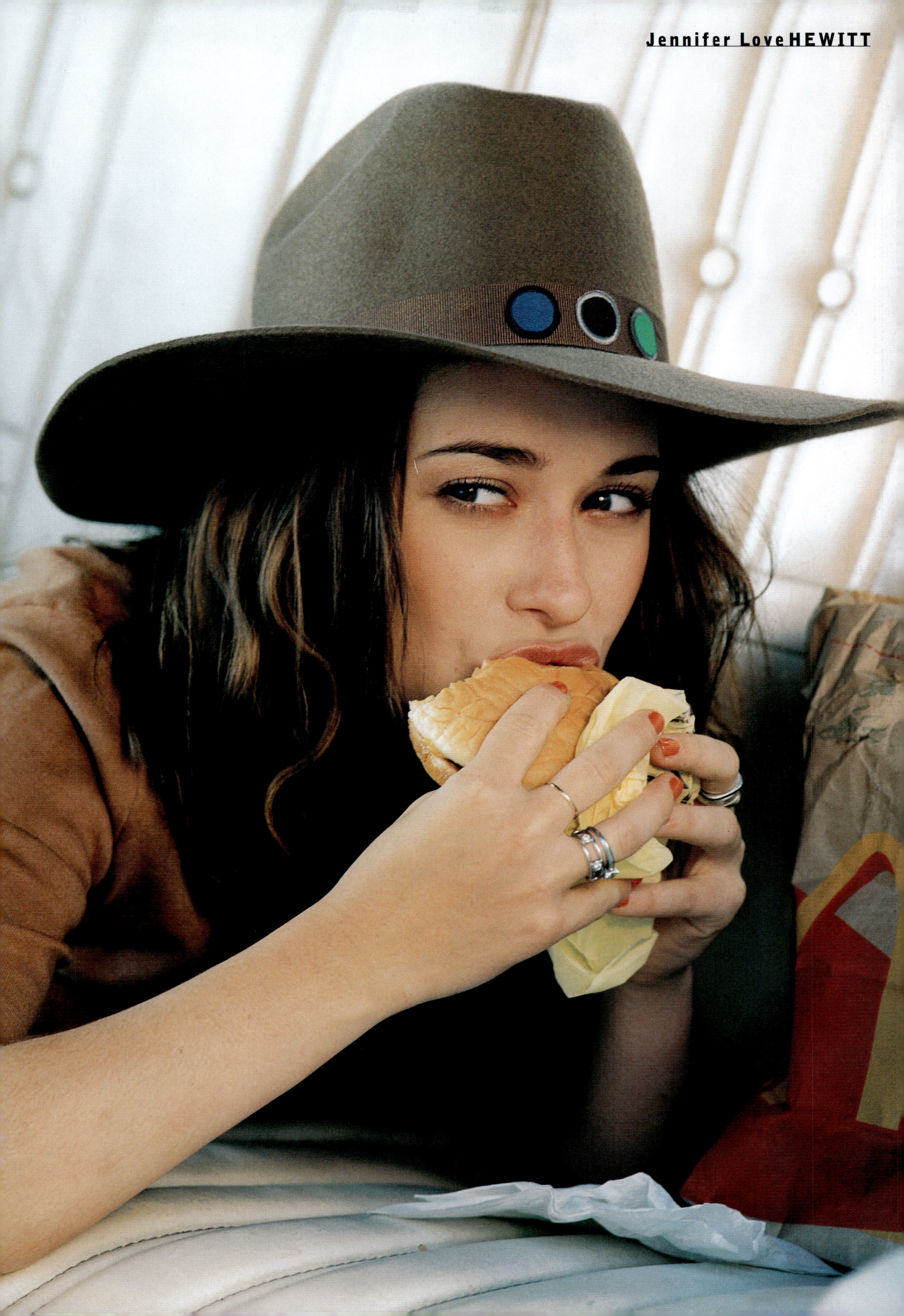

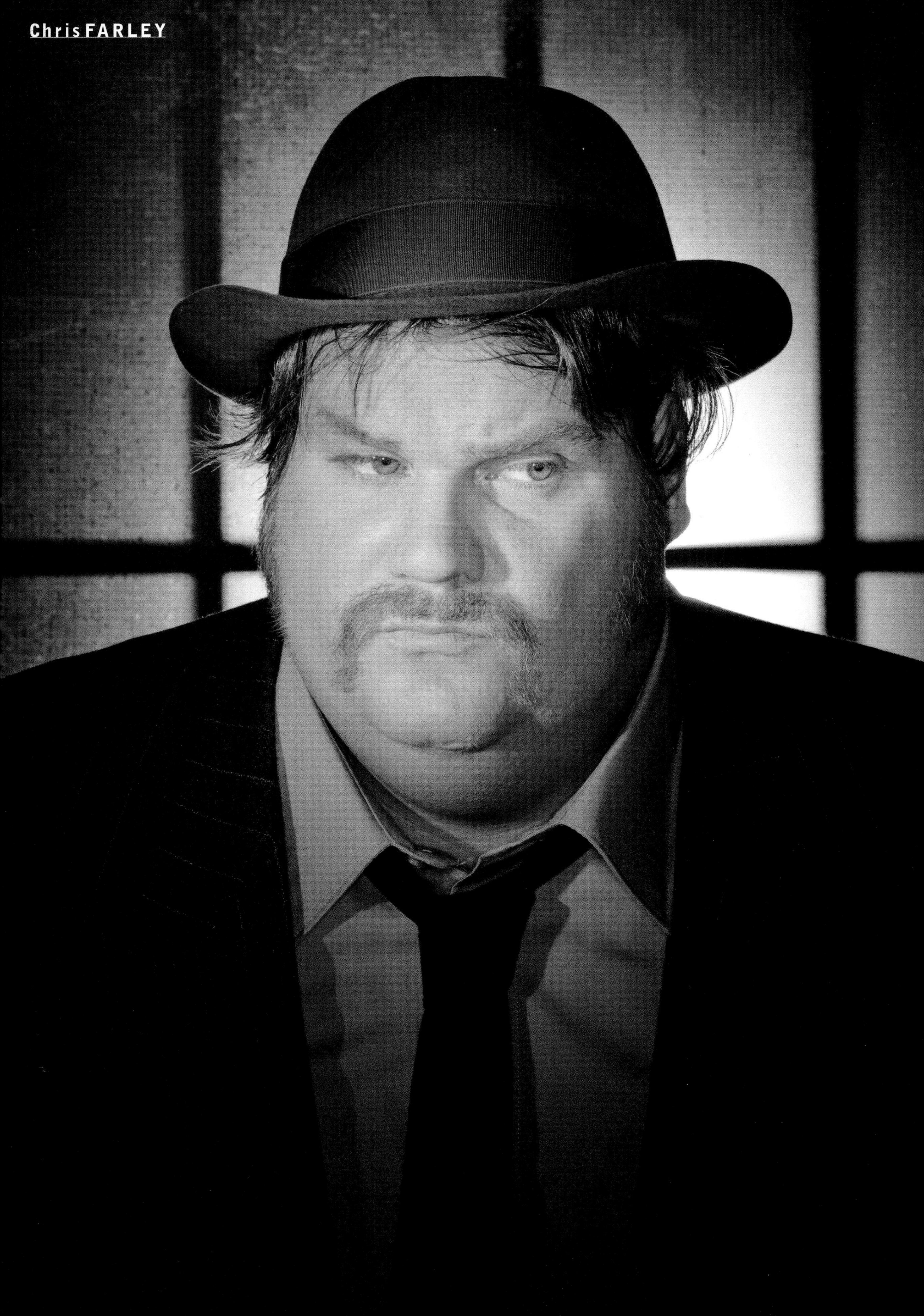

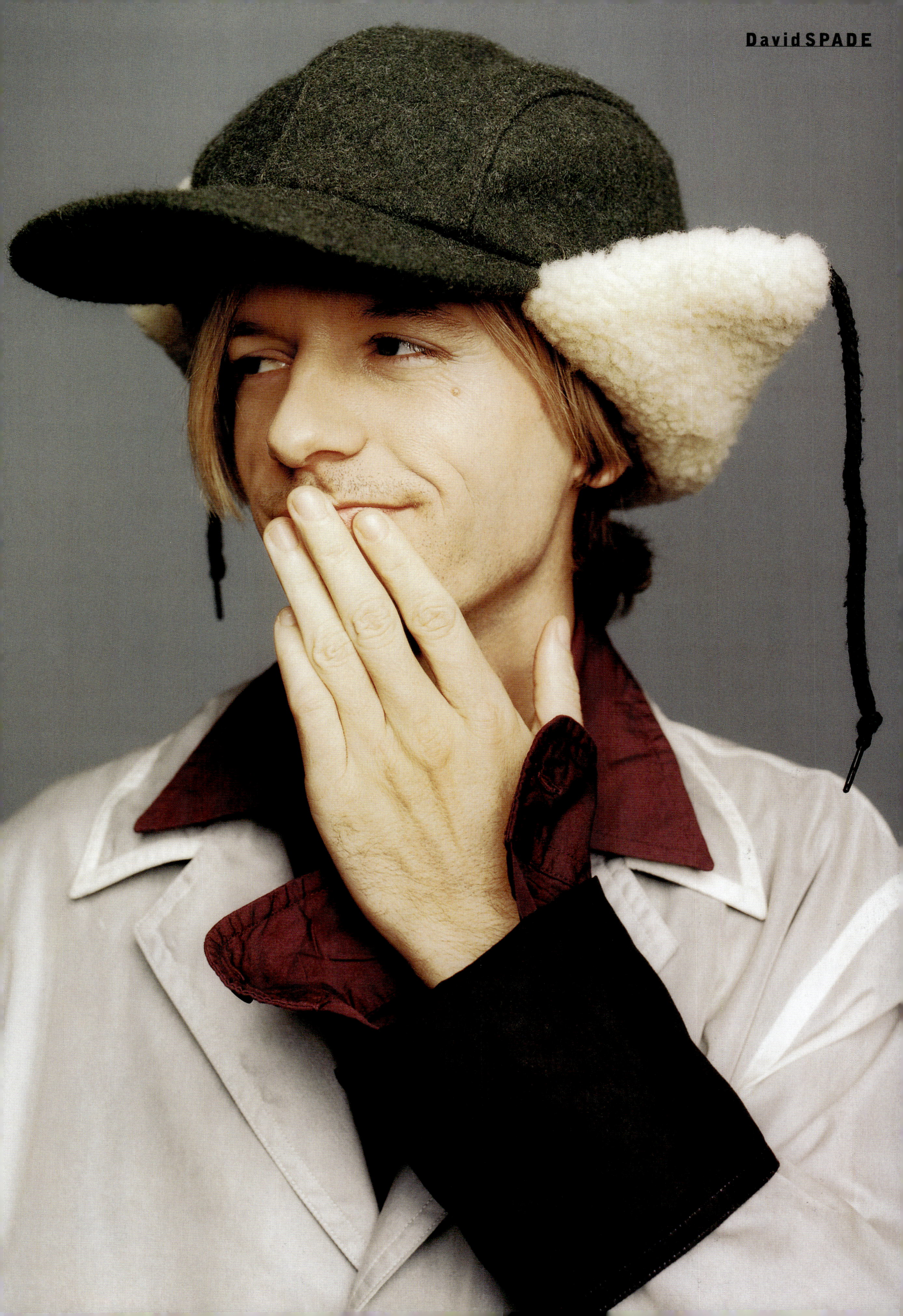

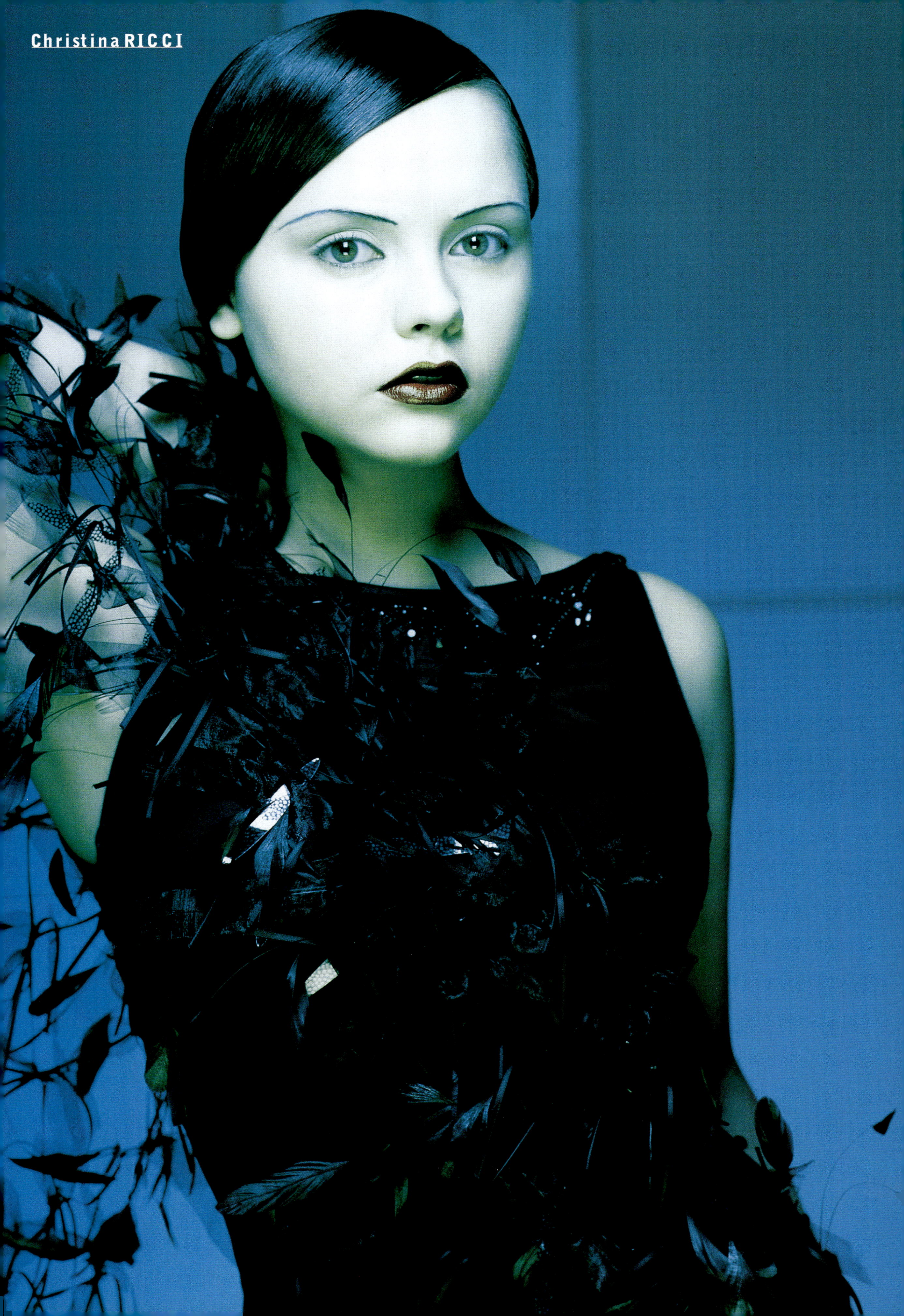

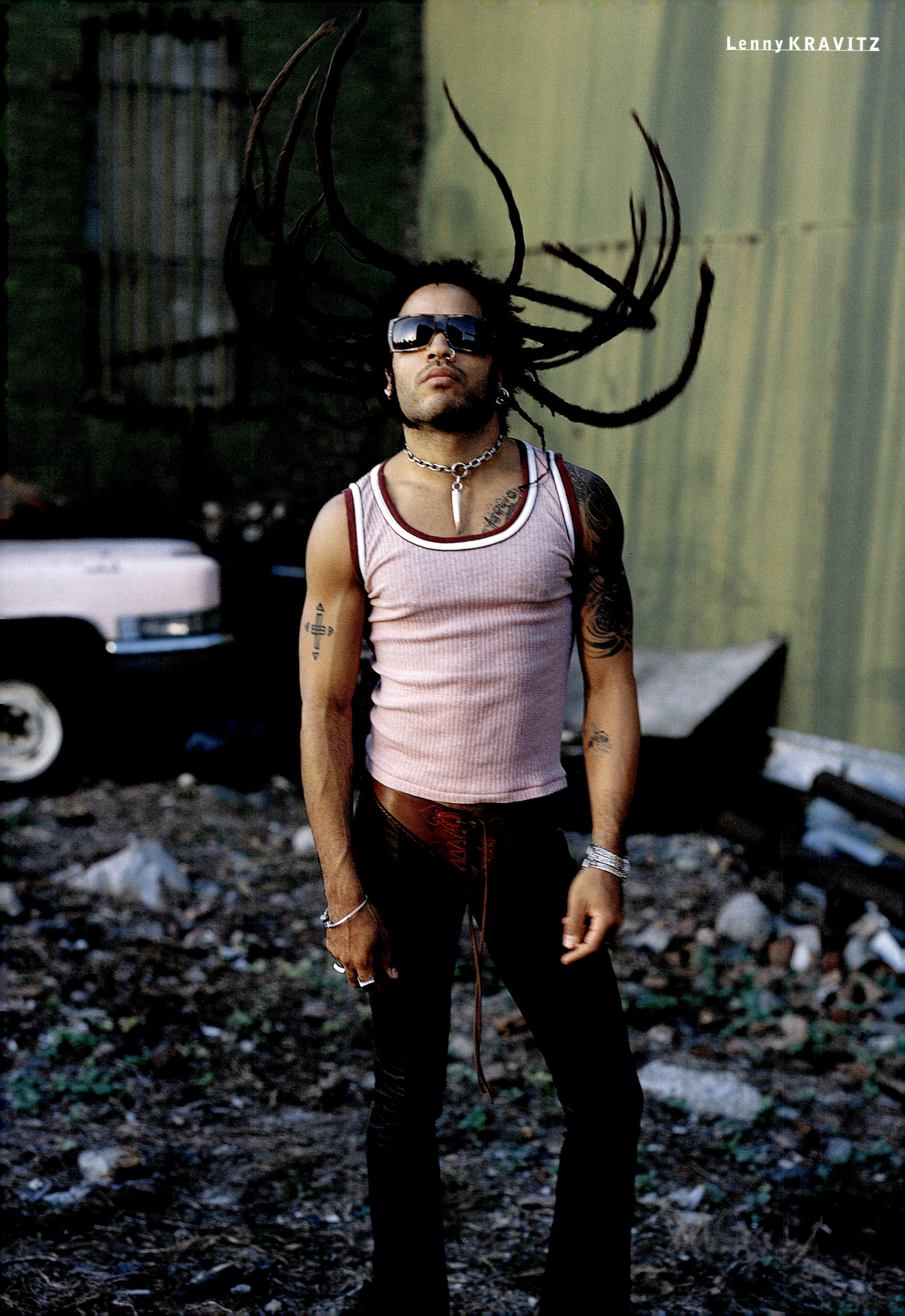

Madonna»

How often does the press get to you personally?

I suppose it depends on the subject. I pretty much can let most stuff roll off. One thing I read that really, really, *really* irked me, where I did have to take a couple of deep breaths, was a little blurb during that minute there when everybody was making a big deal about the Clintons and their maybe wanting to adopt a baby. It said something like: 'Hillary wants to adopt a baby; Madonna has one available.' You know, implying that I was completely and utterly disconnected from my pregnancy and could care less about my baby. I really got upset.

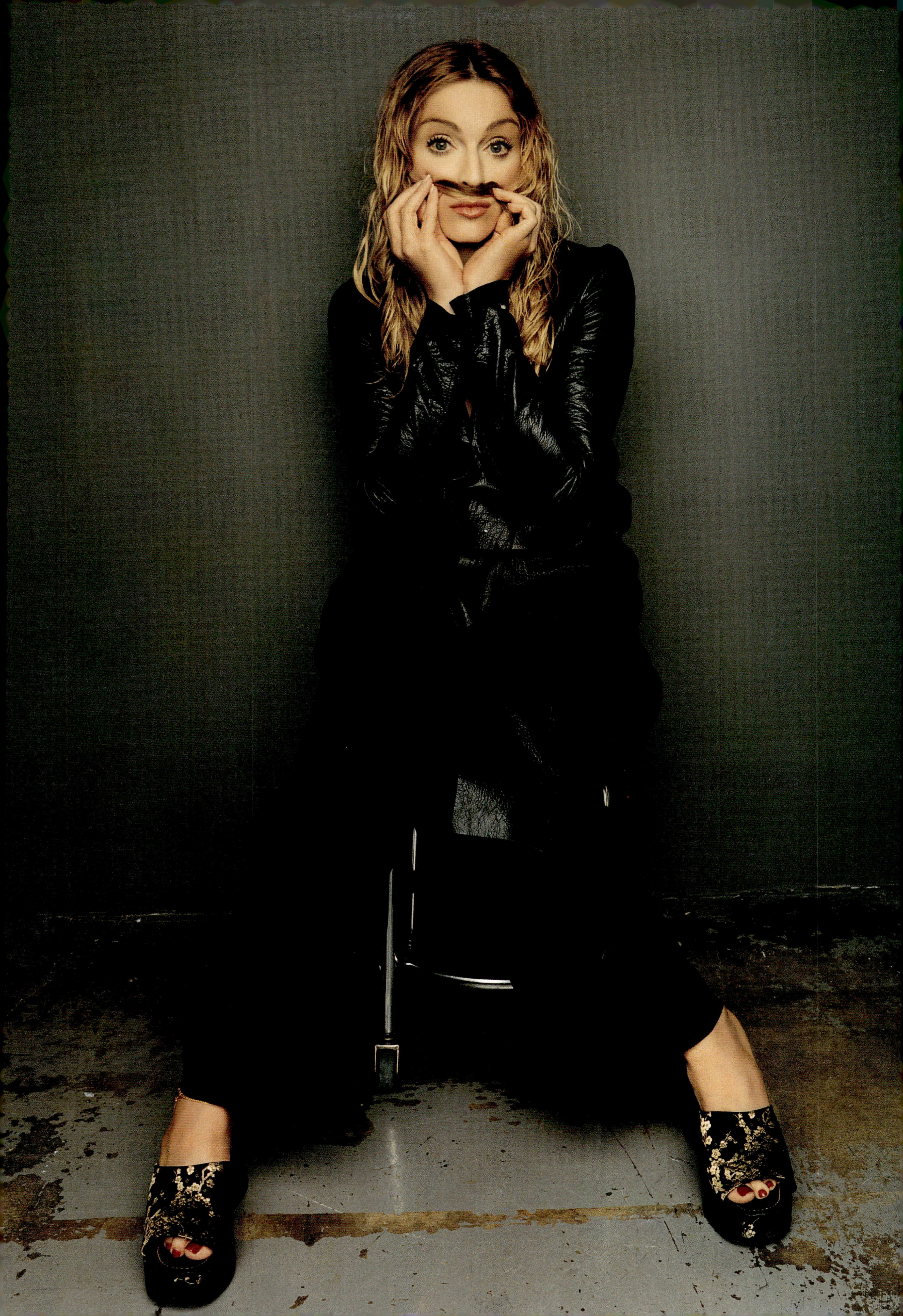

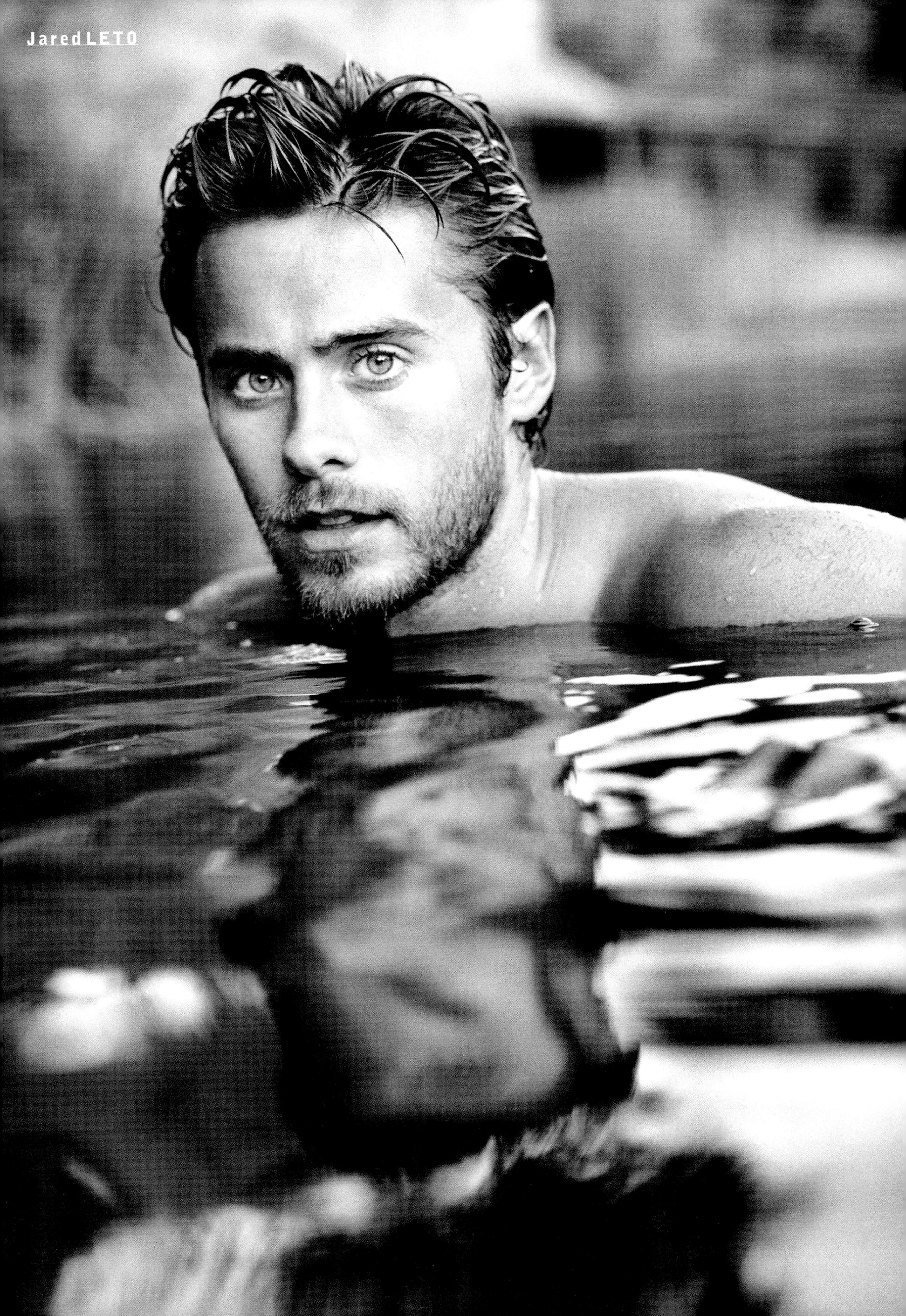

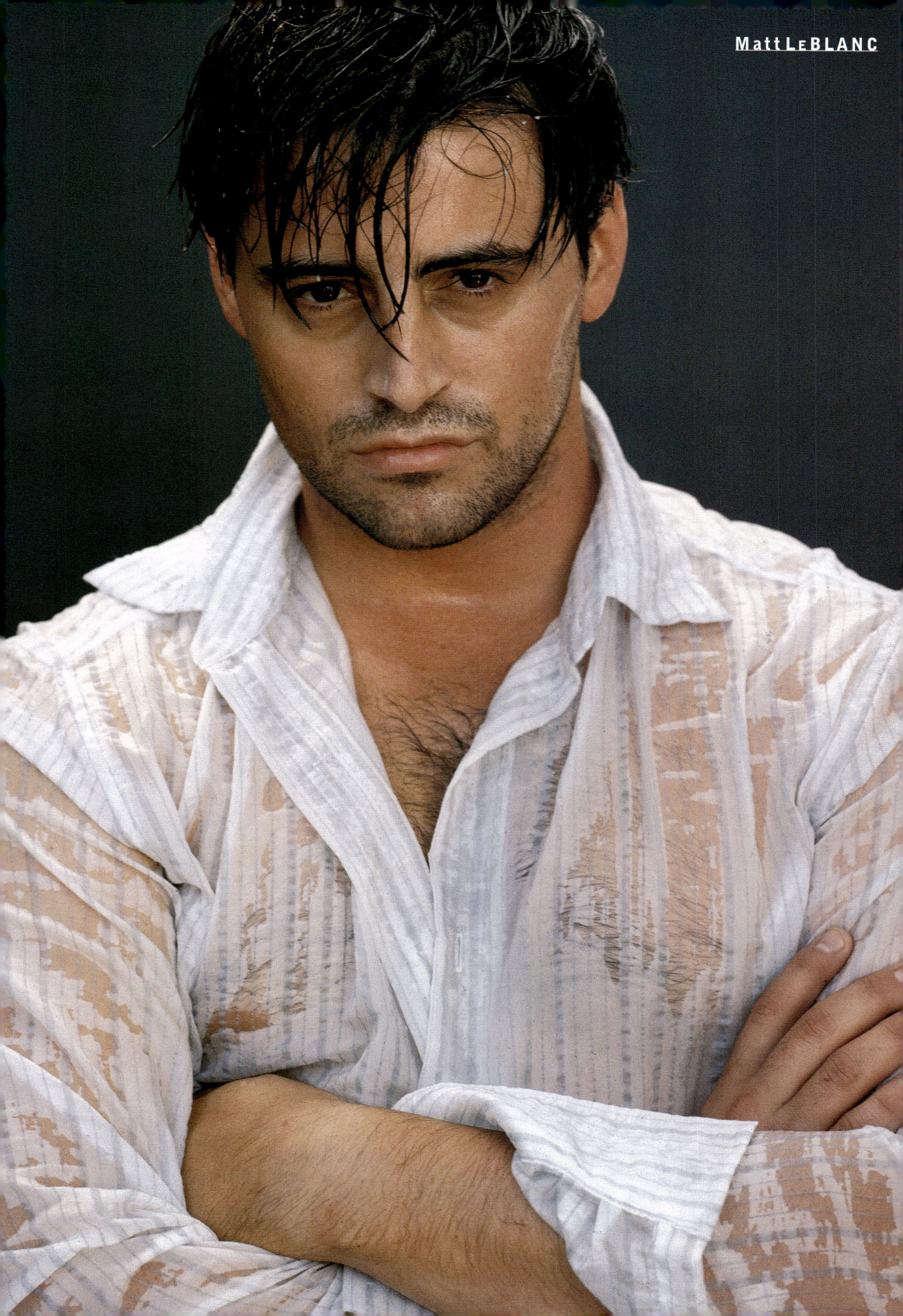

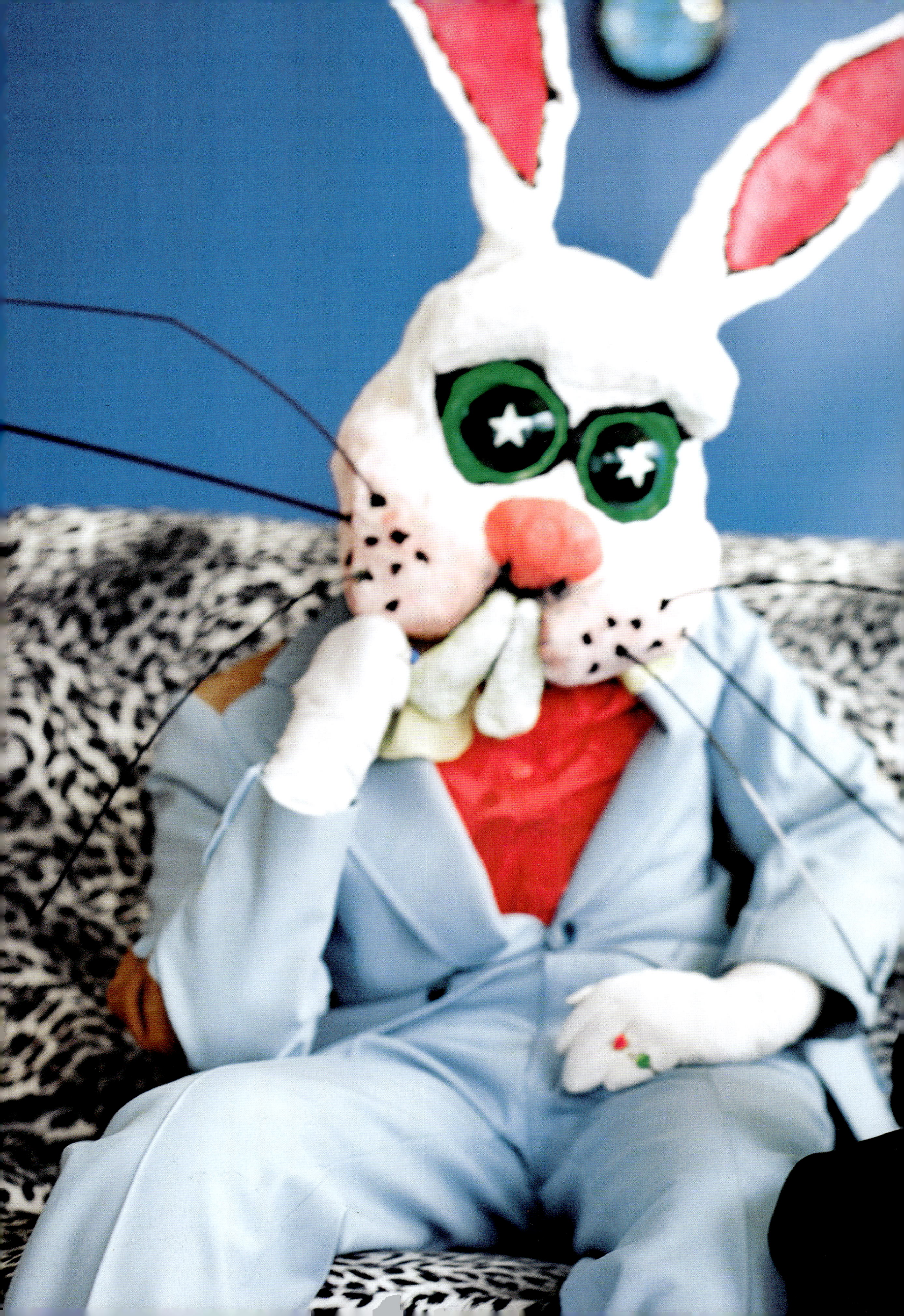

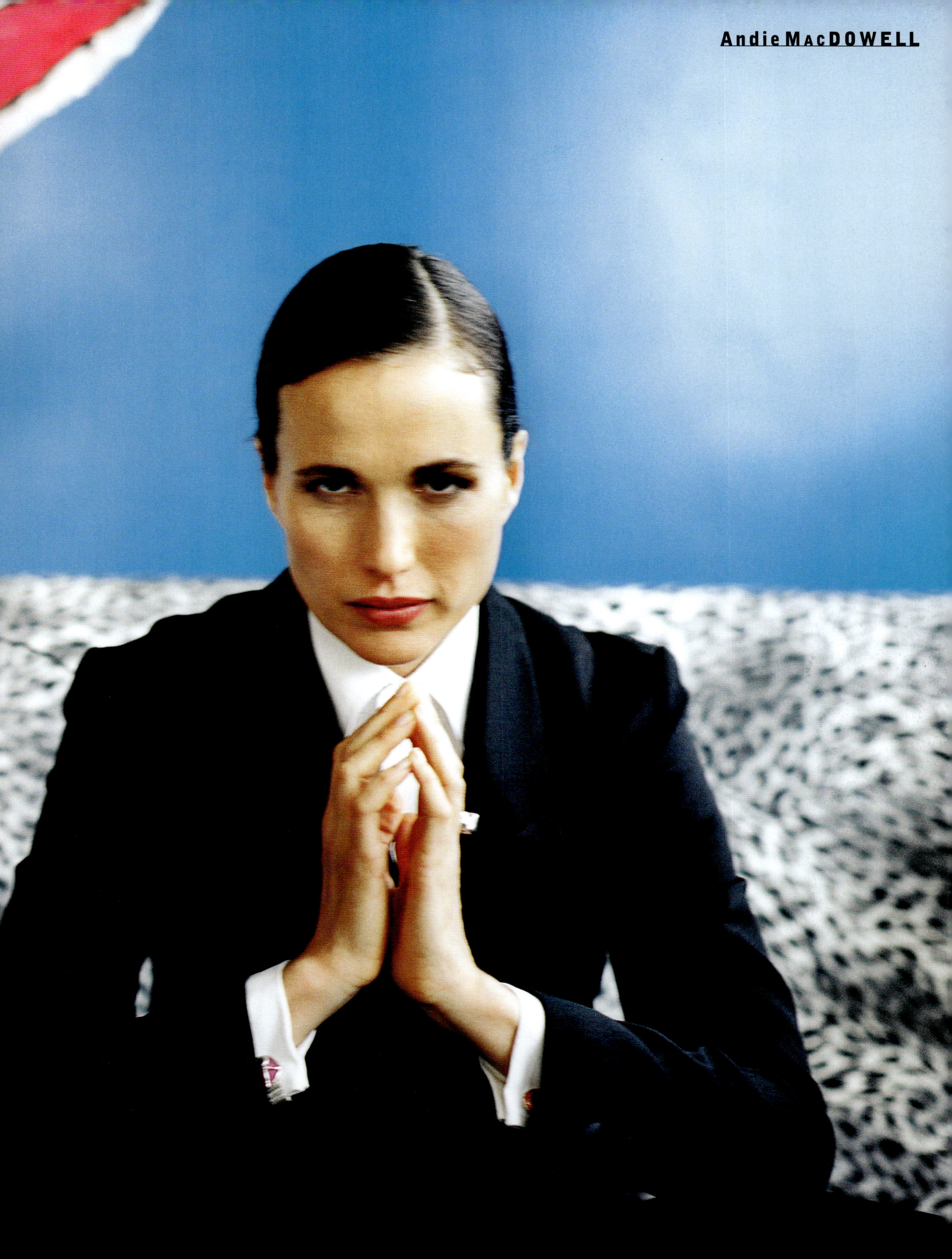

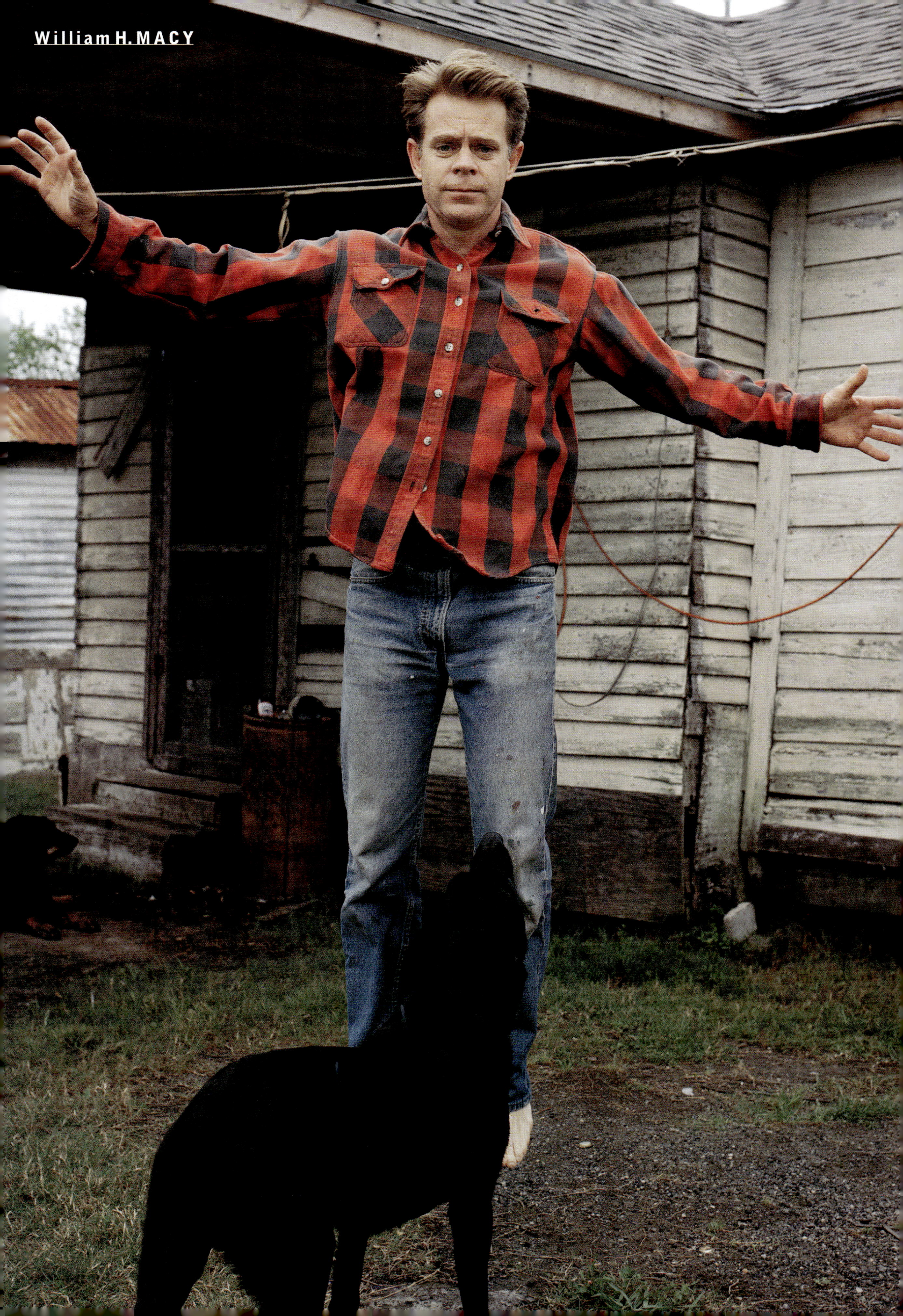

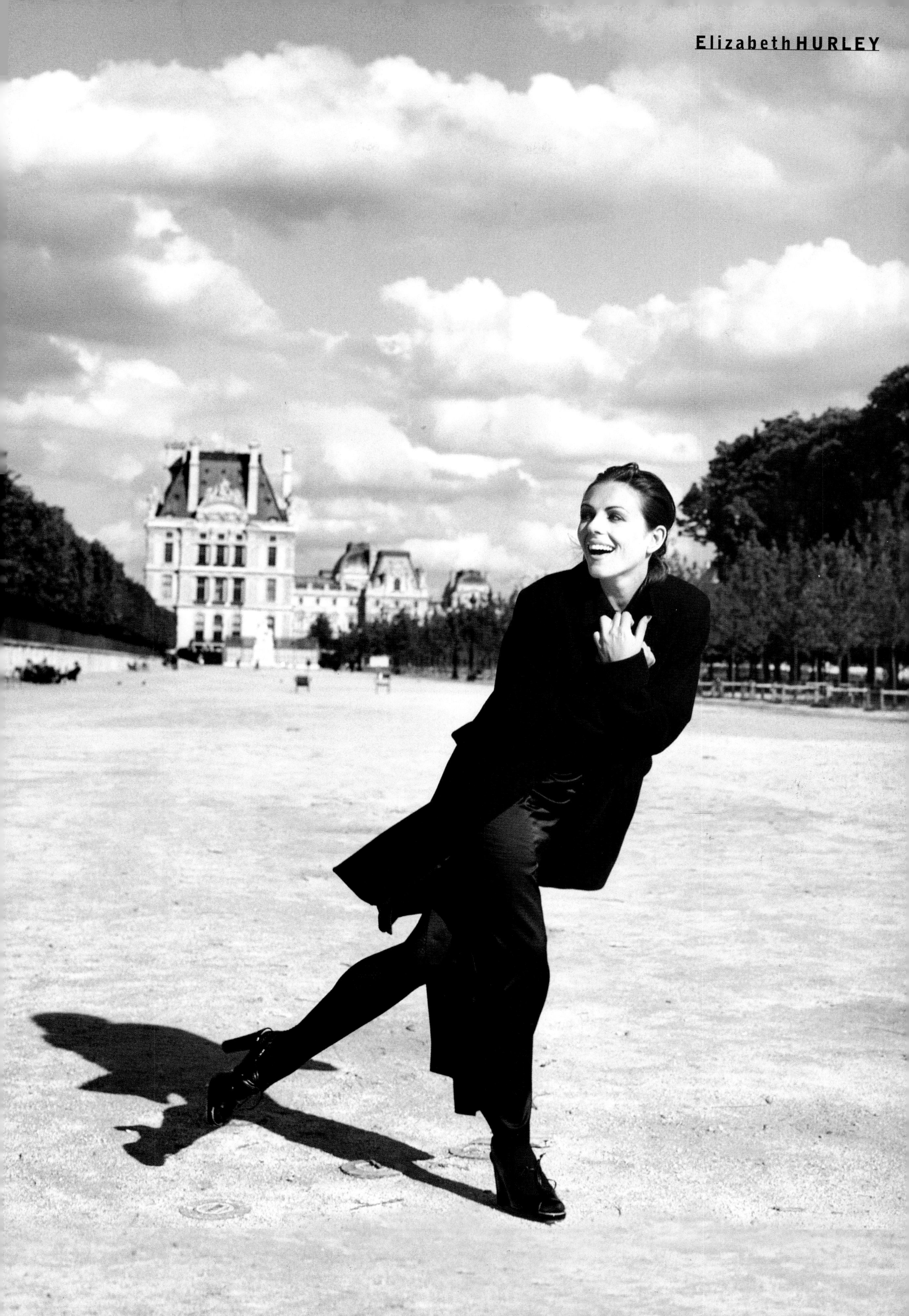

Lisa MARIE & Tim BURTON

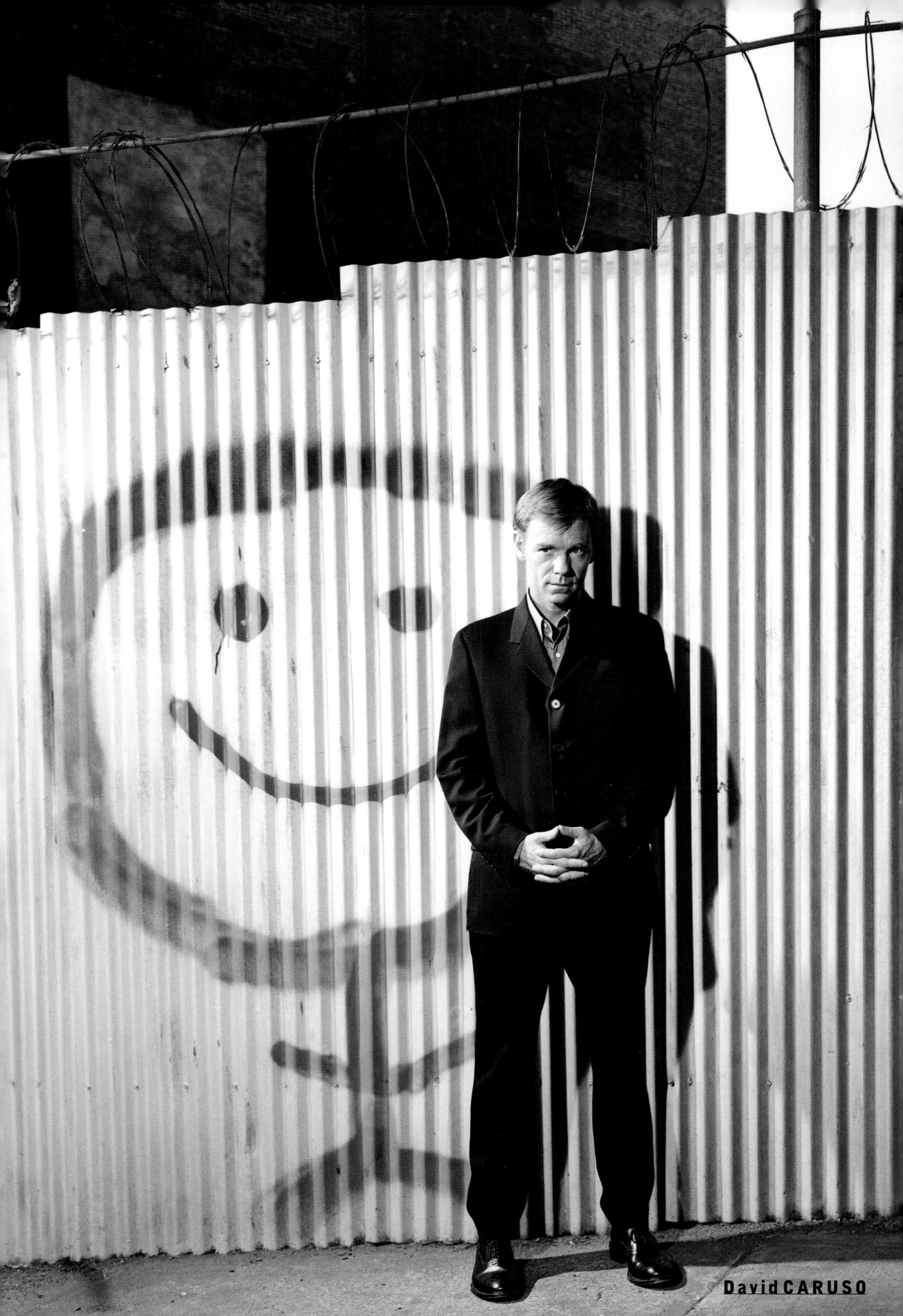

David CARUSO

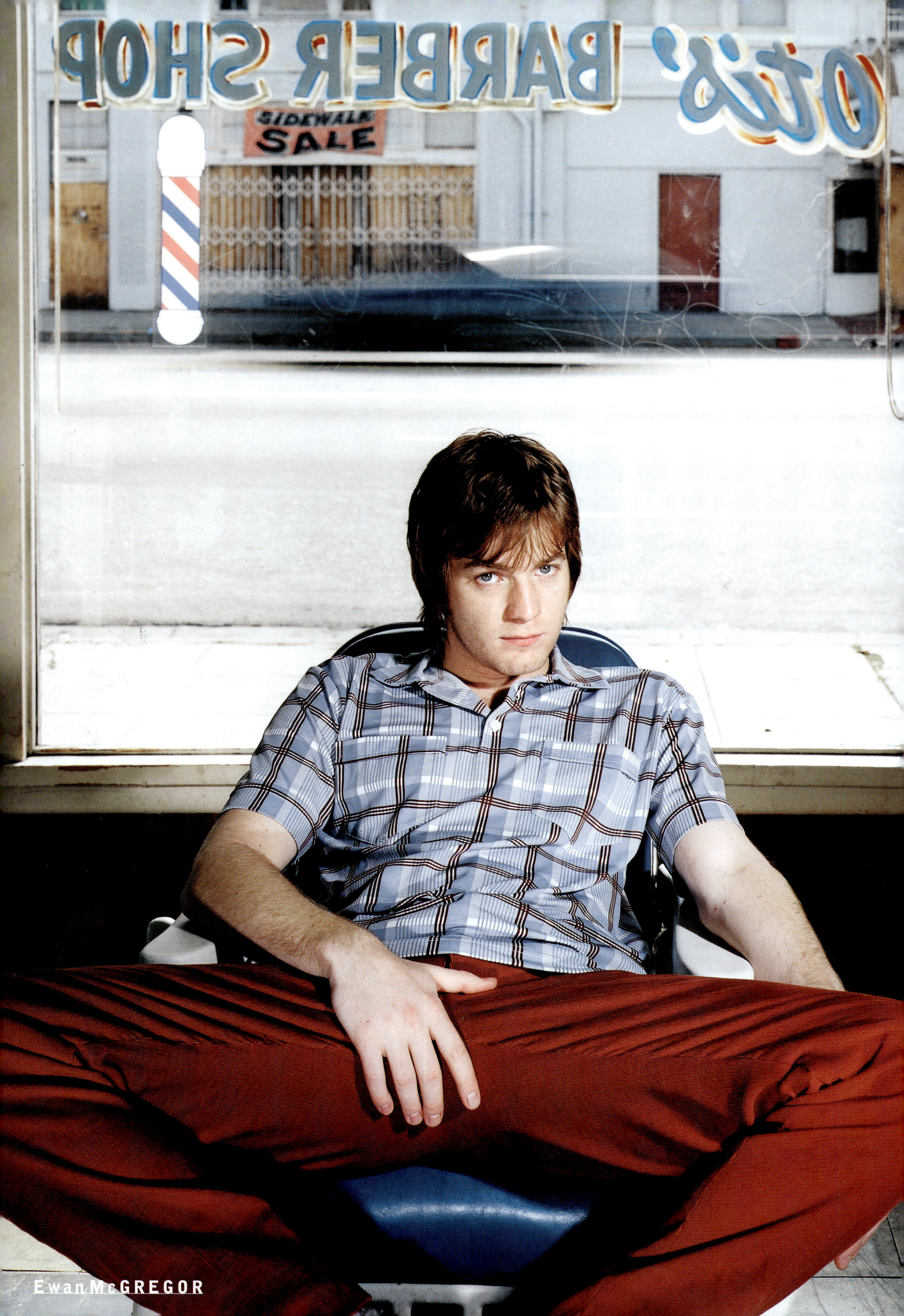

Ewan McGREGOR

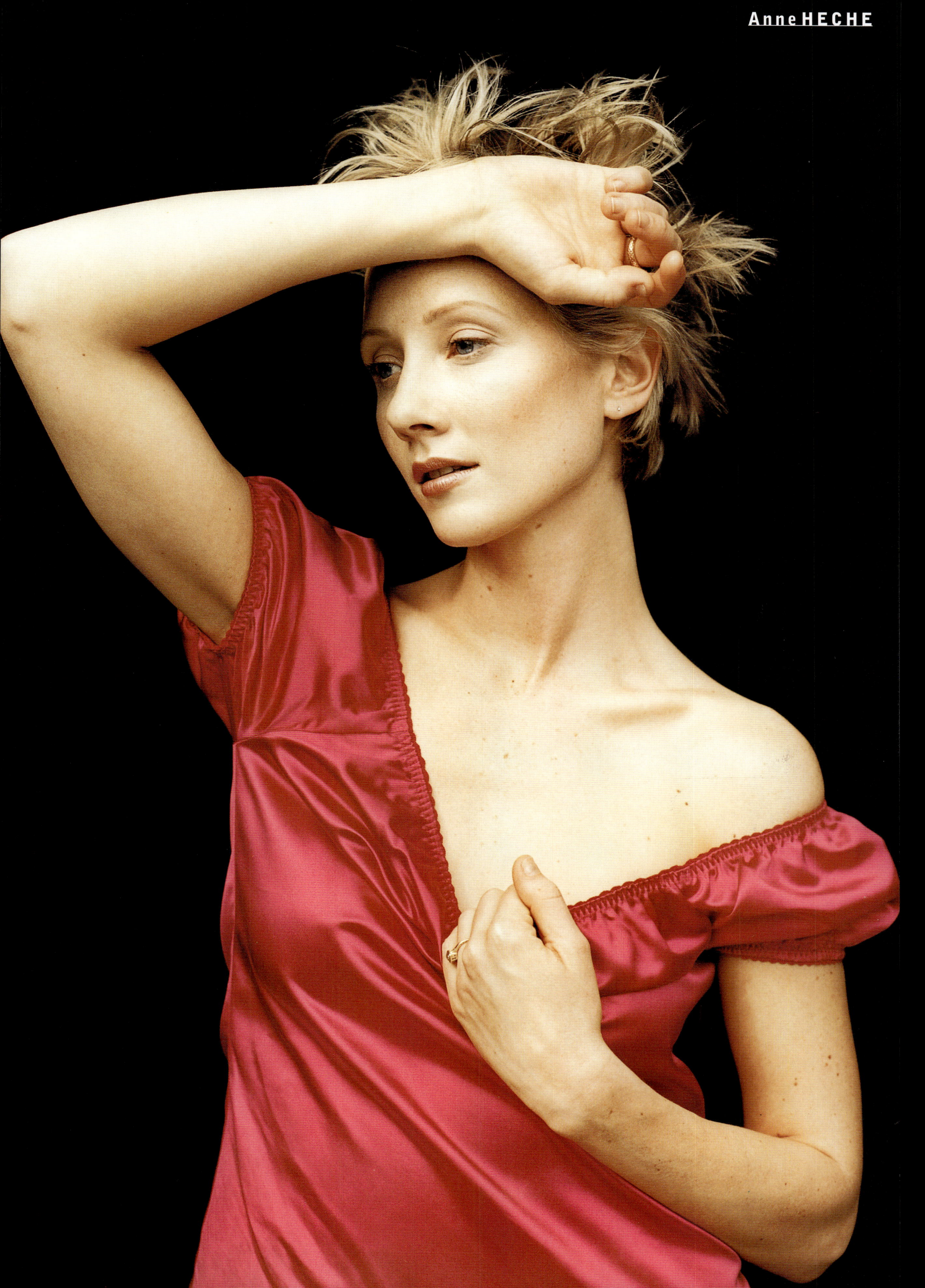

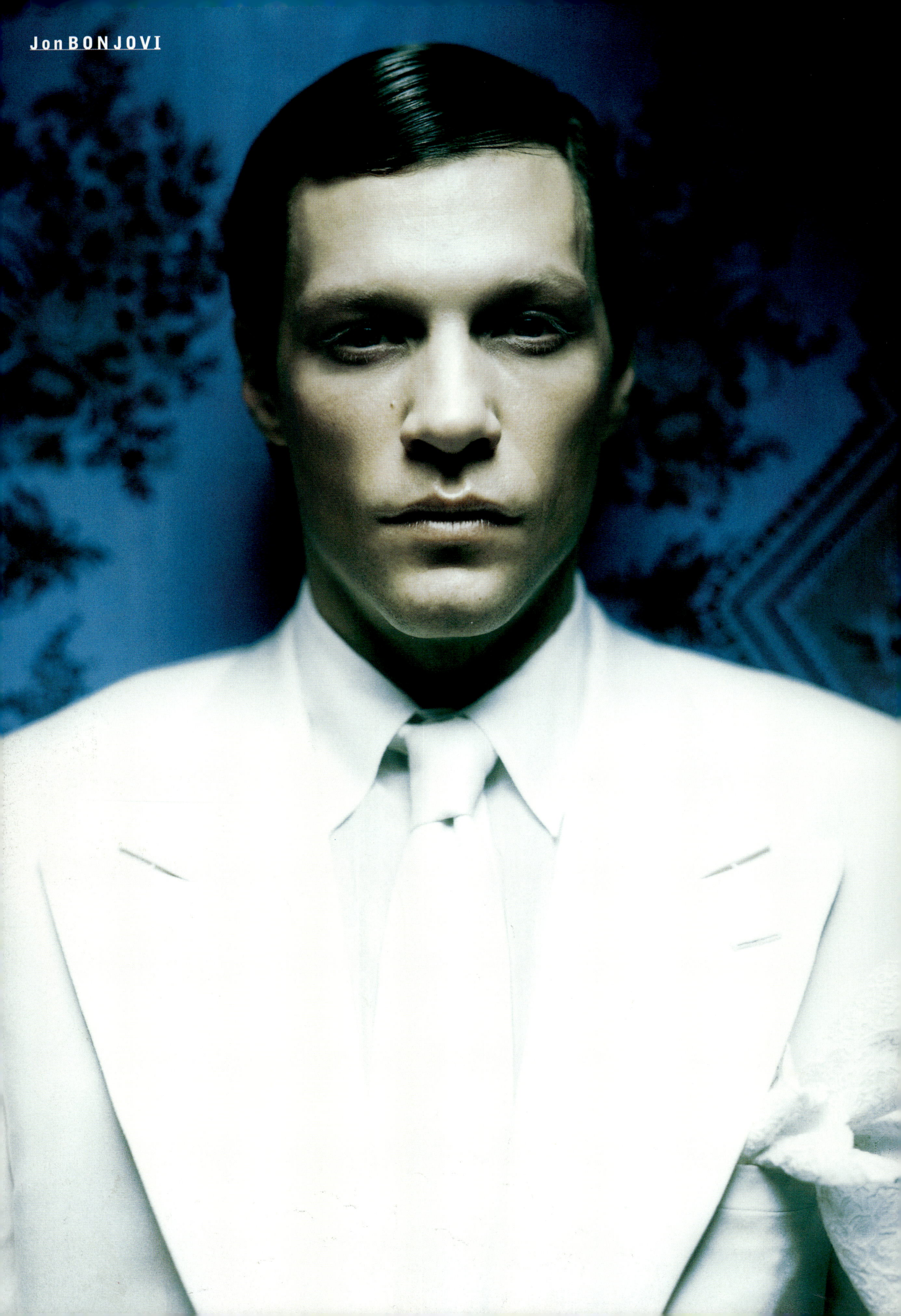

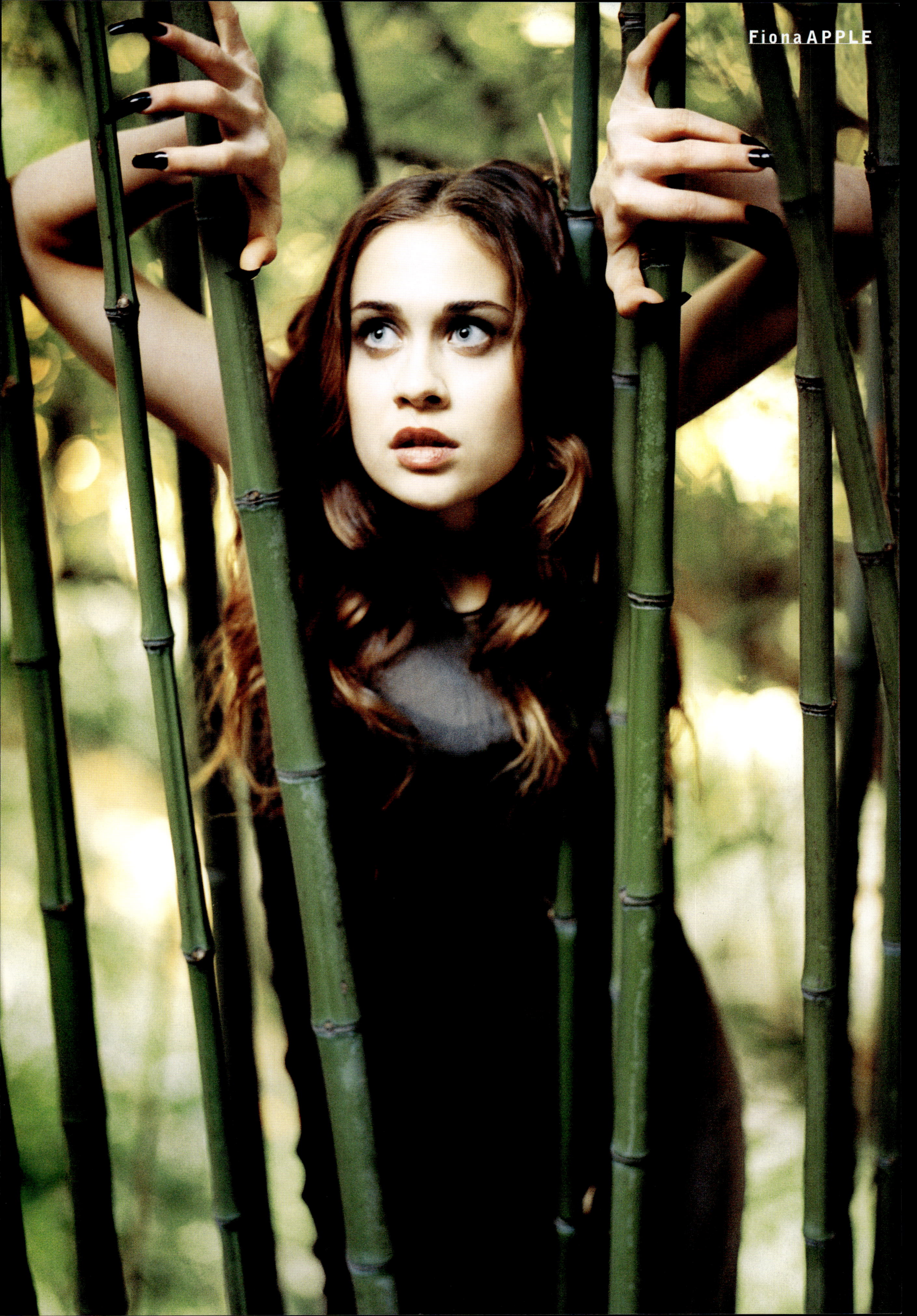

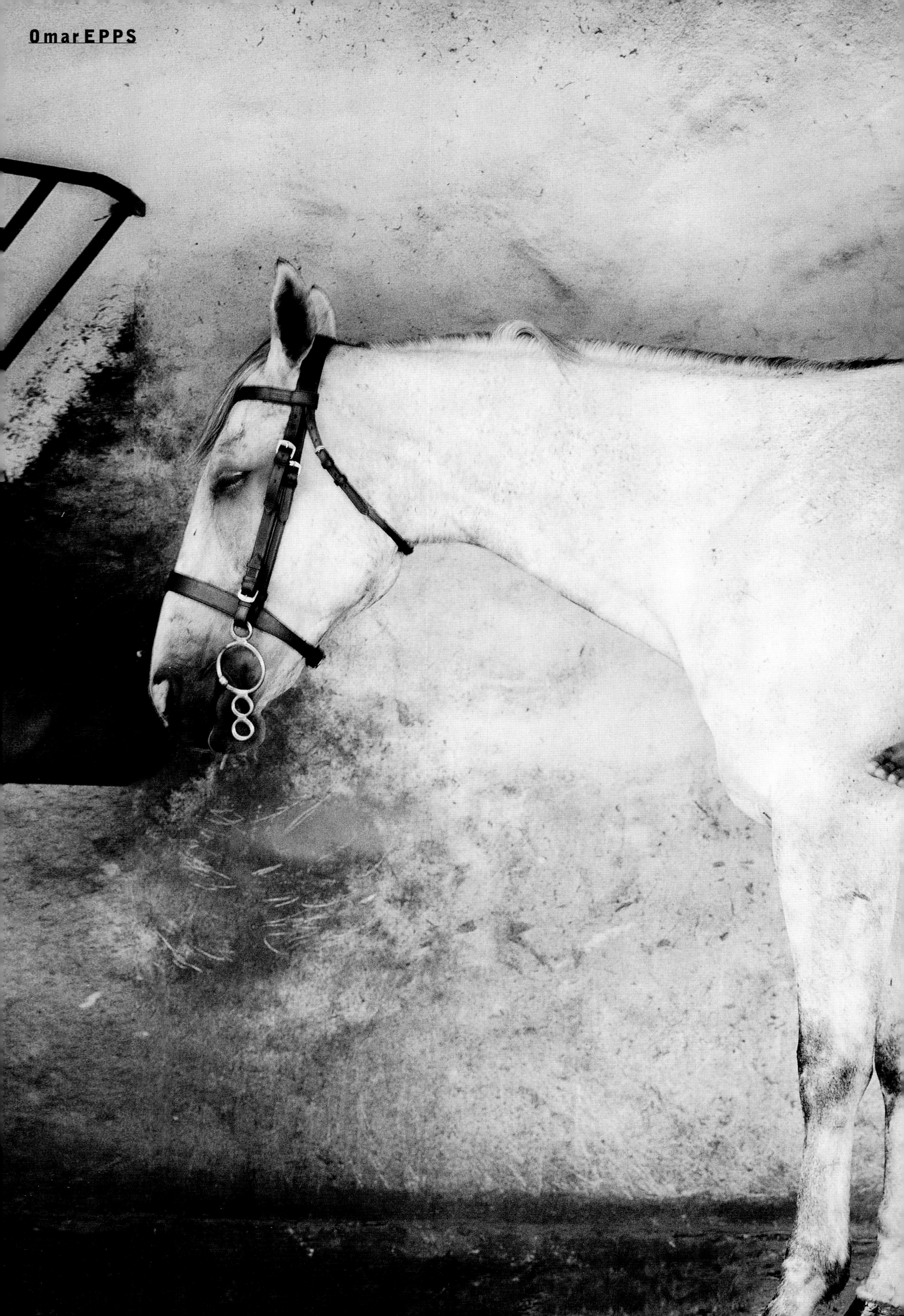

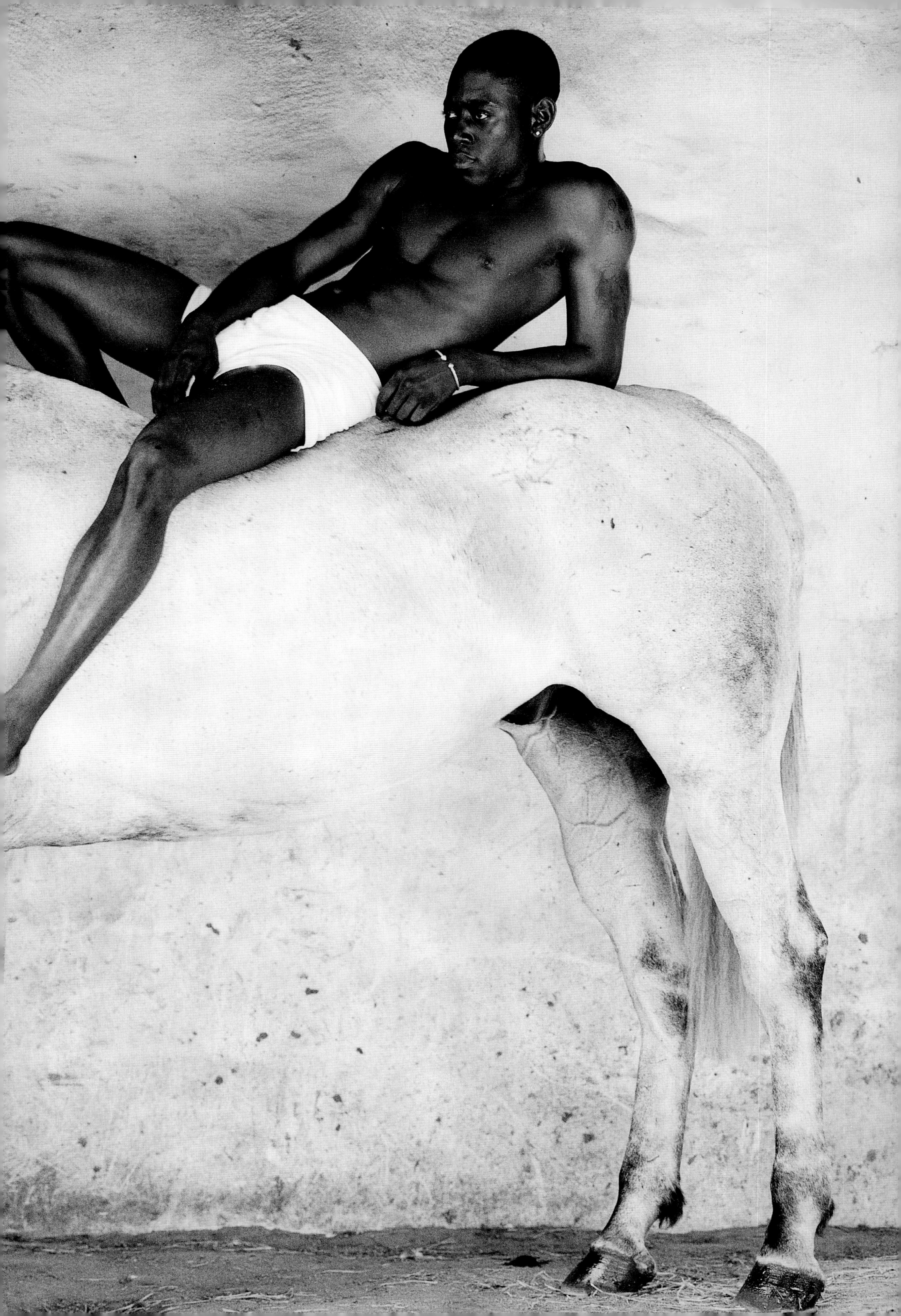

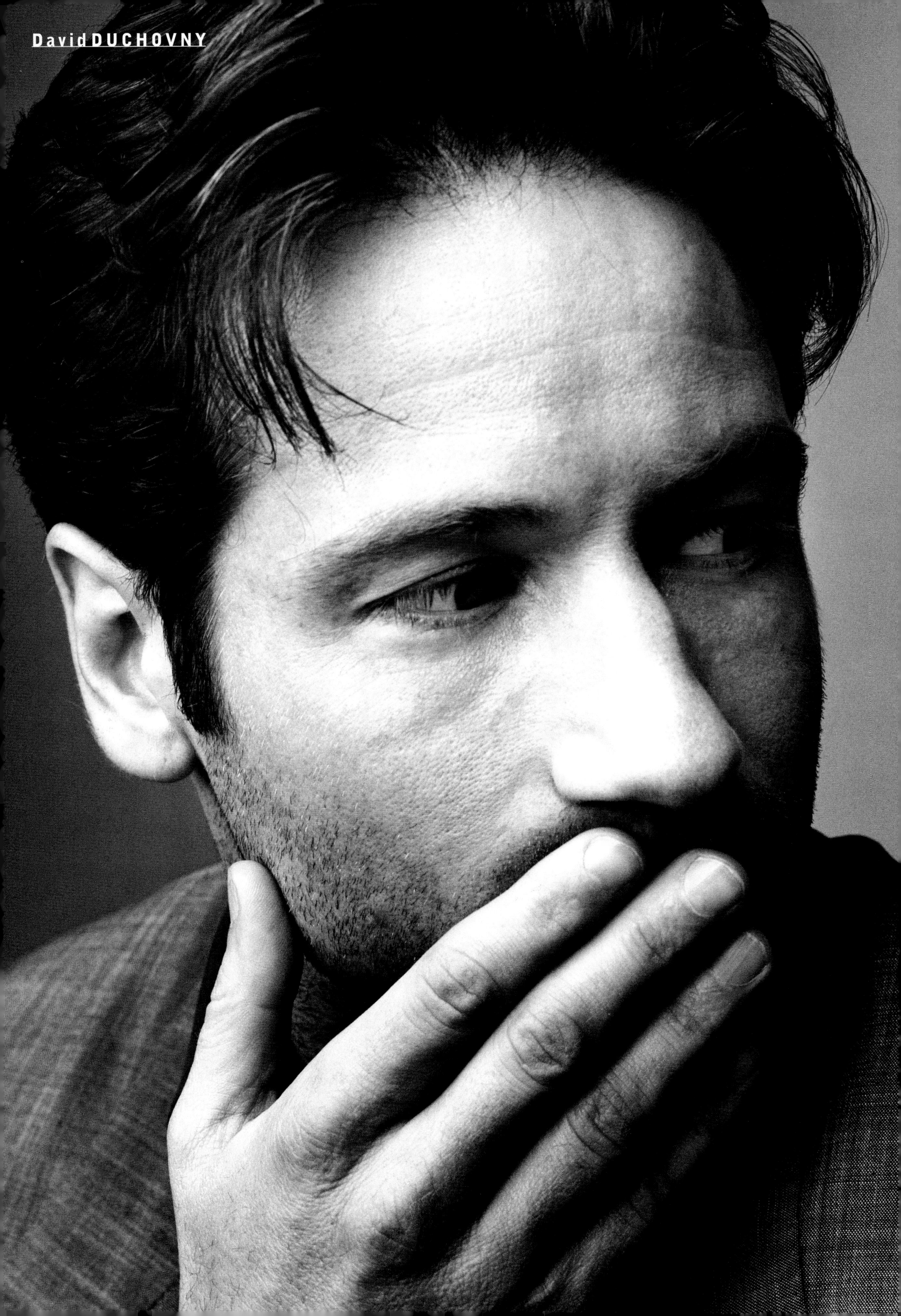

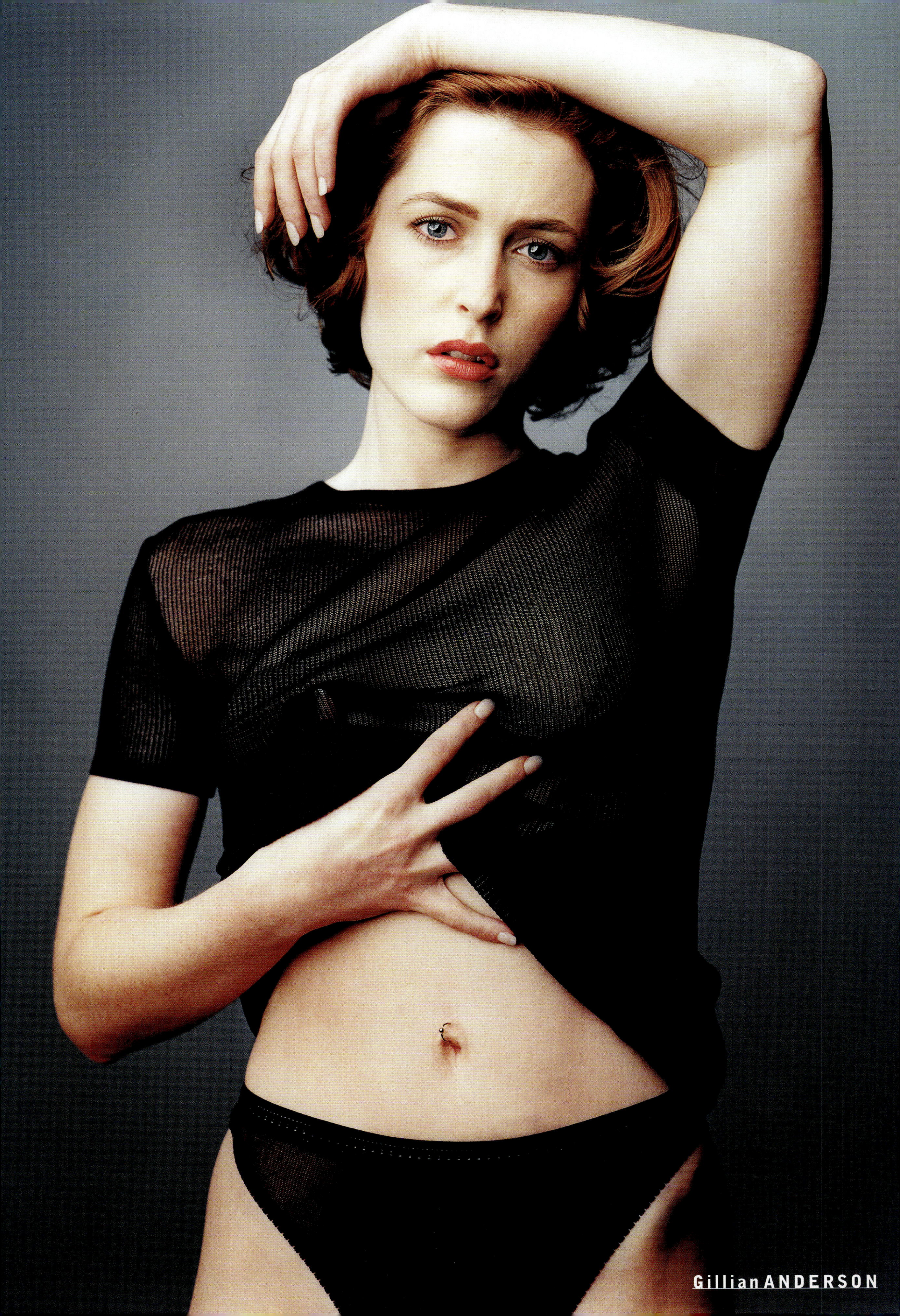
Gillian ANDERSON

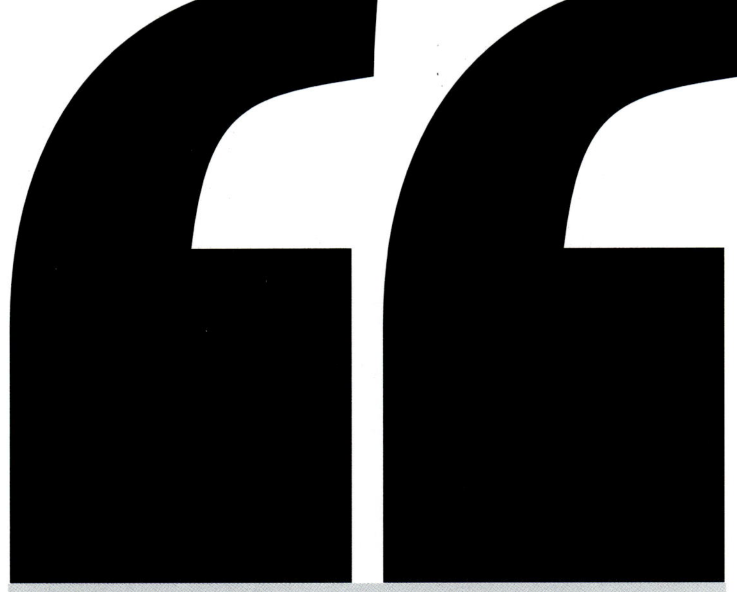

David Duchovny»

What are the oddest rumors you've heard about yourself recently? My driver said somebody warned him not to drive me because I was bisexual. I assured him that I wasn't. Someone said I was going to be the next Batman, and I was going to be in the sequel to 'Men in Black.' That my wife stopped dyeing her hair because she wants to get pregnant. There's one this week in a tabloid that says that the two women in your life – your wife and your costar – are fighting over you. It doesn't even mention [my dog] Blue? Let me read you a little: 'It's Hollywood's nastiest catfight! Wife and costar bare their claws over "X-Files" hunk!' That'd be me. ' "X-Files" heartthrob David Duchovny –' 'Hunk' *and* 'heart-throb' – so far, I like it! '– is caught in the middle of Tinseltown's nastiest catfight, between his wife, Téa Leoni, and his costar, Gillian Anderson. "Naked Truth" cutie Téa –' 'Cutie?' Nah. She's better than that. The tabloids also suggested that you and Gillian don't get on because you had a fling when the series started. Well. [Chuckles] That's a good theory. At least that shows some storytelling. So, tell me: What would David Duchovny never do? I don't think I'd ever be cruel to an animal. And I would never sing in public. Because I've got a horrible voice. I mean, Téa claims to like to hear me sing, and I think it's because I enjoy it so much. We sing in the car. She made me sing that song 'I'd Really Love to See You Tonight.' And I sing Bad Company's 'Ready for Love' and 'Feel Like Makin' Love.' So, basically you now specialize in bad 'Hey I'm ready for the sack, baby' Seventies songs? Yeah. And she air-drums. This is why we have tinted windows. A lot of people think it's because we're making fools of ourselves.

You're the eldest of three children. How often did you wish your parents had stopped procreating after you came along? For twelve years of my life I was an only child and received all the attention there was to give. Then that attention was split. Now, that was difficult. I suggest to any parent who is thinking about having another child to do it before your child reaches puberty. Because that's a point in a young adult's life where they need all the love and understanding they can get. It's a confusing, scary time. When most kids start feeling those changes is when they pick up drugs and act out. And thus, your now-famous period of adolescent rebellion? Well, yeah. That was part of it. That was part of my way of dealing with the fact that I felt like I'd been abandoned. Your daughter is a fixture on the 'X-Files' set. Does it encourage or inhibit her creative mind to know that bogeymen are made in a makeup trailer? Piper's curious about life in general. I think that comes in part from being around such a creative environment. We have prosthetic people and aliens walking around all the time. She wants to touch them, wants them to hold her. If there's someone who has an eyeball hanging out of their face, she'll reach out and say, 'Can I touch?' and they say [sympathetically], '*Ohhh*. I'm sorry.' Are there ways she reminds you of yourself? Well, Piper's very outgoing. When I was six or seven, something switched and I closed down quite a bit. But I have a very strong memory of myself at her age as being very alive and happy and social. And she's that way. She also likes to get away with things. There's this mischievousness about her that I completely identify with myself as a kid. Do you know that, except when you laugh, you always have a serious look on your face? People are always saying, 'You look so serious.' You know, I laugh a lot. But I take life very seriously. There are so many thoughts going on in my head at one time. If I allow them to run their gamut, they can take over. Part of my survival mechanism is about quieting those voices. When I'm looking that way, I'm either thinking or I'm in a space where I'm purposely not thinking.

Gillian Anderson»

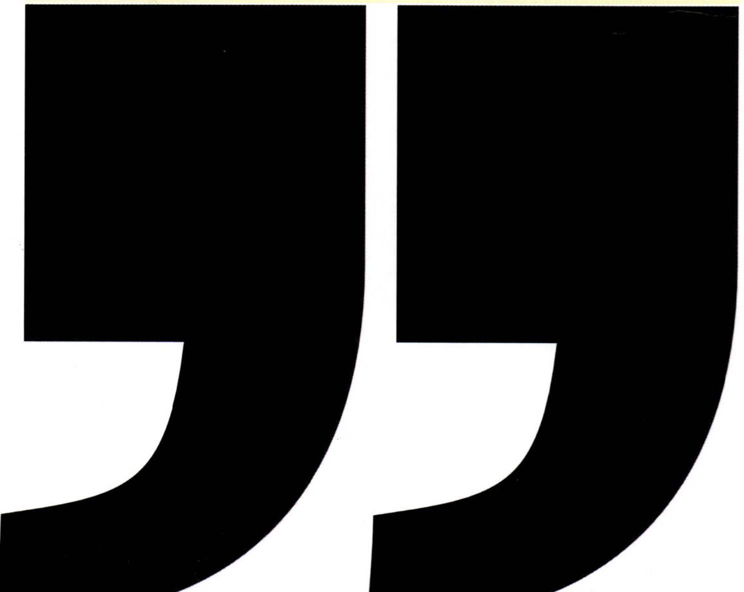

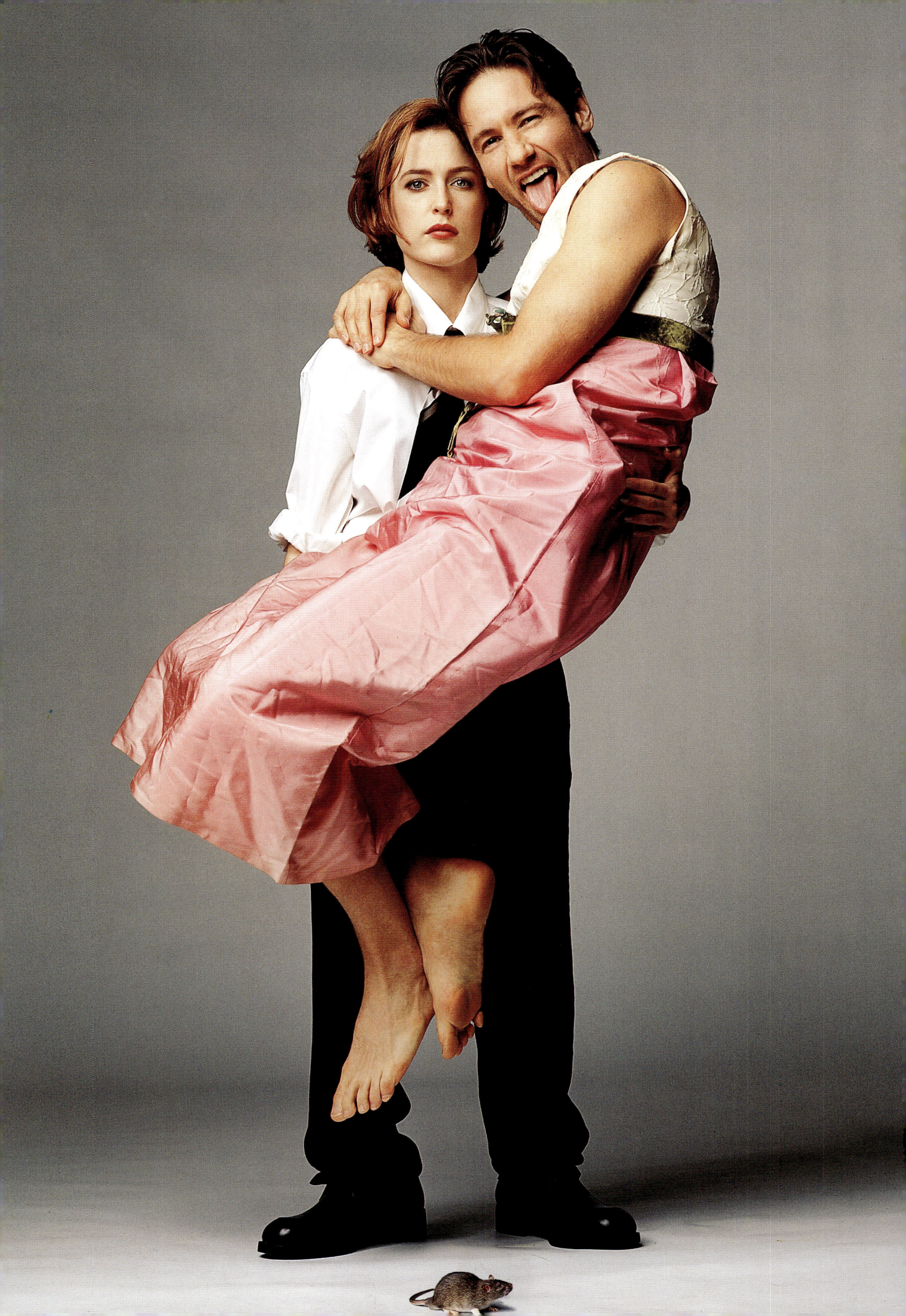

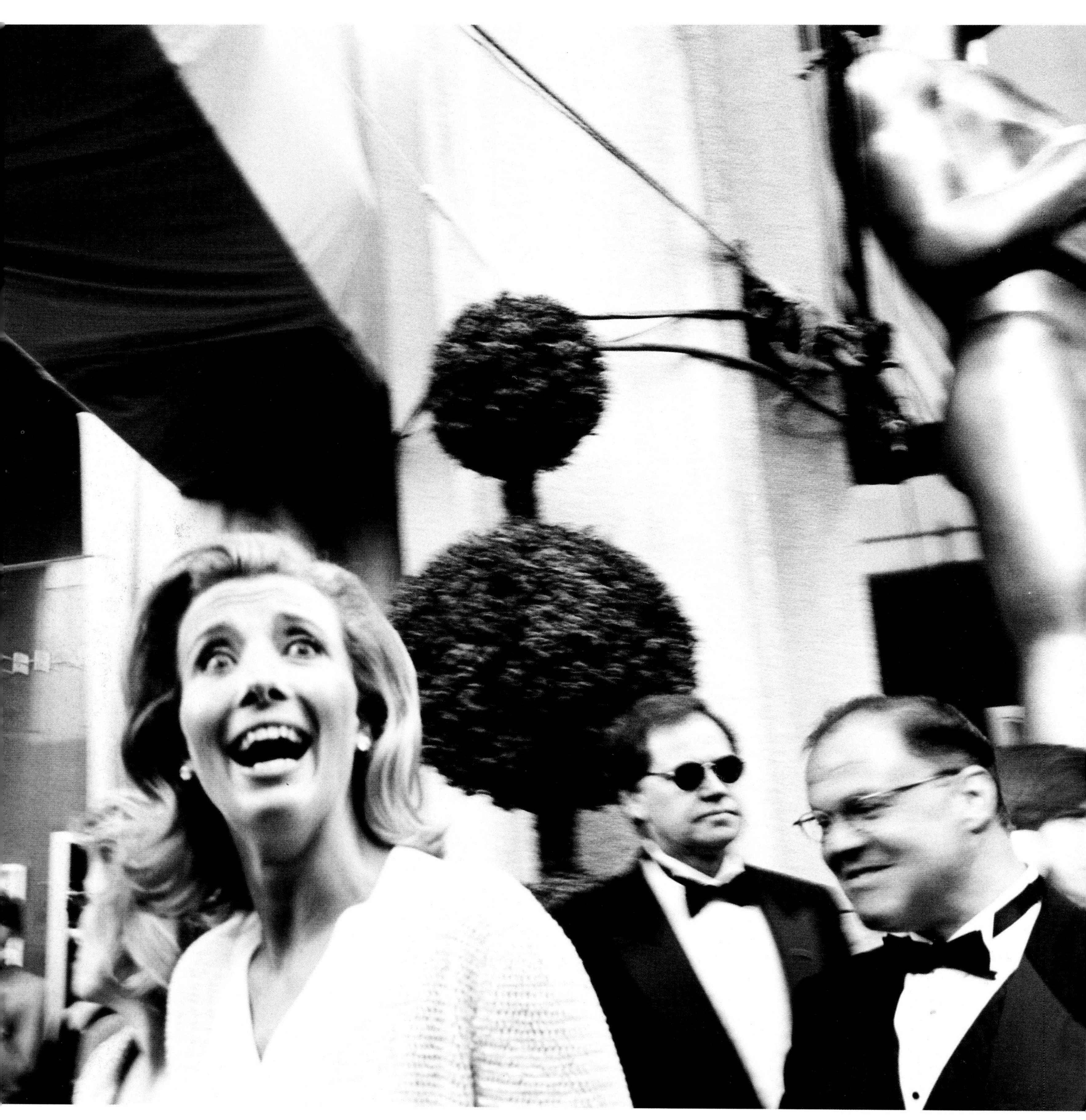

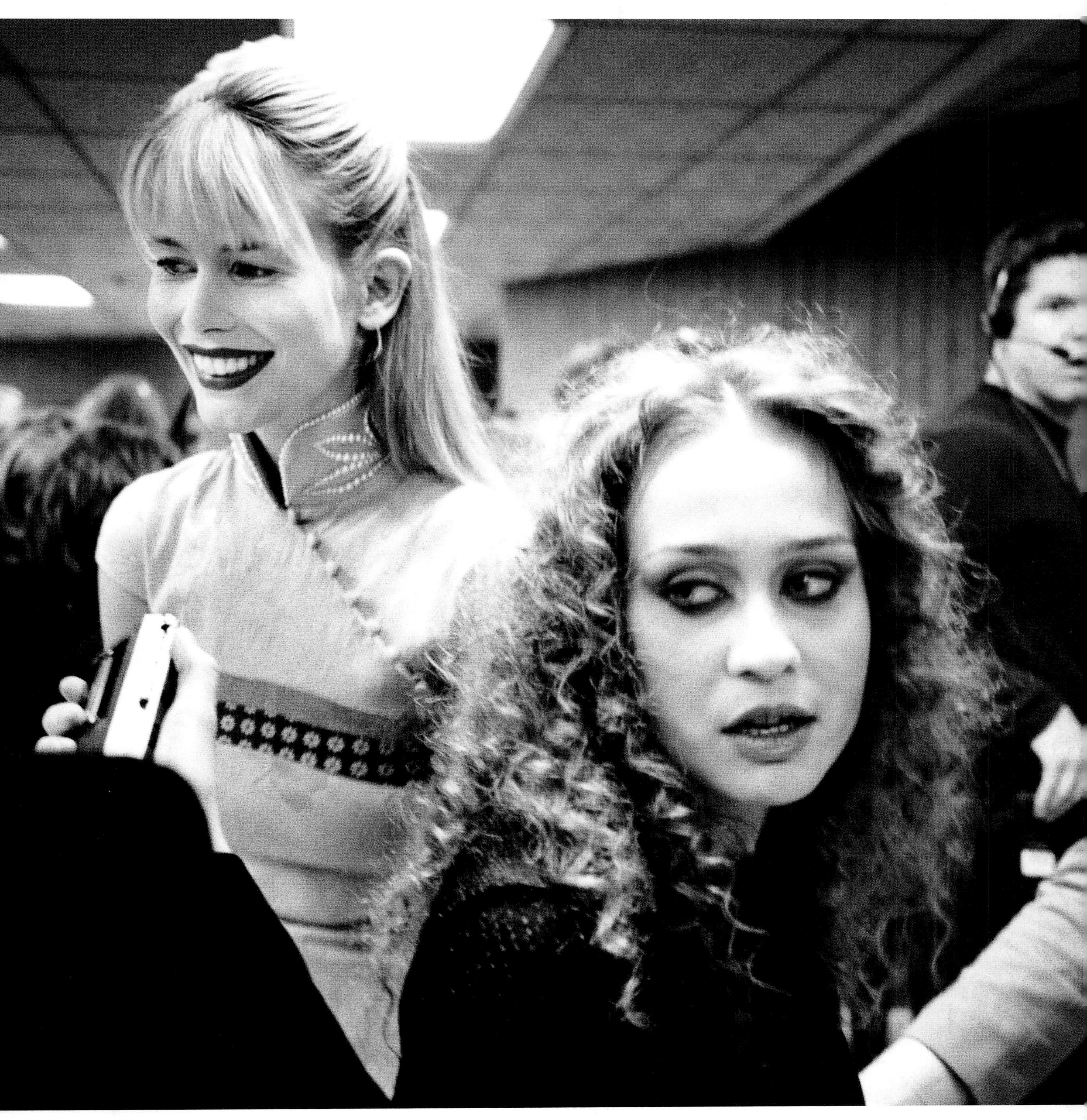

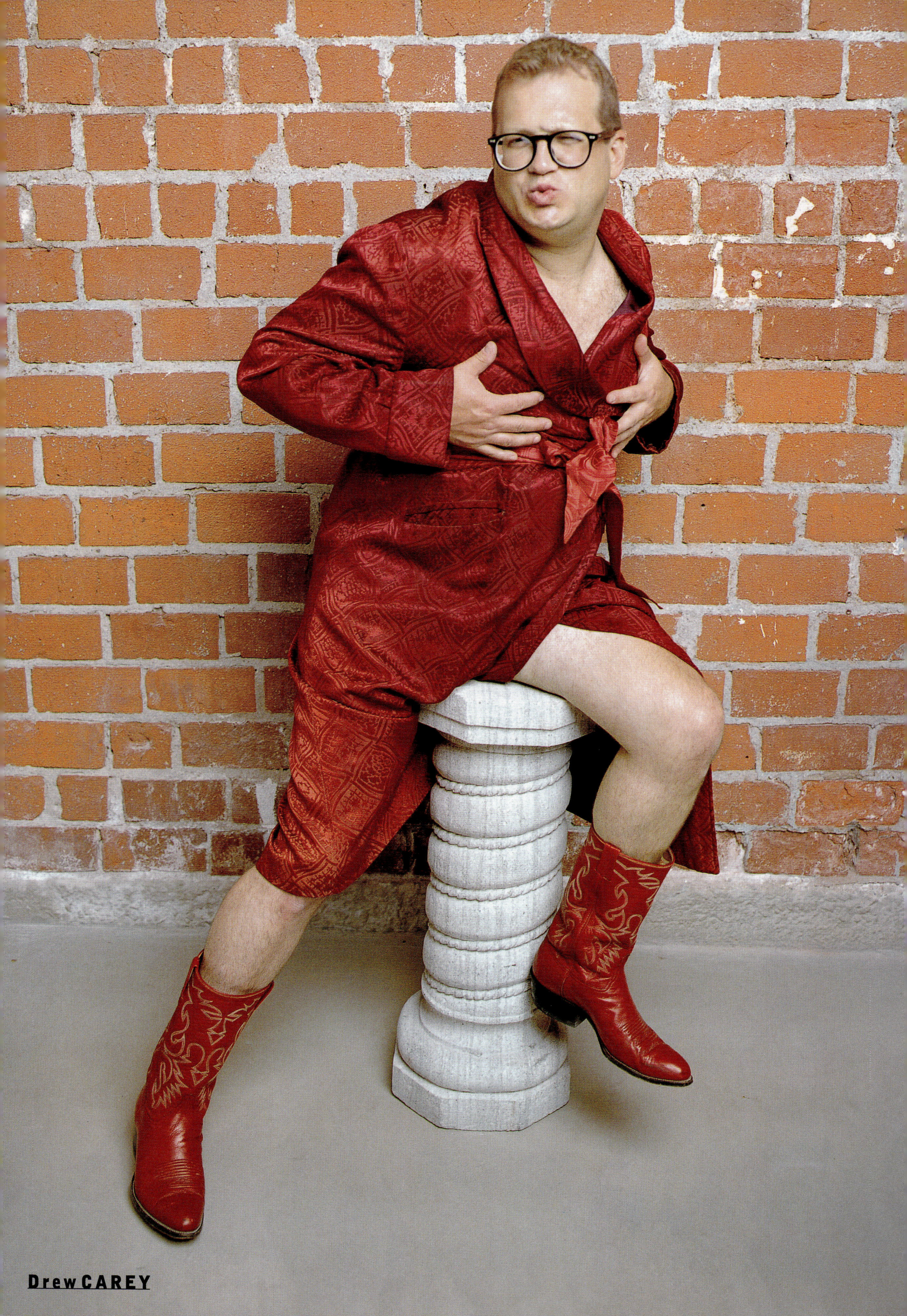

DrewCAREY

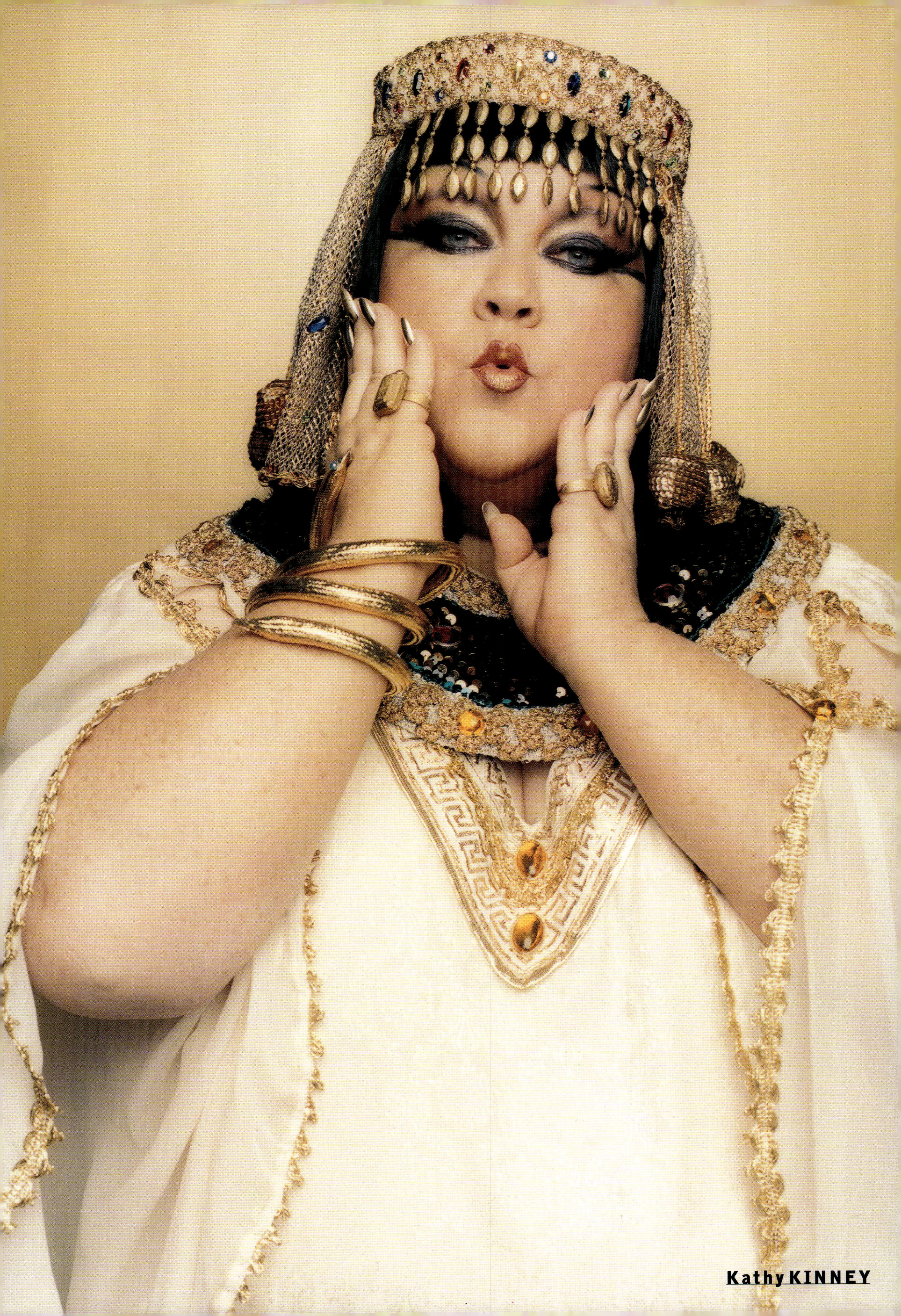

Kathy KINNEY

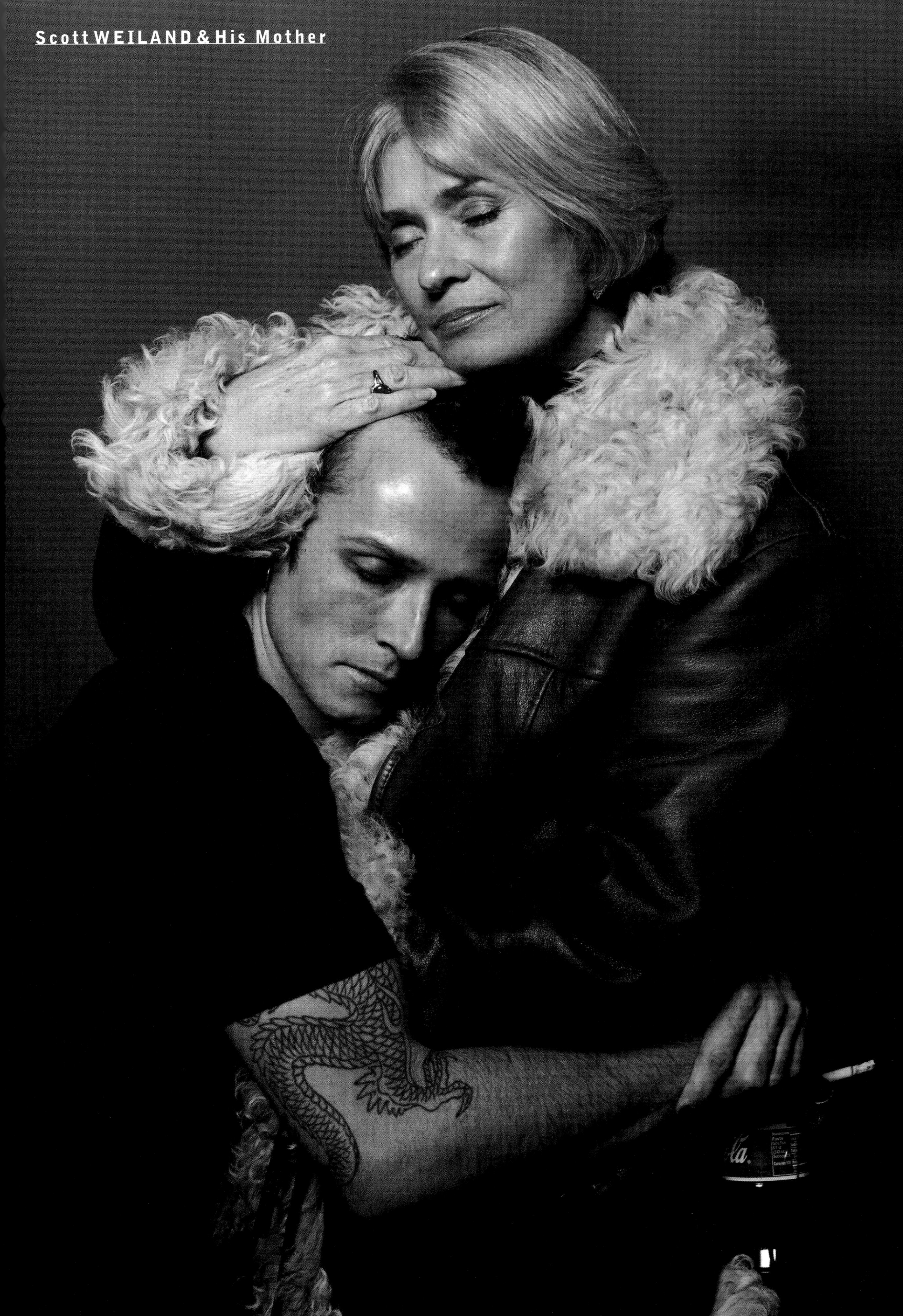

Scott WEILAND & His Mother

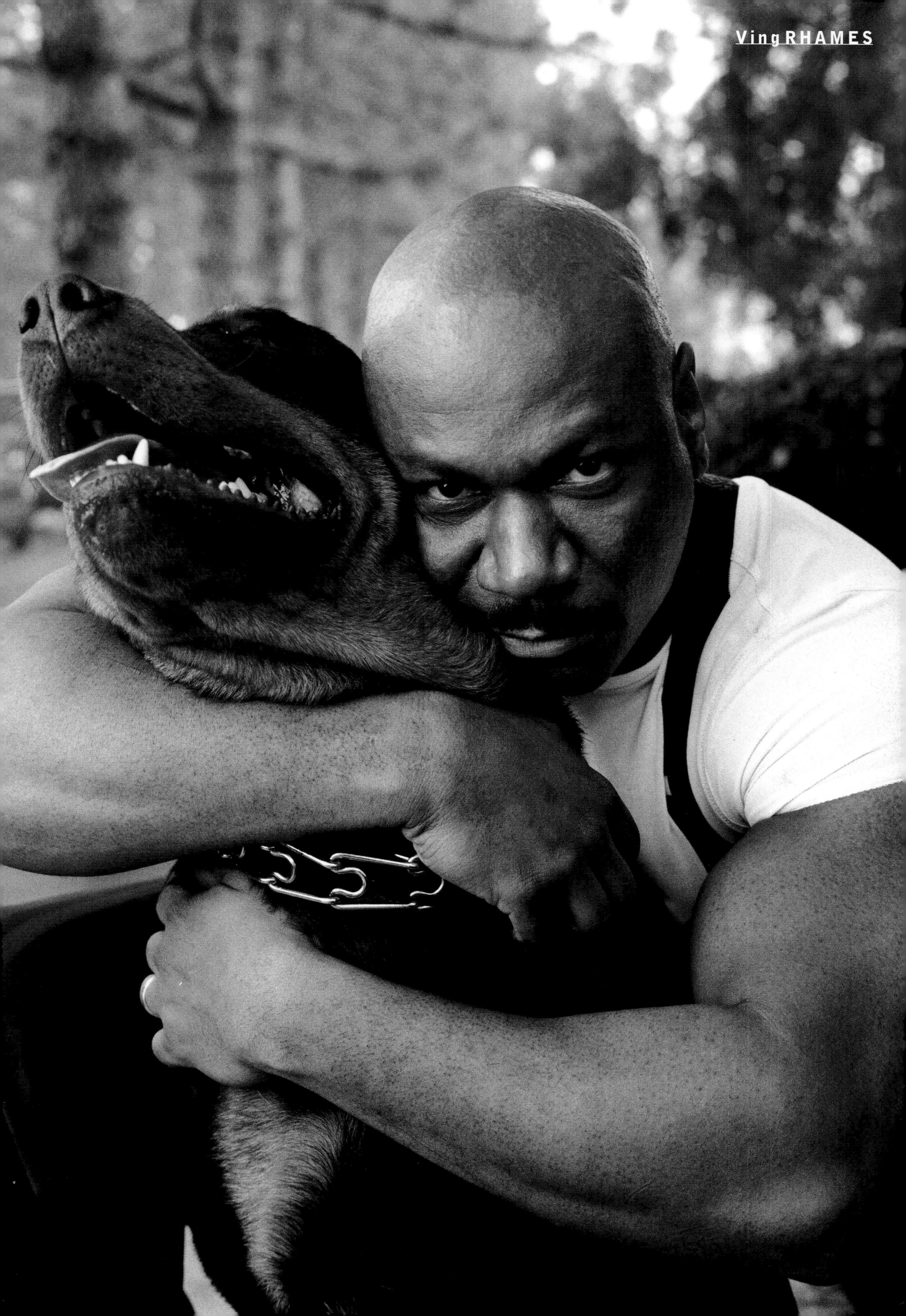

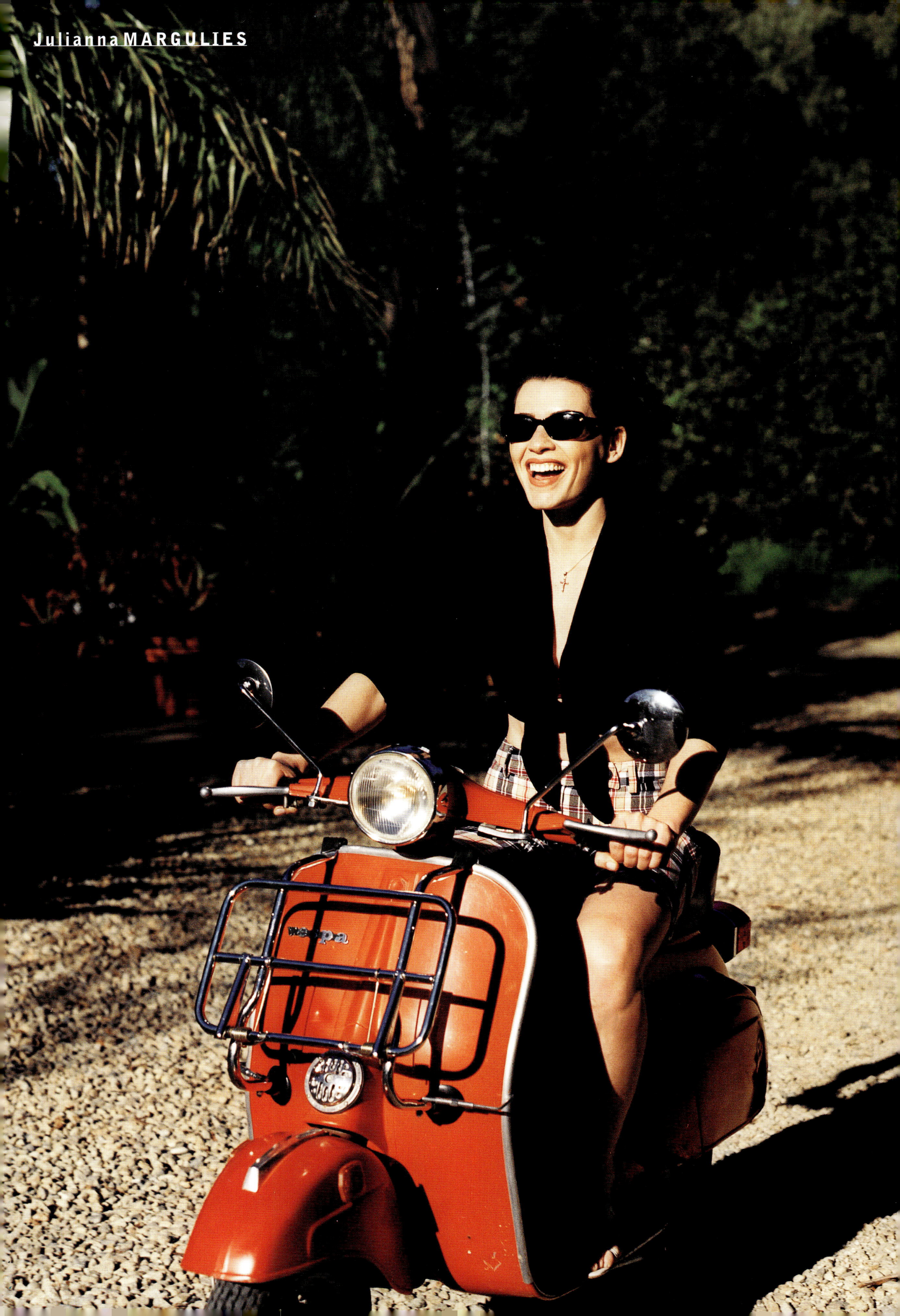
vespa

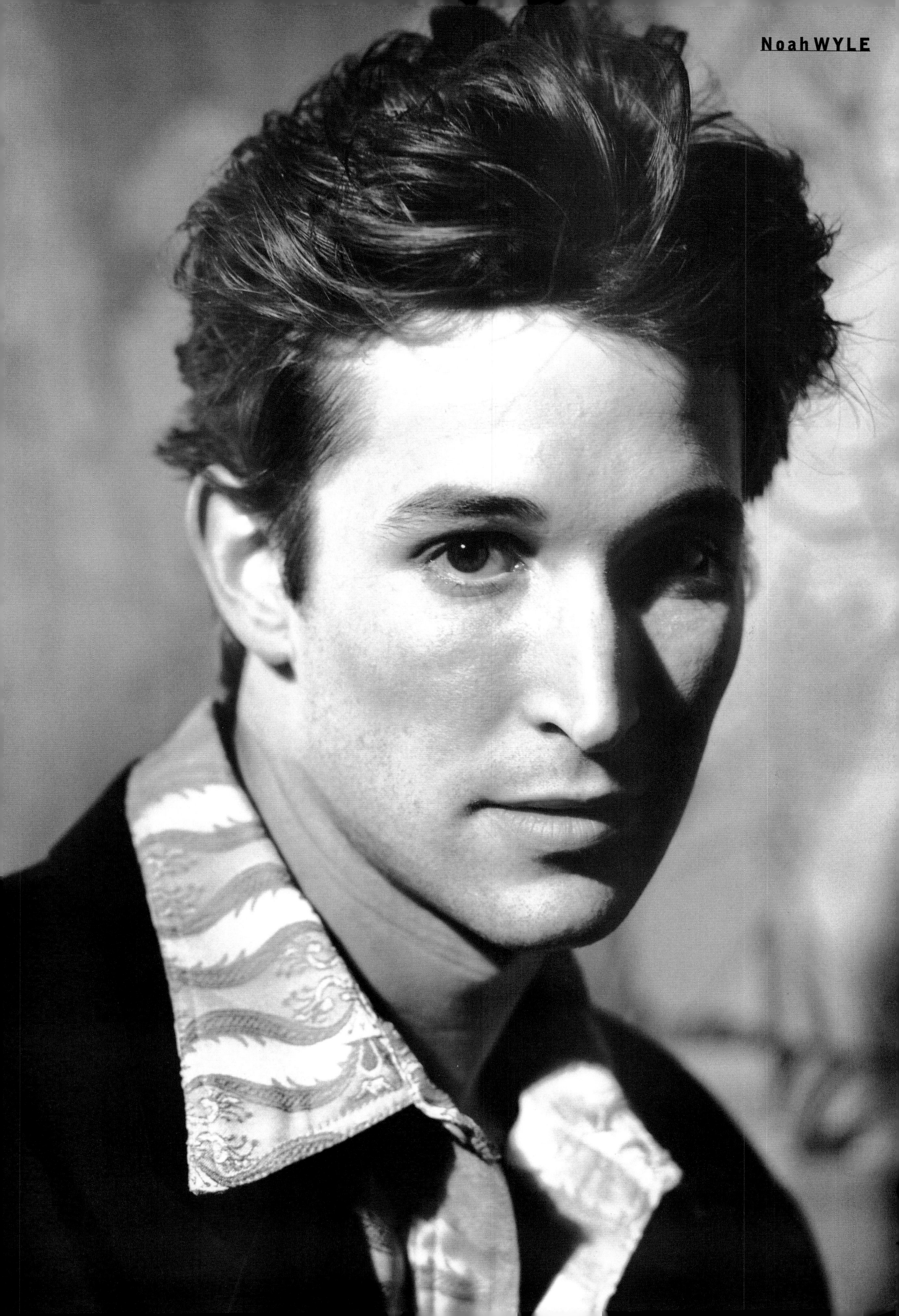

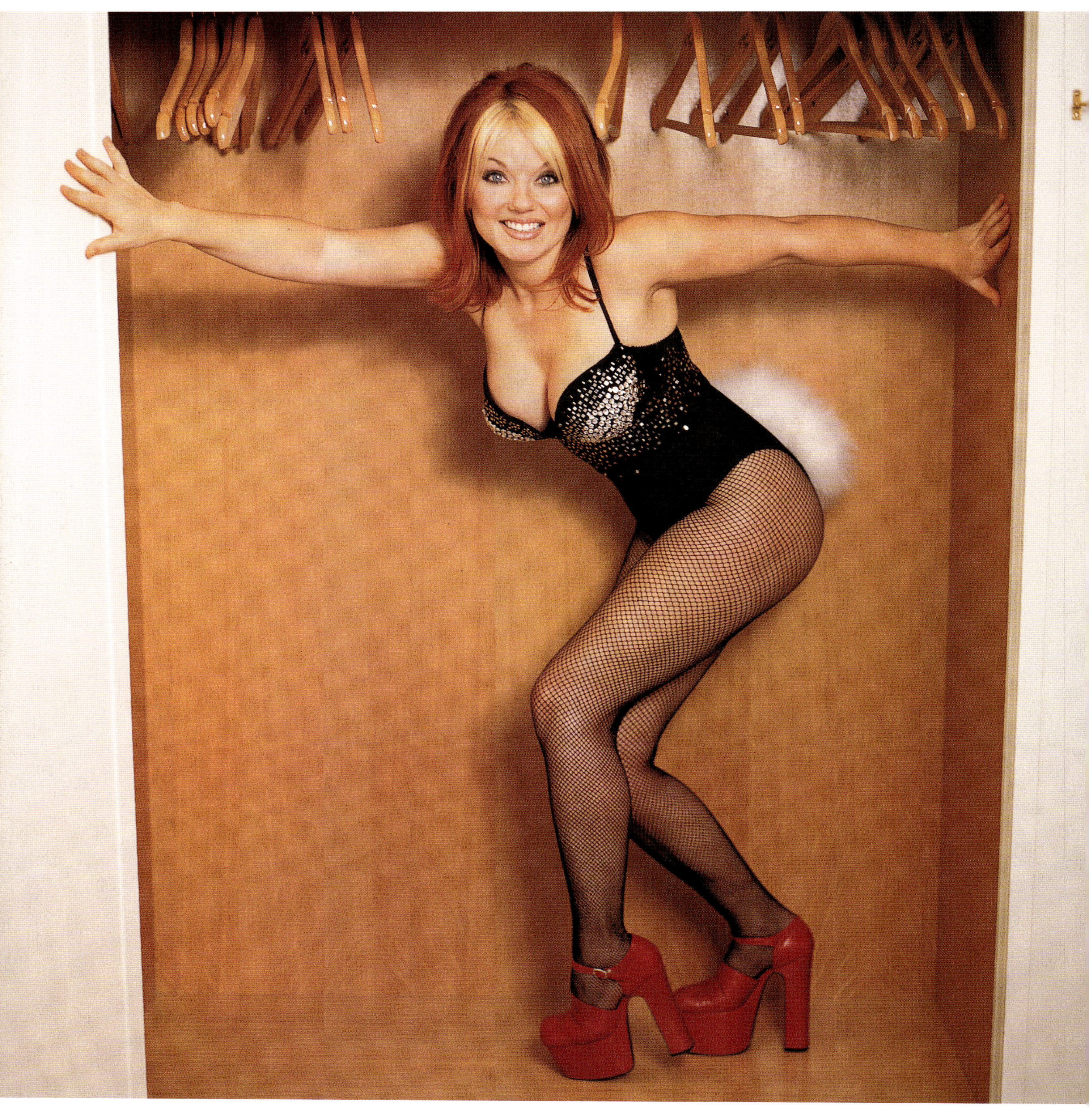

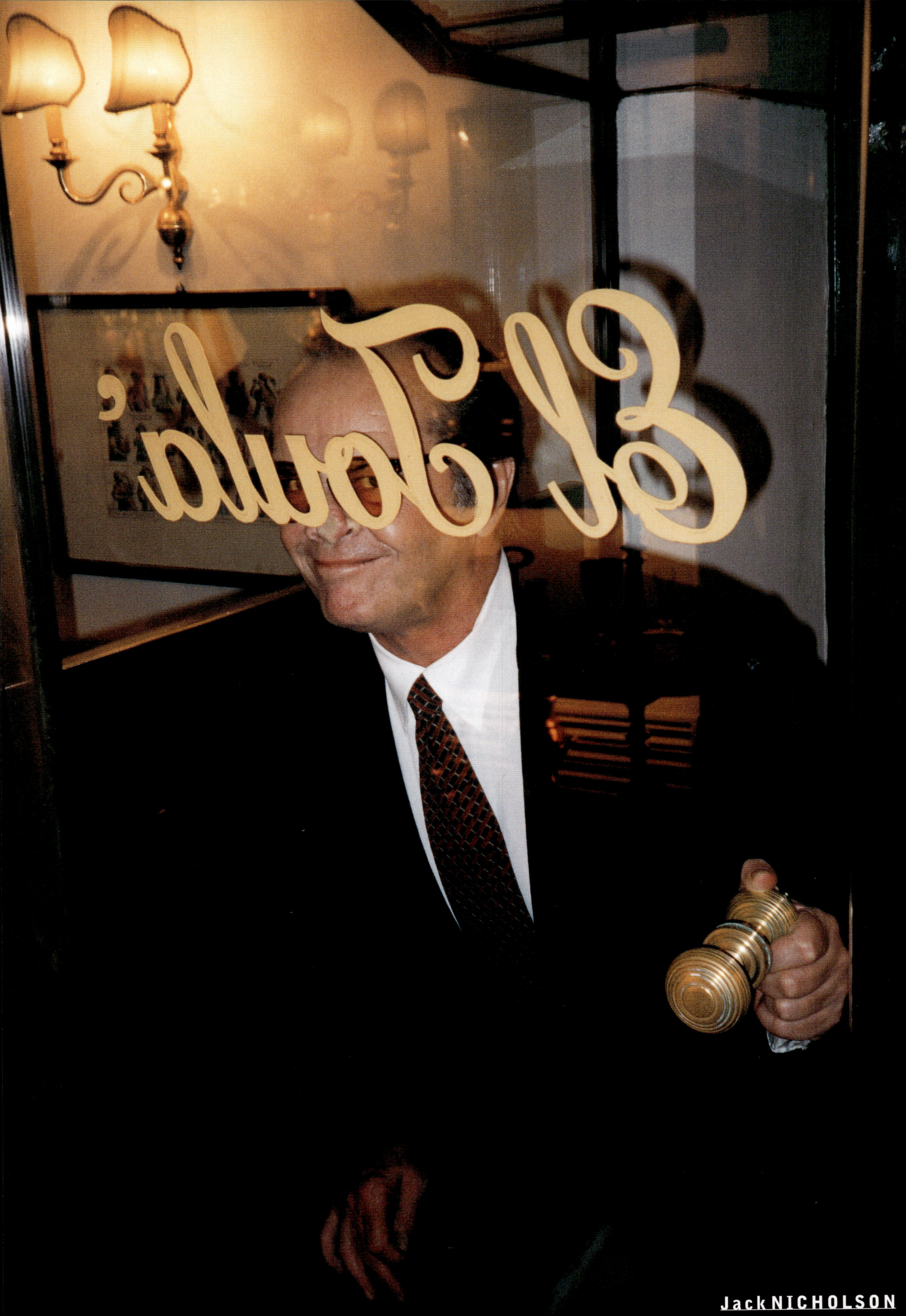

Jack NICHOLSON

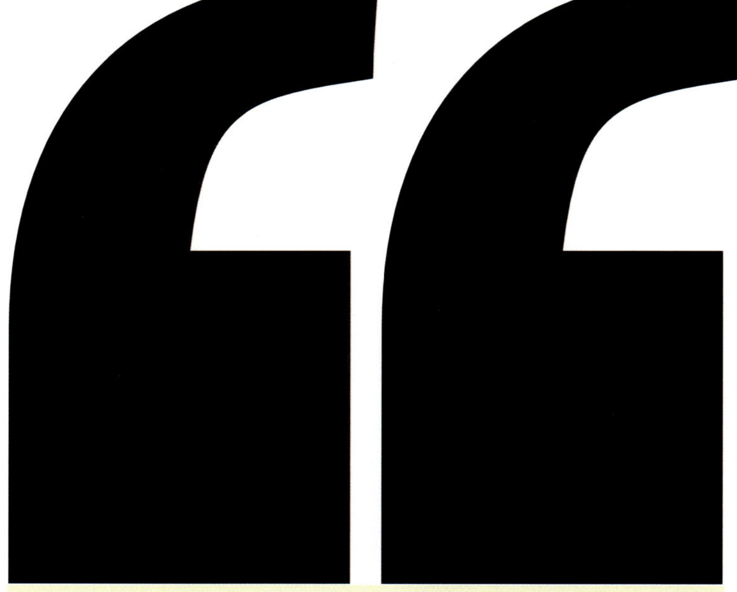

You're a guy who lives by his beliefs: You practice Buddhism, you give away a lot of money. And yet you, more than any other celebrity, are dogged by persistent, nasty rumors. Why? You can explain everything by karma. Whatever happens to me is the fruit of some previous action of mine. **My God, what did you do?** I don't know. But it's a great tool for learning. If what's being said is true, and it's negative, change your life. If it's totally untrue, it has no effect on me. **Most of the rumors are about sex. Do you think that you pose a sexual threat to some people?** I don't know. I just do my job. **You don't have an opinion about it?** You can't see what you represent to other people. You can't. The magician sees the trick, not the magic. **There was a period in your life when you chose sexually charged roles, in 'Looking for Mr. Goodbar,' 'American Gigolo'...** What twenty-five-year-old is not interested in exploring sexuality? **But you did it publicly.** Well, that's my job. Anything I do is public. Why shouldn't I make movies about what I'm actually going through? Just don't assume the actor is the character. My characters were constructs. It wasn't like I walked in off the street and that's who I was at the time. **But you did cultivate a bad-boy reputation for a while there.** I think it's probably true of all actors, in the beginning, that the instinct to act is that you really want to be somebody else. So you give yourself totally to it. And you've got to do the twenty-four-hour-a-day thing where you are the character, you're intoxicated with him, and it does become your obvious, surface self much more. There's a certain limitation to it. **Why did you want to be someone else?** I think most actors go into acting because there's a lot of self-loathing and confusion. The usual. Any impulse to be someone else is a distrust of who you are. **What did you loathe about yourself?** [Laughs darkly] You're into borderline questions here. You are someone I met ten minutes ago, and now you want to get into the deep, dark questions about my being? It's just universal stuff. It's hormonal; it's in society itself. Things aren't as they appear to be. They're not as you're told they are. And that tension creates a lot of anxiety. **Do you think that, in the Nineties, people still fear sexual expression?** I don't know. That was a long time ago that I did those movies; I think it ran its course. People don't want to see it anymore. It's curious, there was fairly little actual sex in 'American Gigolo.' It's quite a chaste little film. It's more the *idea* of it, the job description. That character, a hooker, is traditionally played by a woman. I think men did get really bent, and challenged, and threatened, that I played a traditionally female role. But I could identify with that character. He wanted to be more than he is. **Did being married change you?** You know what it made me realize? I really was good at it. Which surprised me. All the fear that I had was about loss – loss of self, loss of identity, loss of individuality, loss of freedom. In fact, the things I gave up, I gave up willingly. And I never felt better in myself. That doesn't mean the marriage was any good. But making the commitments, and living up to them, I felt great about it. And it does conserve energy, for sure. It defines things clearly. The marriage vow is essentially the same as a celibacy vow. **That usually happens much later in a marriage.** [Soberly] I'm talking about the nature of a vow, of making a real, serious

Richard Gere »

commitment. Essentially, I was never more of a monk – meaning focused and clear – than when I was married. Although we clearly had a sexual relationship. But the level of commitment for me was just the same as if I had made a vow to be a monk. **Because it's a vow to cut out all other women?** Because it's vowing to spiritualize everything. That's the way I saw it. To become selfless within that commitment. In many ways, I did some of my best work creatively when I was married. Although I was miserable. But the focusing of energy was curious. **It was miserable?** [Hedging] No, no. *Masterful.* **I'm a little confused about something. Isn't the end result of Buddhist practice to become a monk?** No. Being a monk is a strategy. There's nothing that's inherently higher about becoming a monk than anything else. In fact, it's easier, because you can harness internal energies, chakras, more easily if you're not in a sexual relationship. But it's impossible for me. I've never been strong enough to say, 'I'm going to be celibate for the rest of my life.' That would be a joke.

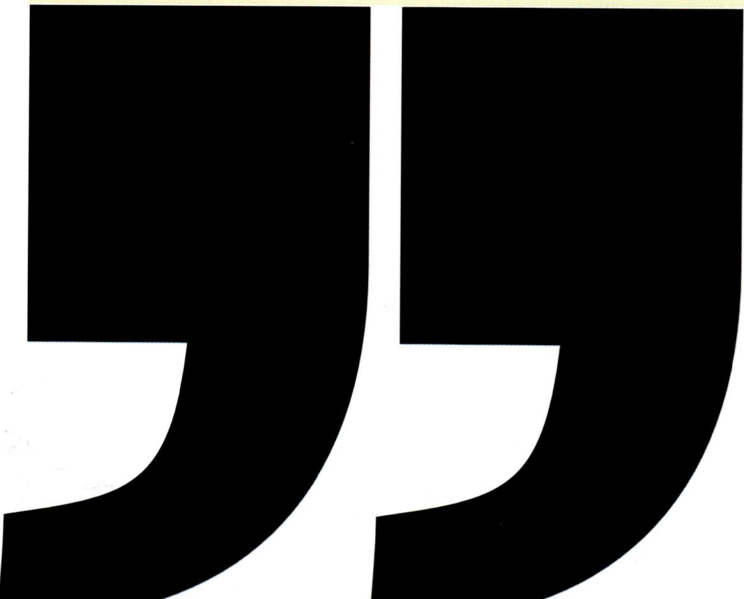

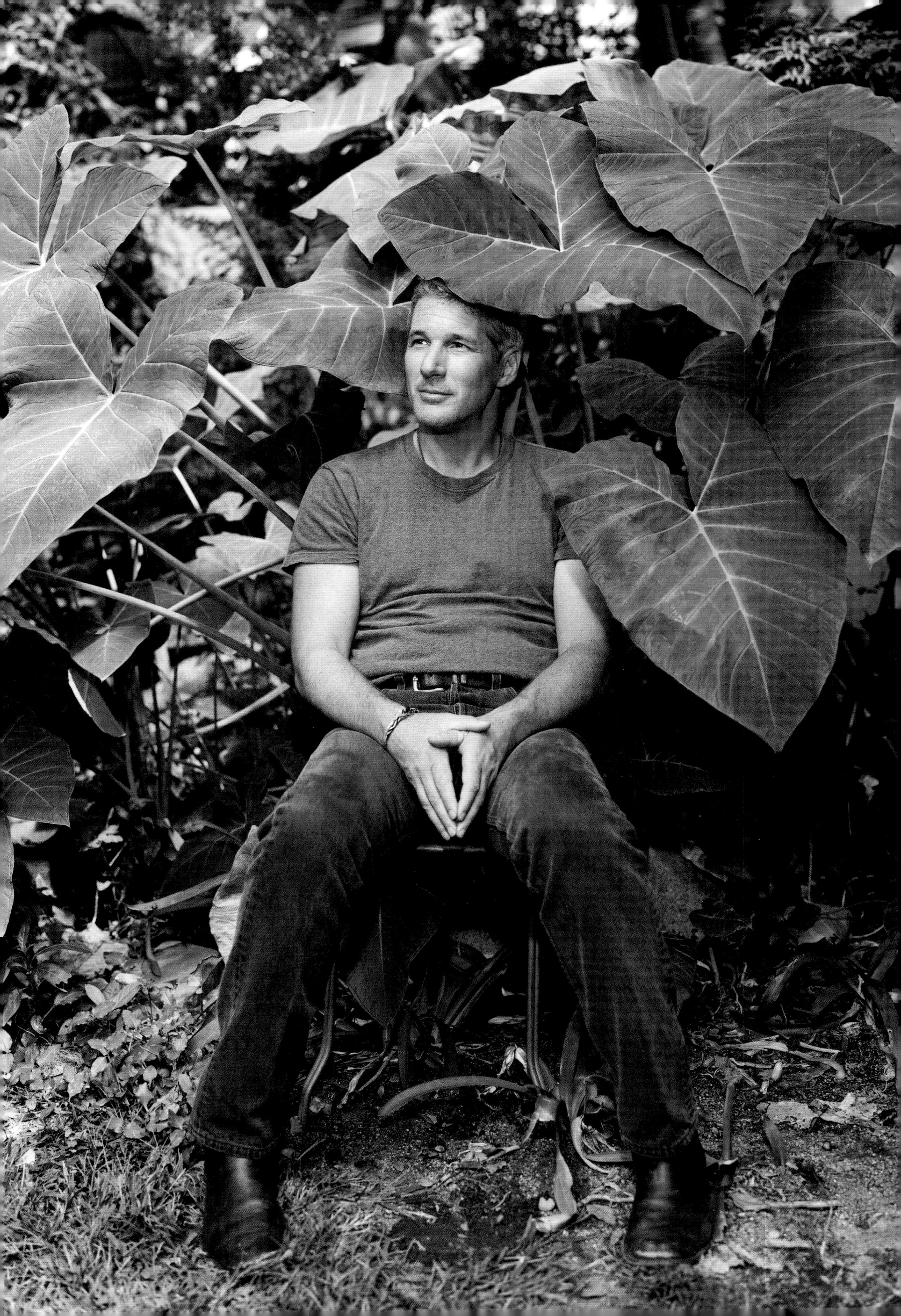

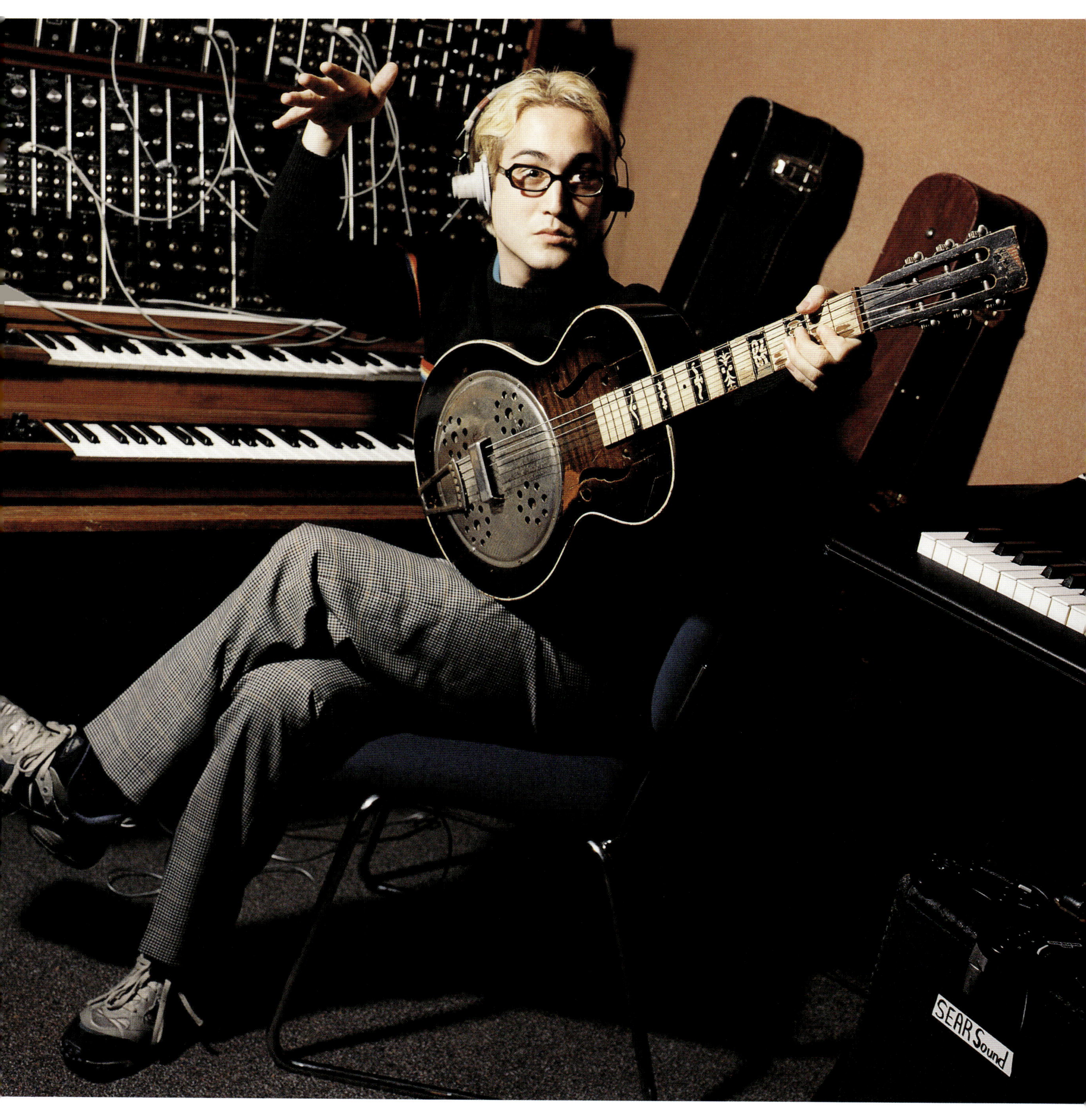
SEAR Sound

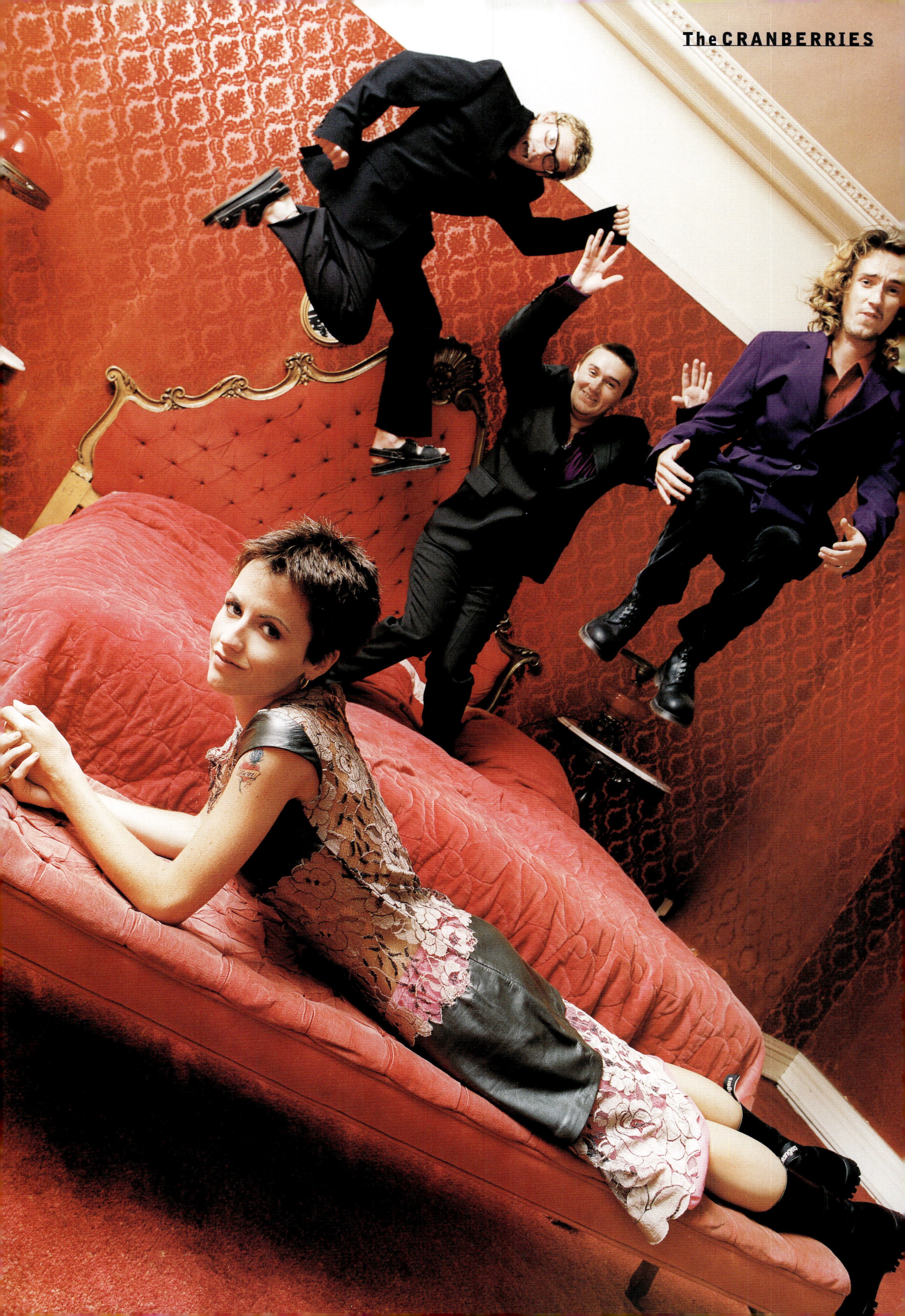

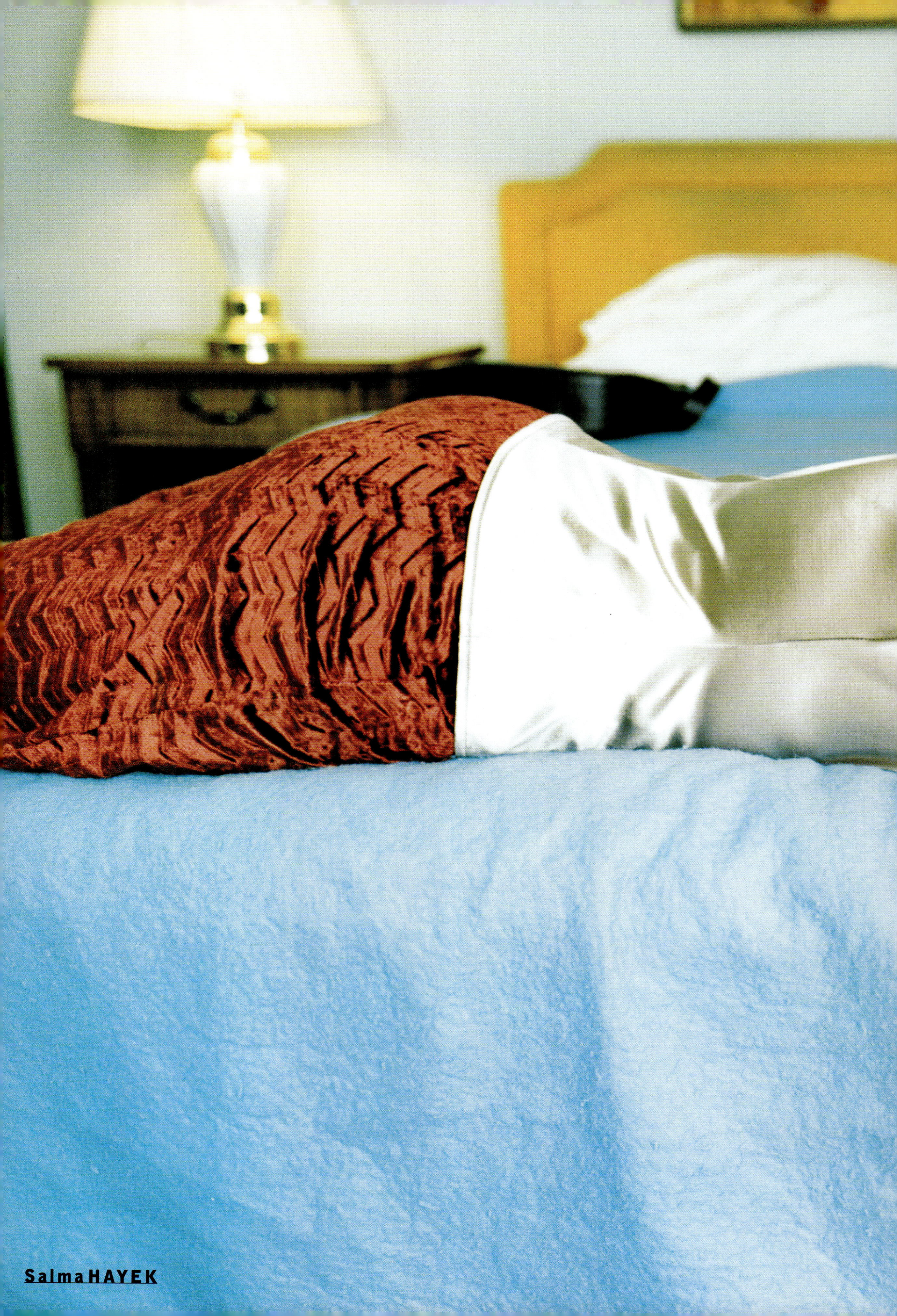

Salma HAYEK

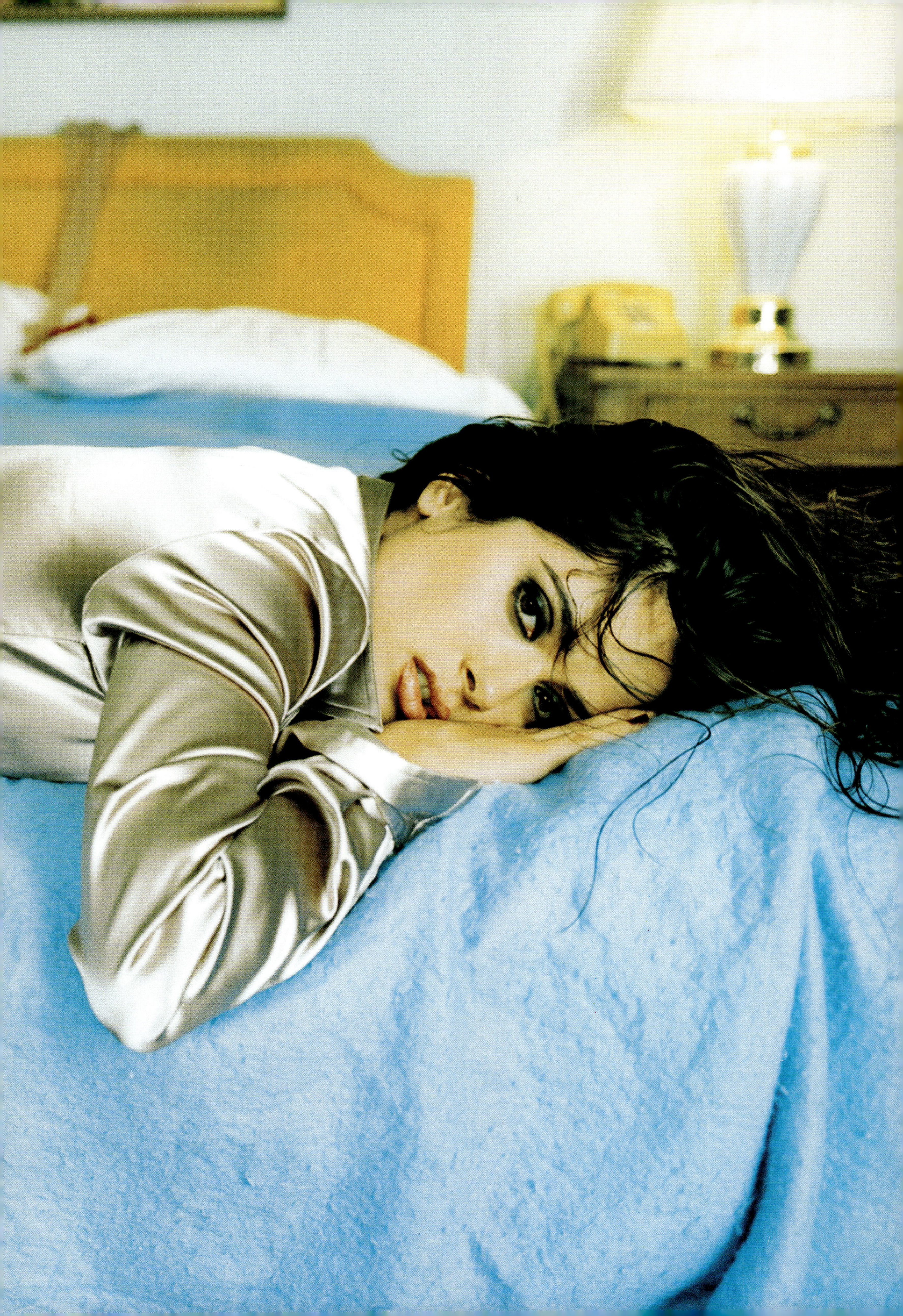

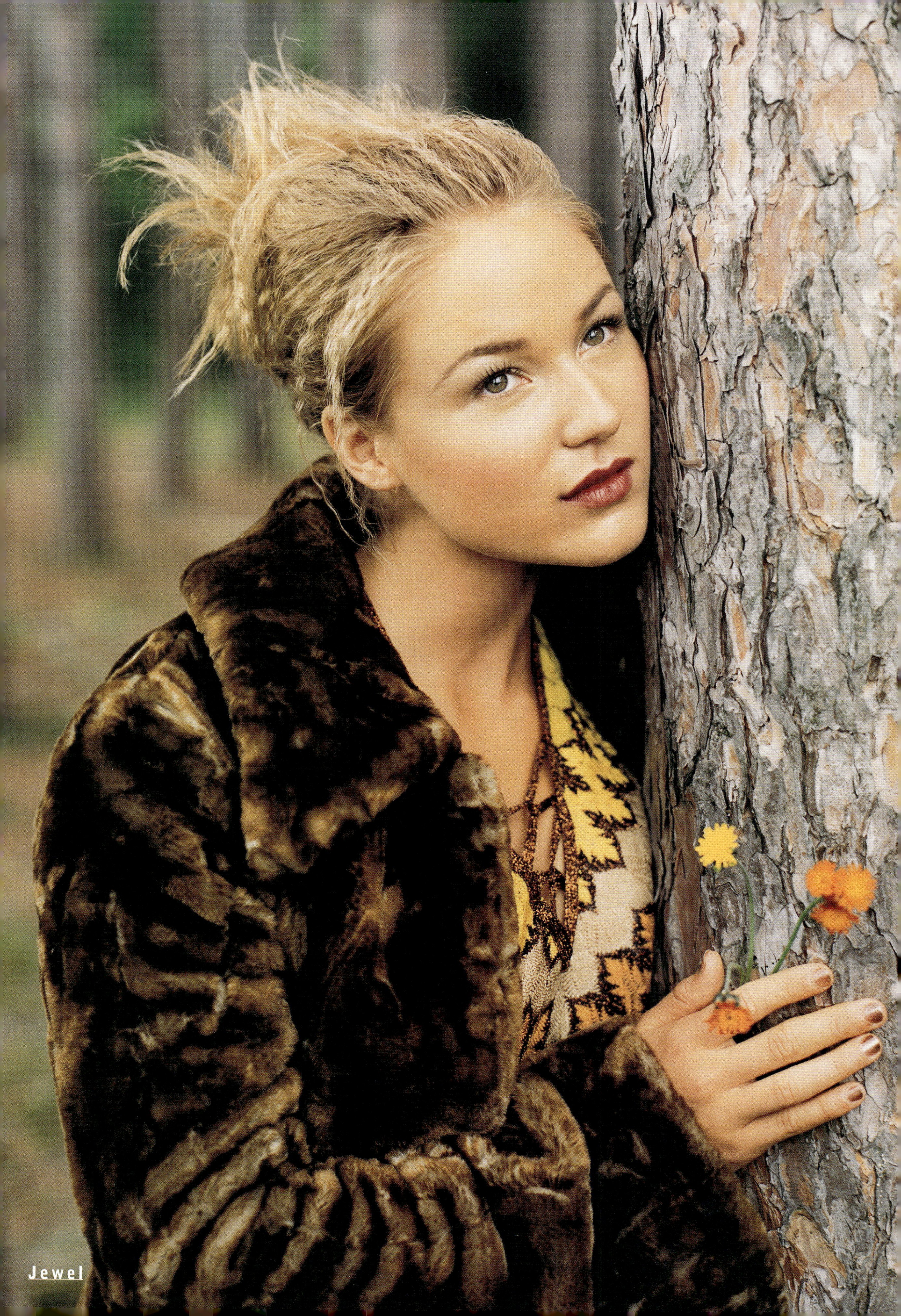

Jewel

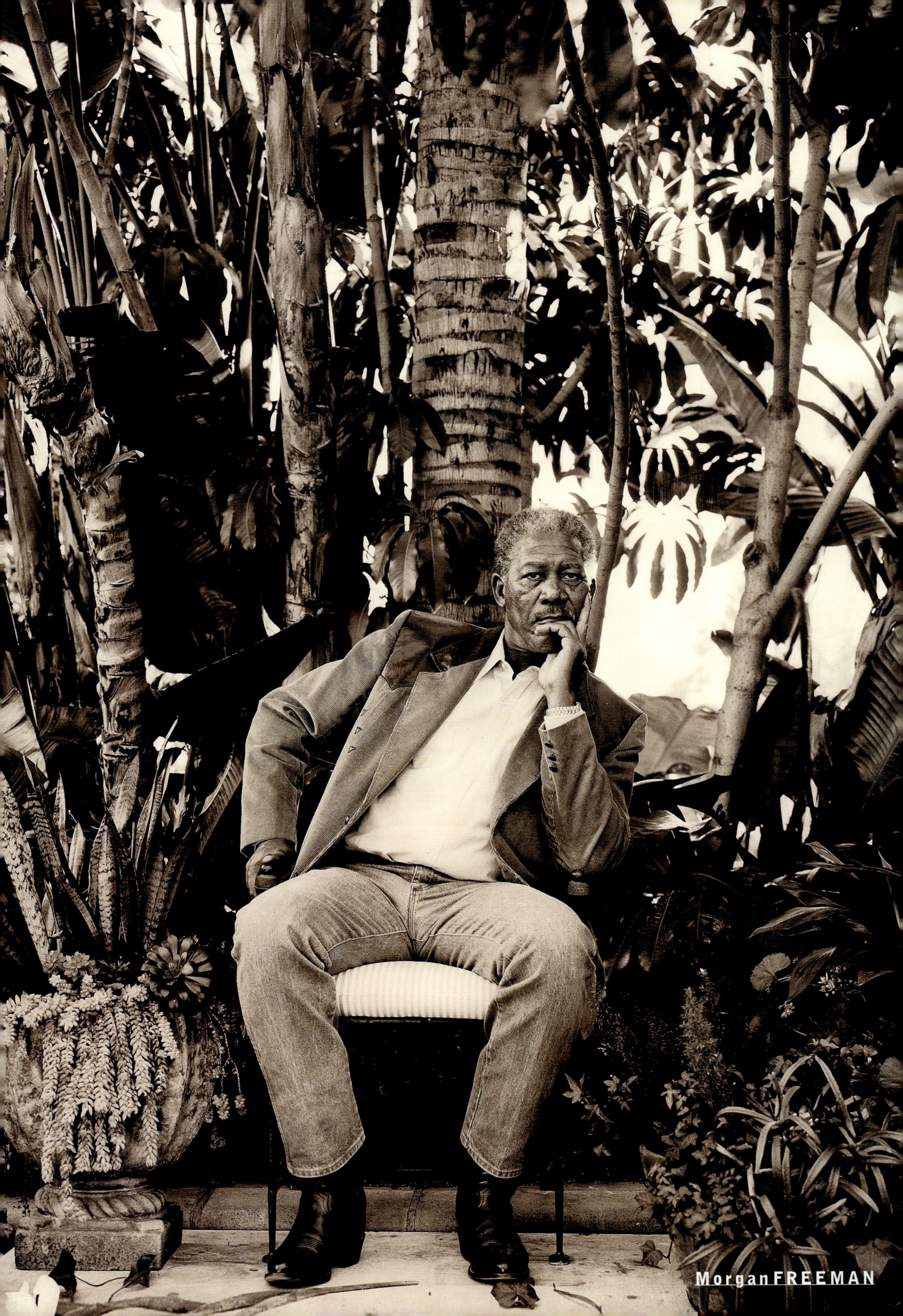

Morgan FREEMAN

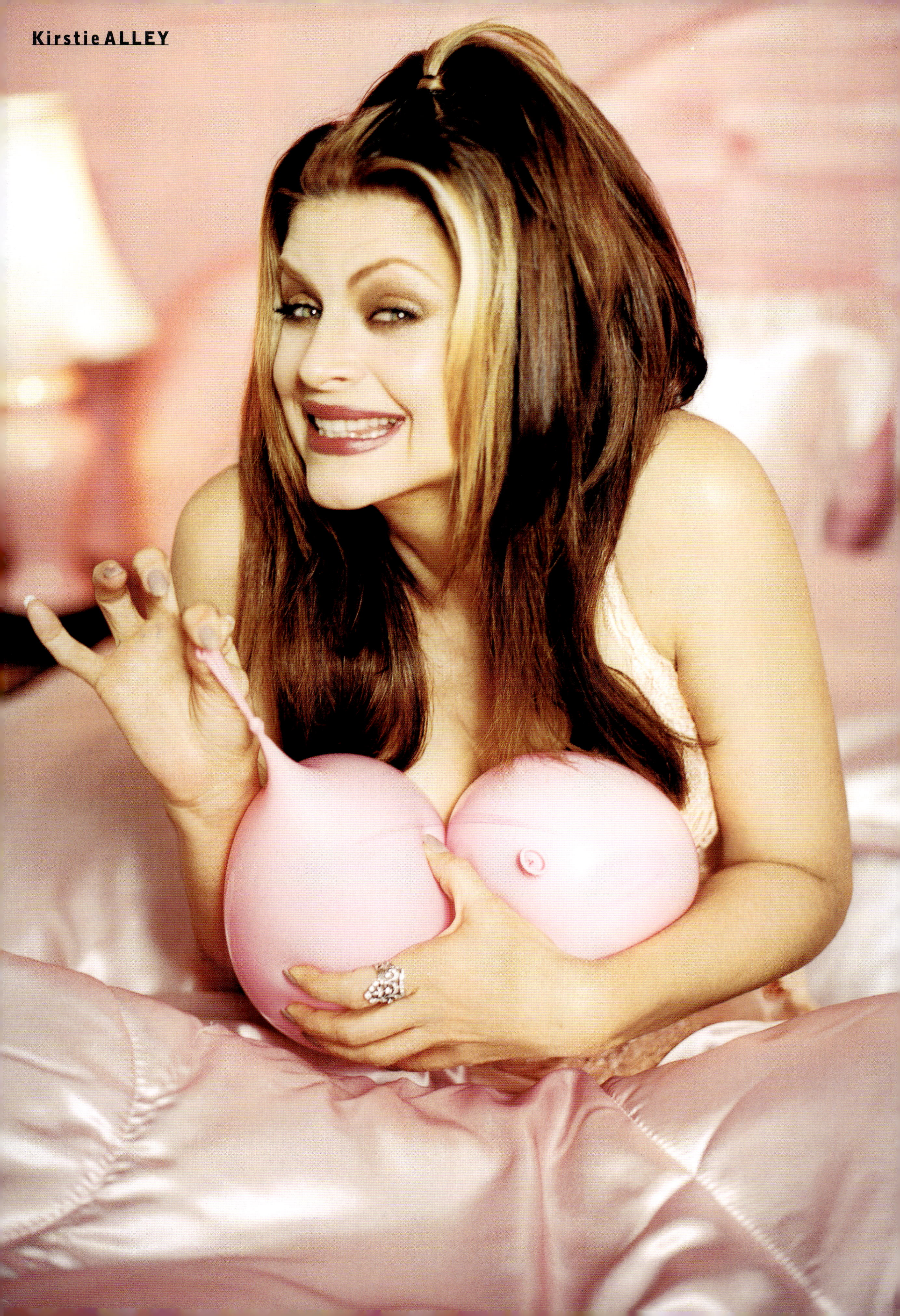

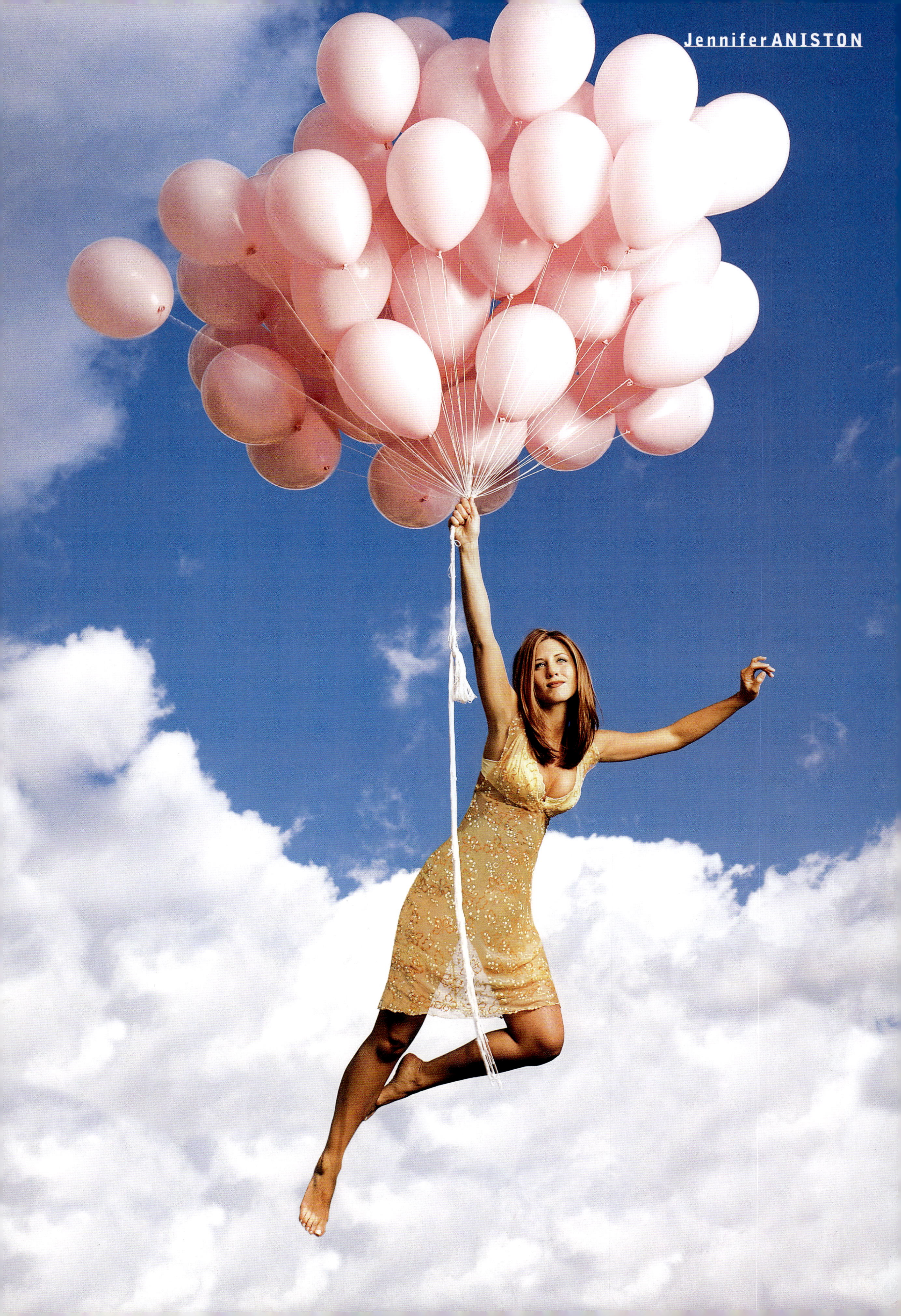

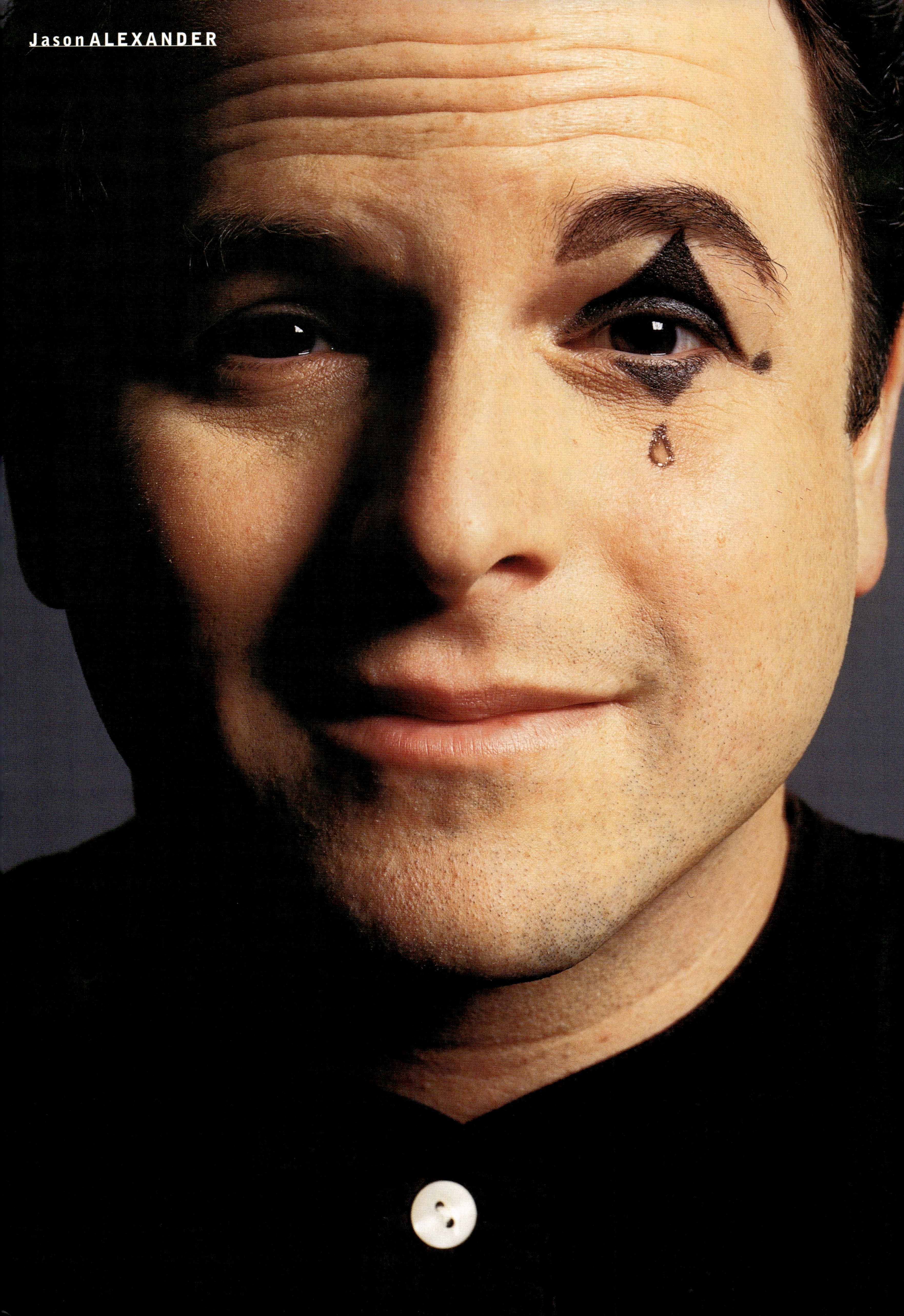

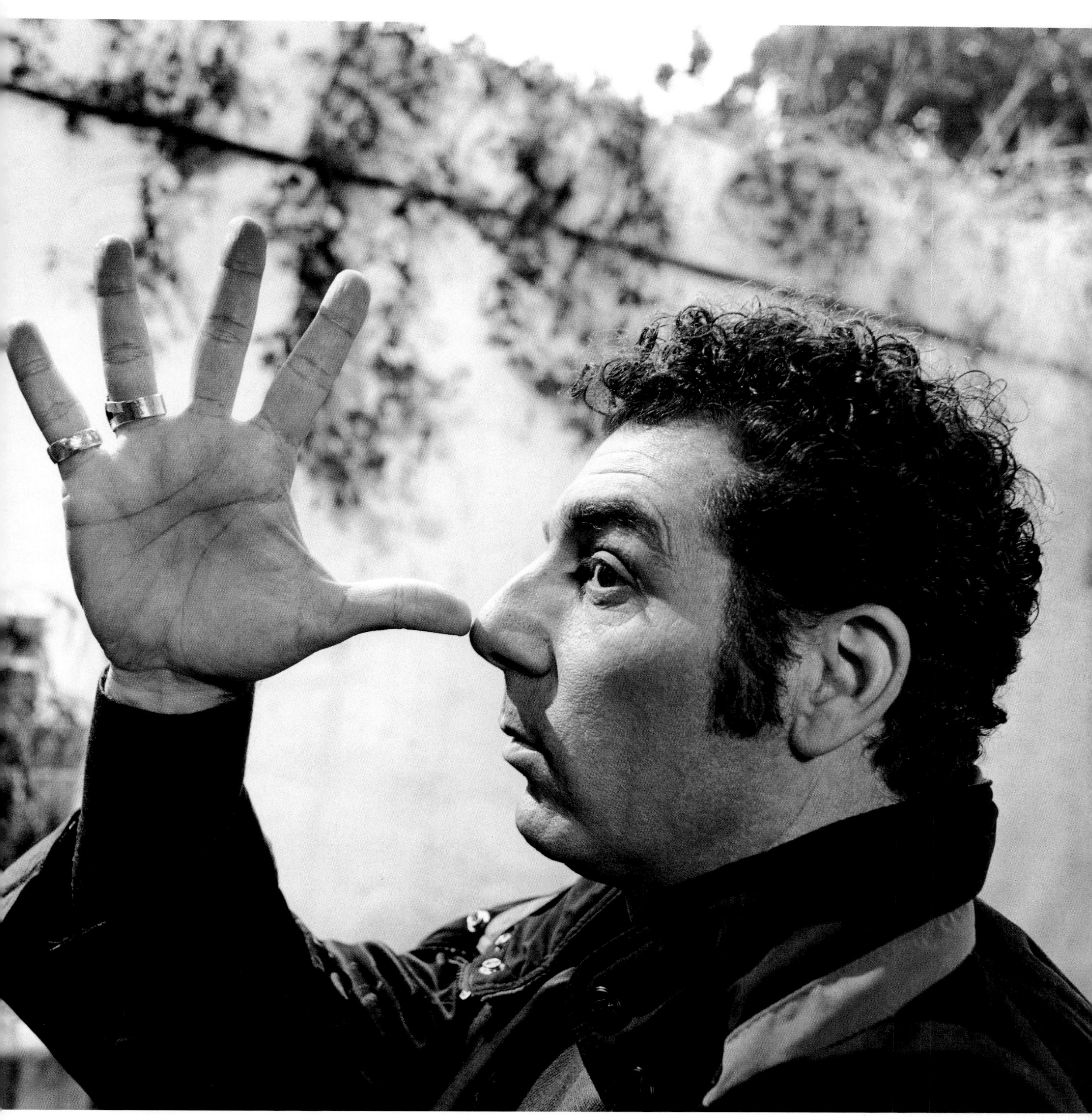

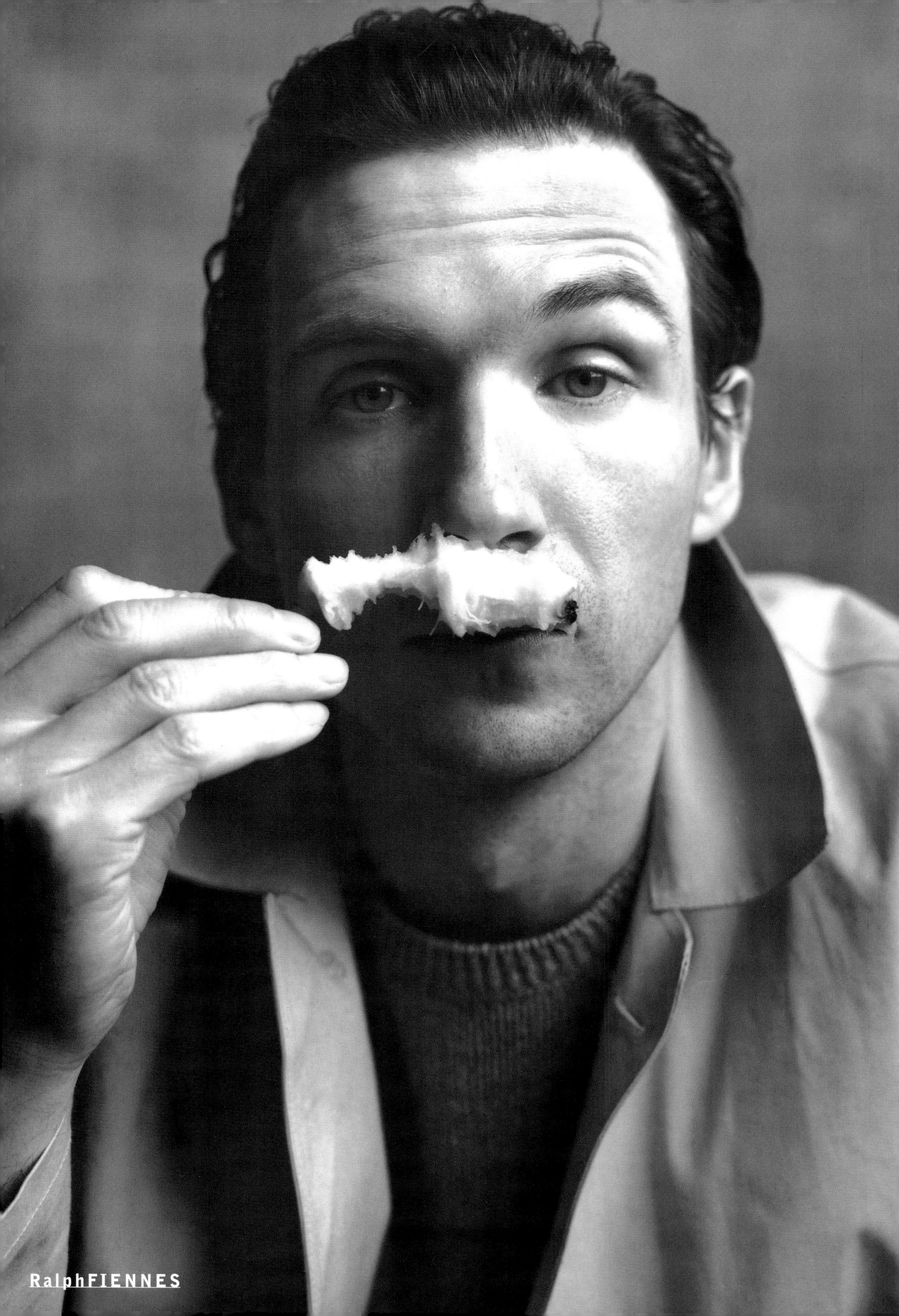

RalphFIENNES

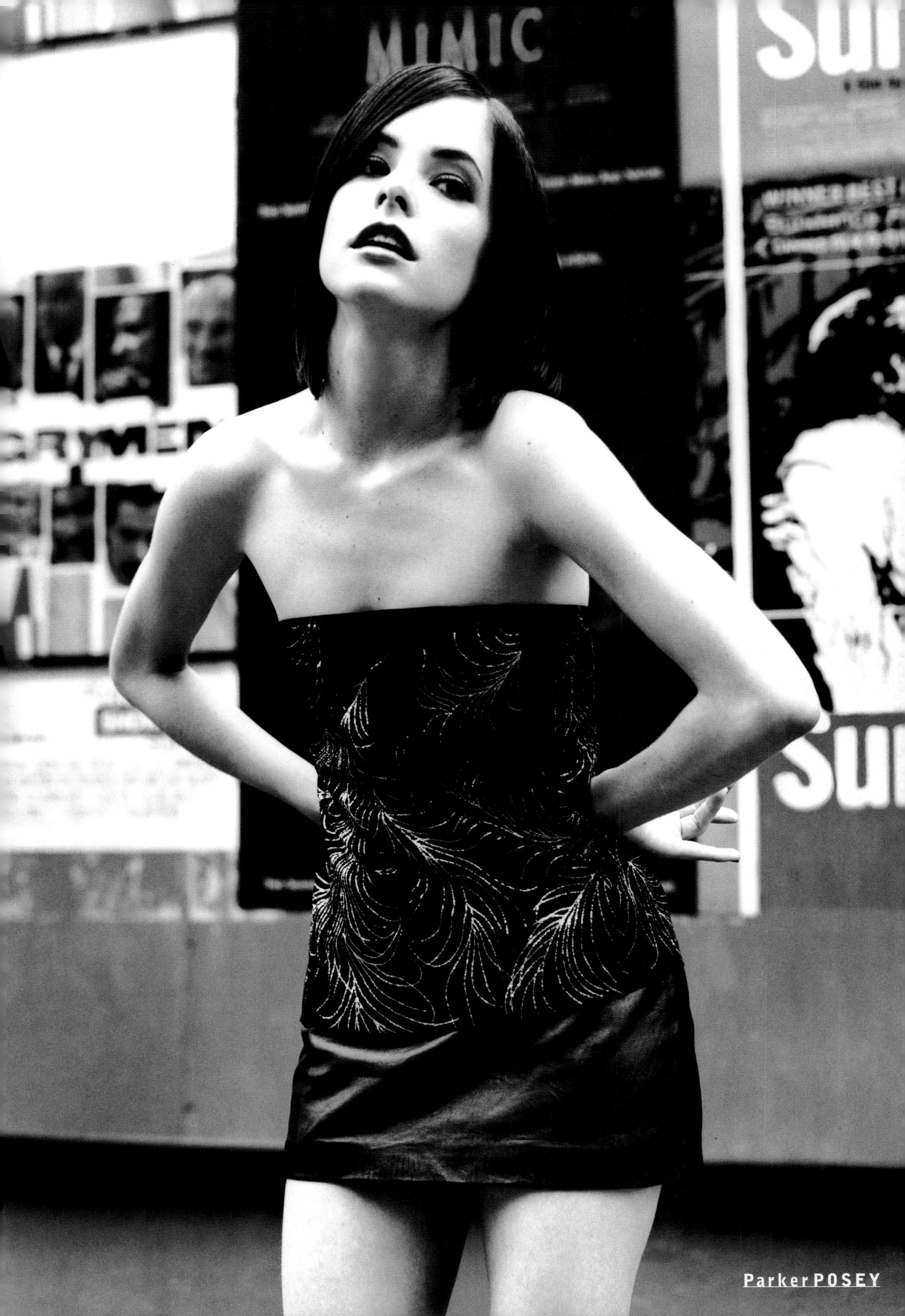

Parker POSEY

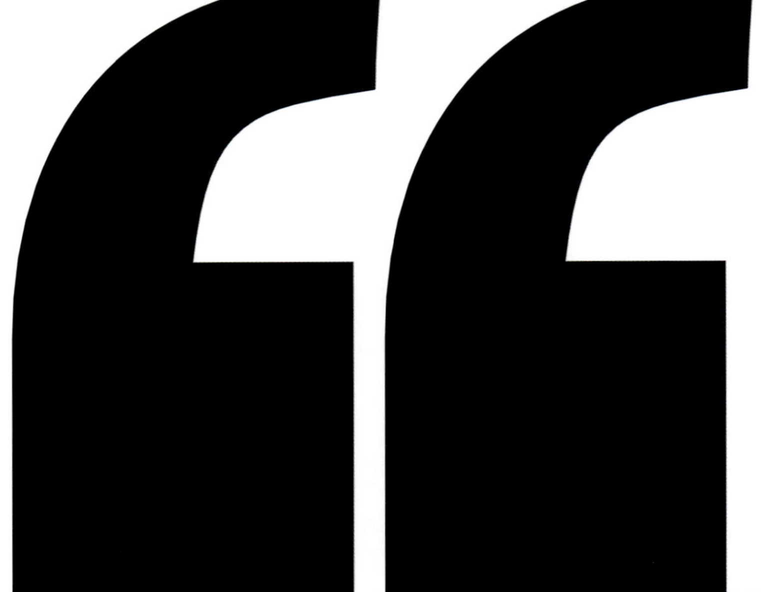

Mel Gibson »

I have had many challenging roles: actor, director, producer, father and kaiser. But today I face my most challenging roles to date: those of interviewer and interviewee. Is it all right if I call you Mel? No. I just want to say I'm a really big fan and I love everything you've done, even 'Bird on a Wire.' Thanks. [Peels bill from large roll] Here's a hundred bucks. Really? Can I keep it? Sure, I got loads of 'em. Thanks! Well, I guess we should start with your childhood. *I* did. You were born in upstate New York, 1956... Why do you say it like that? Like what? You said 'upstate New York' like it's not to be confused with New York City. [Peevish] Why wouldn't you just say 'New York'? What, upstate isn't cool enough for you? Sor-ree. No, no, I'm sorry. I just quit smoking and I'm a little testy. Anyway, then you leave America and move to Australia. Was the move a traumatic experience for you? Oh, yeah. Your sister enrolls you in drama school. What was that like? At first it was horrible. As a freshman I got pushed around. A *lot.* But then I hired this big guy to be my bodyguard, because this one kid kept picking on me. So then *he* hires a bodyguard, too. So while my bodyguard is fighting his bodyguard, I have to fight the guy myself! And I kick his ass! So then I get really popular and... Hold on. Isn't that the plot from the movie 'My Bodyguard'? Yeah. But it's a lot more interesting than, 'I took dance, diction, fencing, dialects, blah, blah, blah.' Come on, this is an interview, damn it! When you were making 'Ransom,' did you ever imagine any of your own kids being kidnapped? You know, to draw from the experience, to give the character depth? [Horrified] No. That's a *terrible* thought. What kind of crazy man would imagine his own kids being kidnapped? What's wrong with you? Nothing. I just thought it was a good question. Did you research the role? [Nods] I had Arnold Schwarzenegger's kid kidnapped. Just for, like, an hour. Then I called him up and asked *him* what it was like. Pretty smart, huh?

Wasn't he mad?

At first, but when I told him why I did it, he understood. We had a big laugh and a stogie over it. He's a great guy. *Really* good sense of humor. Which brings up another good point: your infamous sense of humor. What is the best practical joke you've ever played? Just between you and me? Of course. [Pointing to tape recorder] Is that thing still on? [Lies] No. Well, my youngest boy, Shecky, wanted a pony really badly, so my wife and I drive him all the way to Montana, right? Yeah...? We get to this barn and we tell him, 'The pony's in there.' So he races out of the car and into the barn – and my wife and I take off! Yeah...? That's it. That's it? You just left him there? Yeah. [Wistfully] I wish I could have seen his face when he came out. Wait a minute. You don't have a son named Shecky. Not anymore. But we still have six, and I'll tell ya, nobody has asked for a pony since. Have you seen my shades? Um, no. Did you lose them? I hope not. Maybe they fell under the table. [Disappears under the table for a few minutes, then returns with his sunglasses] Did you just have a cigarette? [Indignant] No! I smell cigarette smoke. [Angrily] I thought you were an interviewer, or a journalist, or whatever you bottom feeders call yourselves these days. I didn't realize you were a reporter *and* a forensic pathologist.

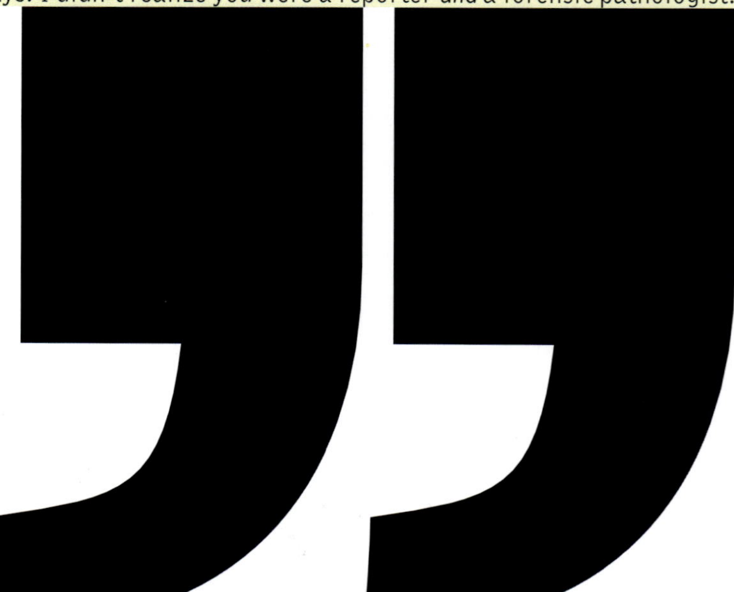

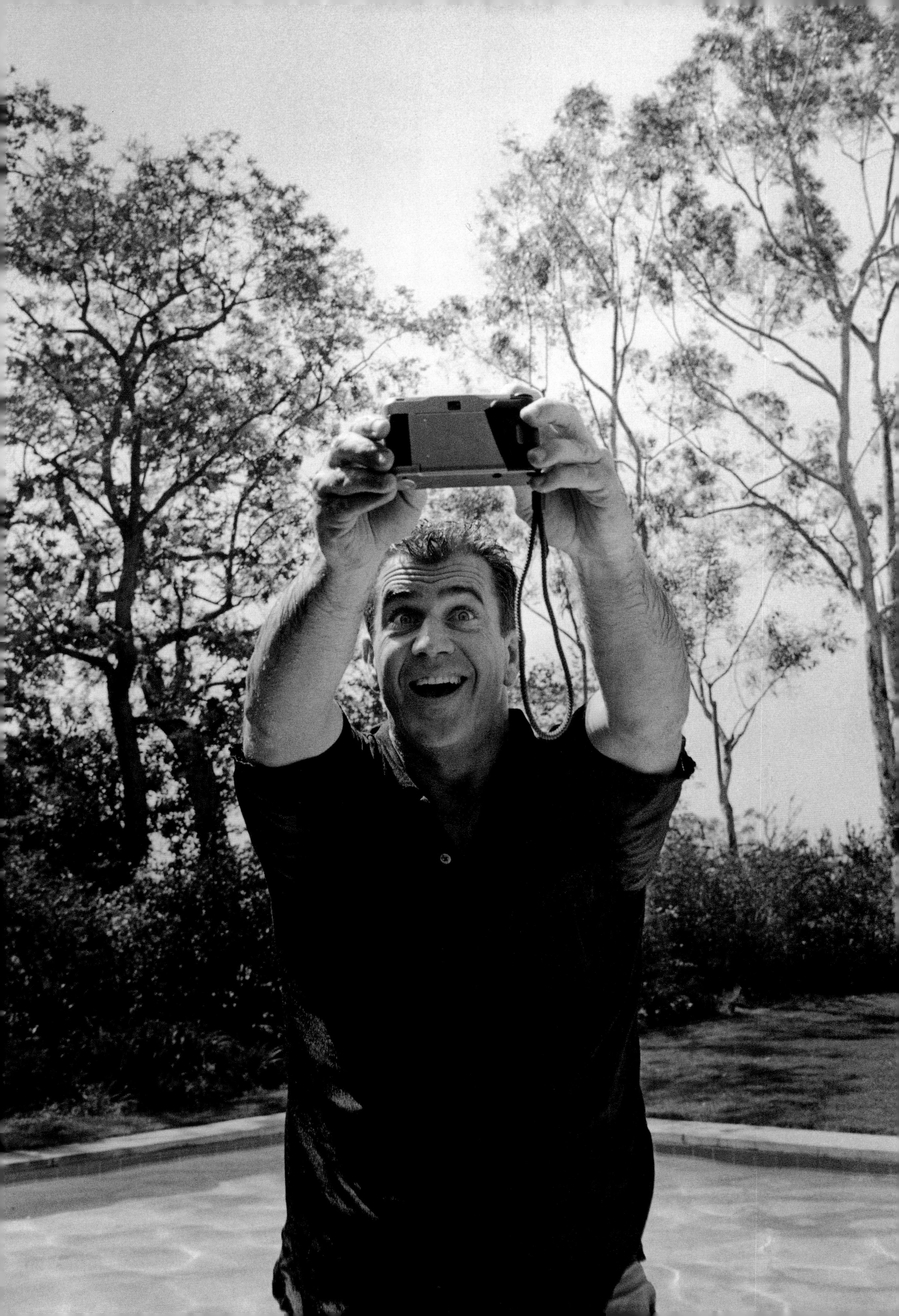

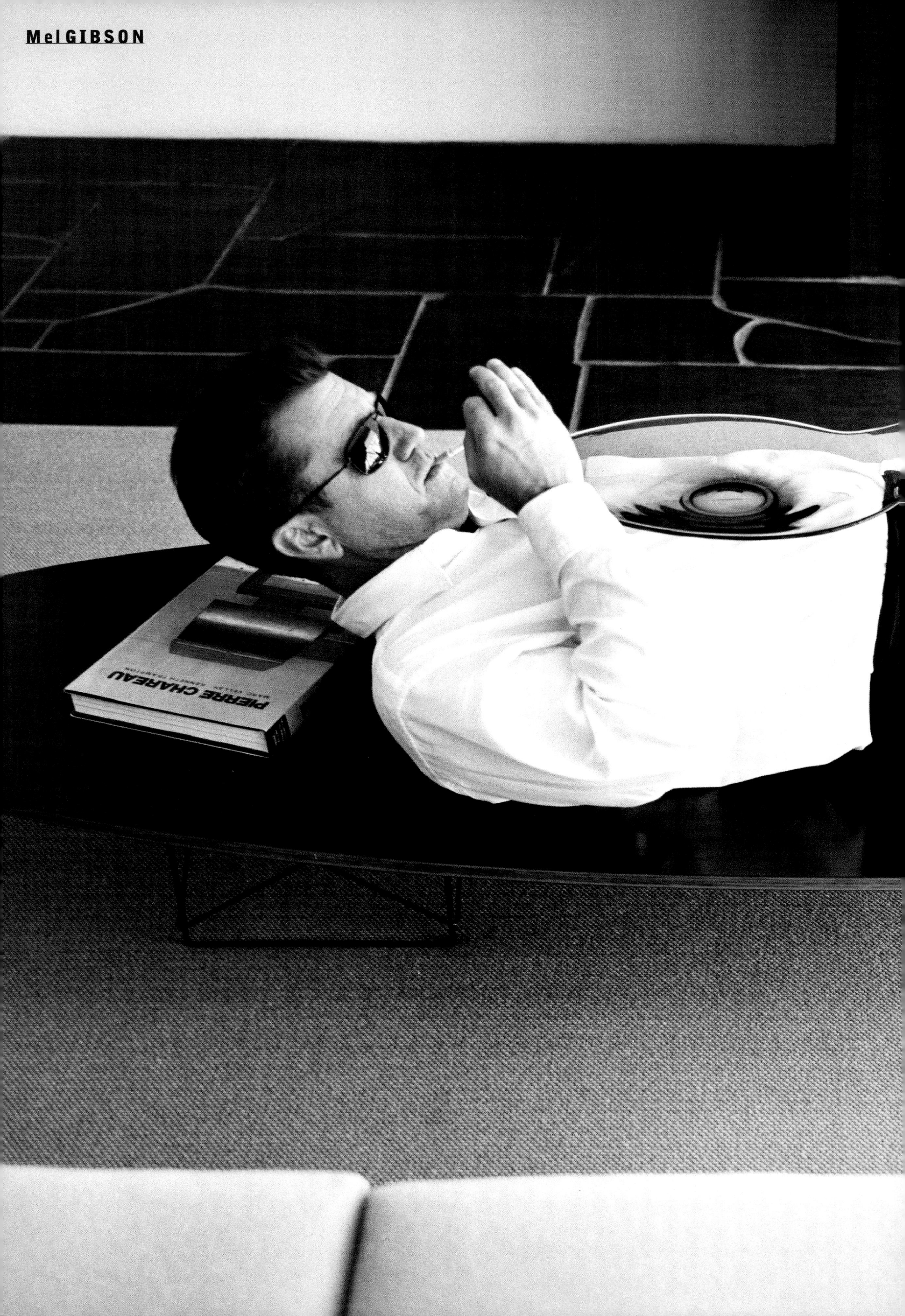
PIERRE CHAREAU

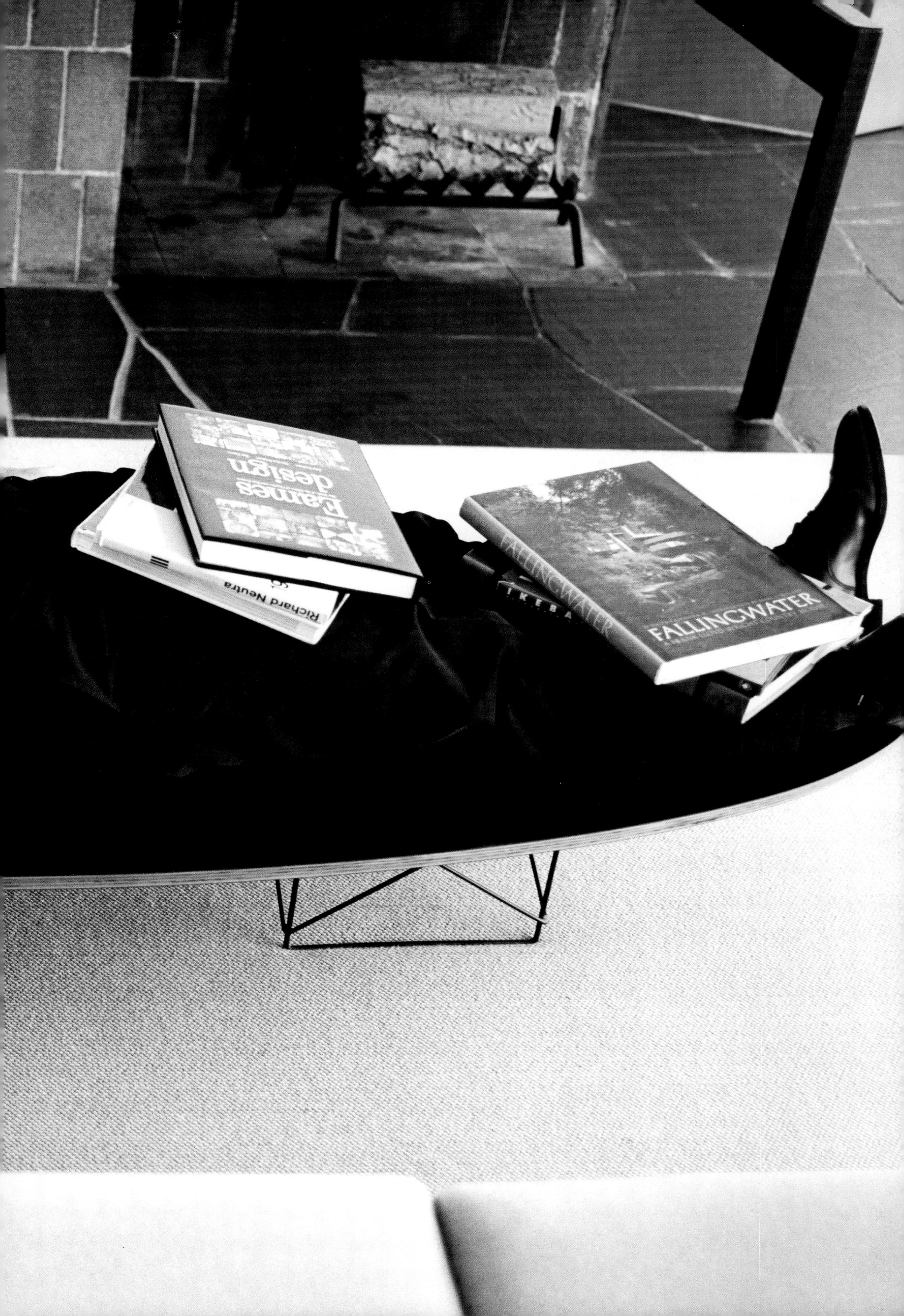
Eames
design
Richard Neutra
FALLINGWATER

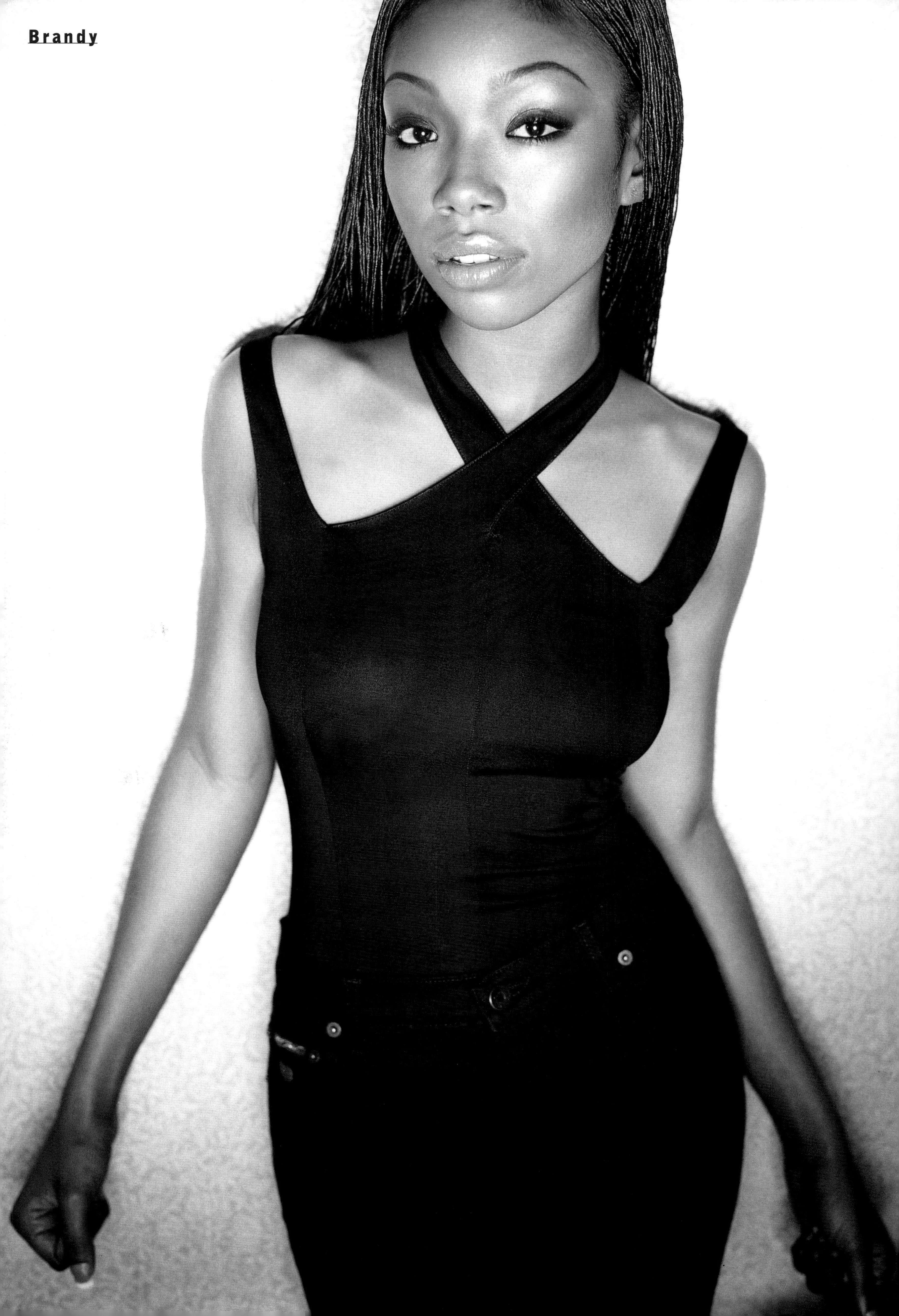

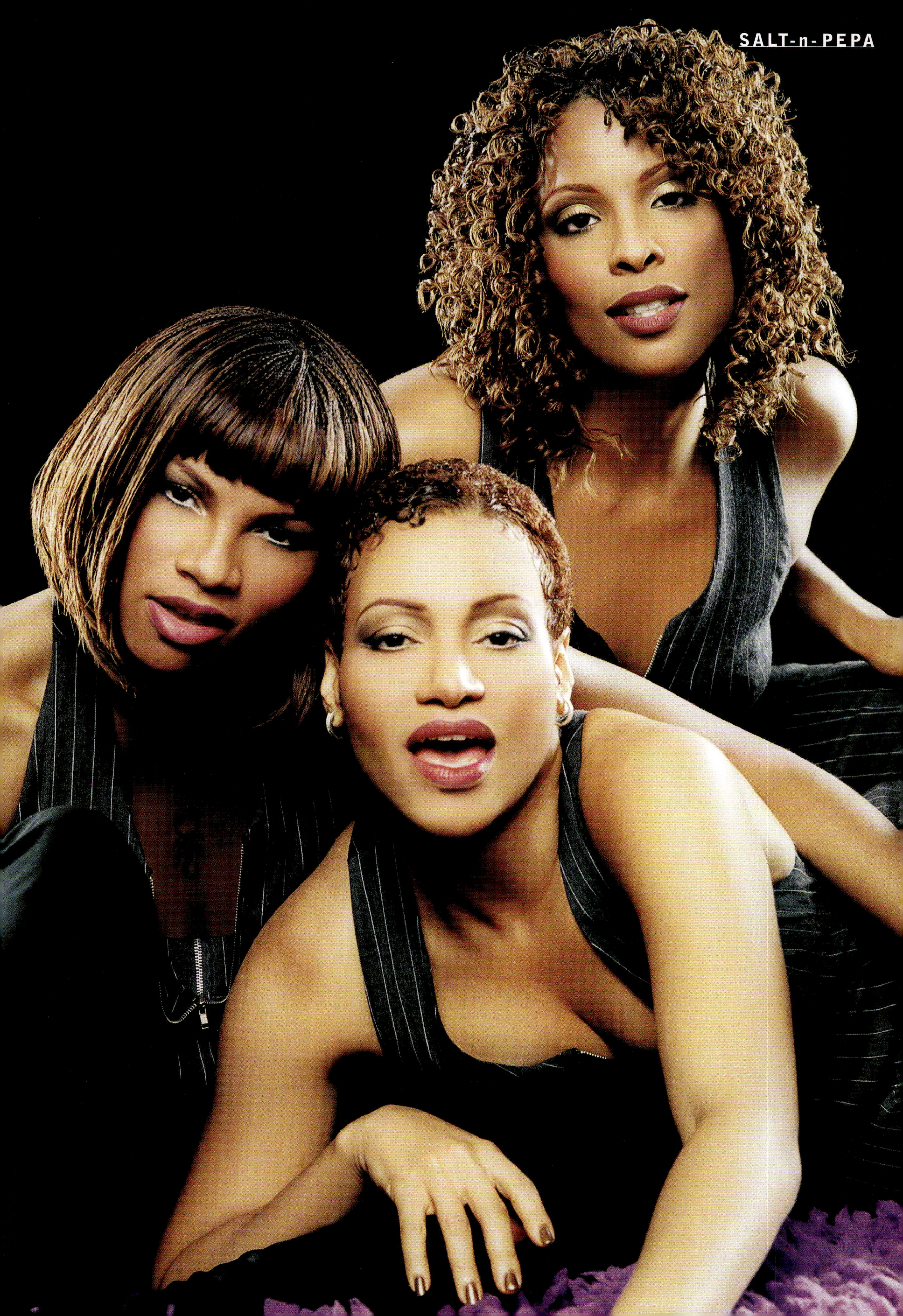

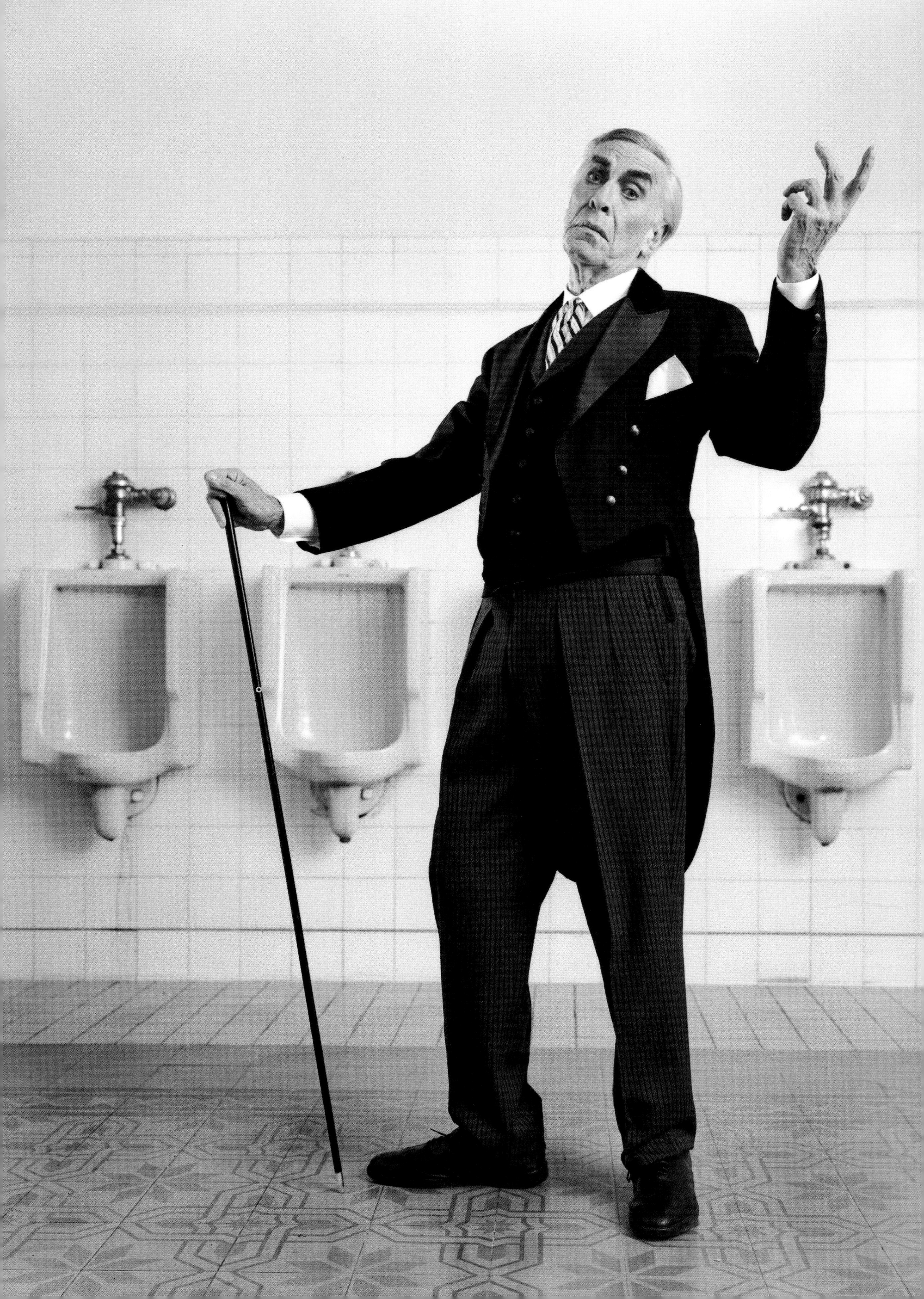

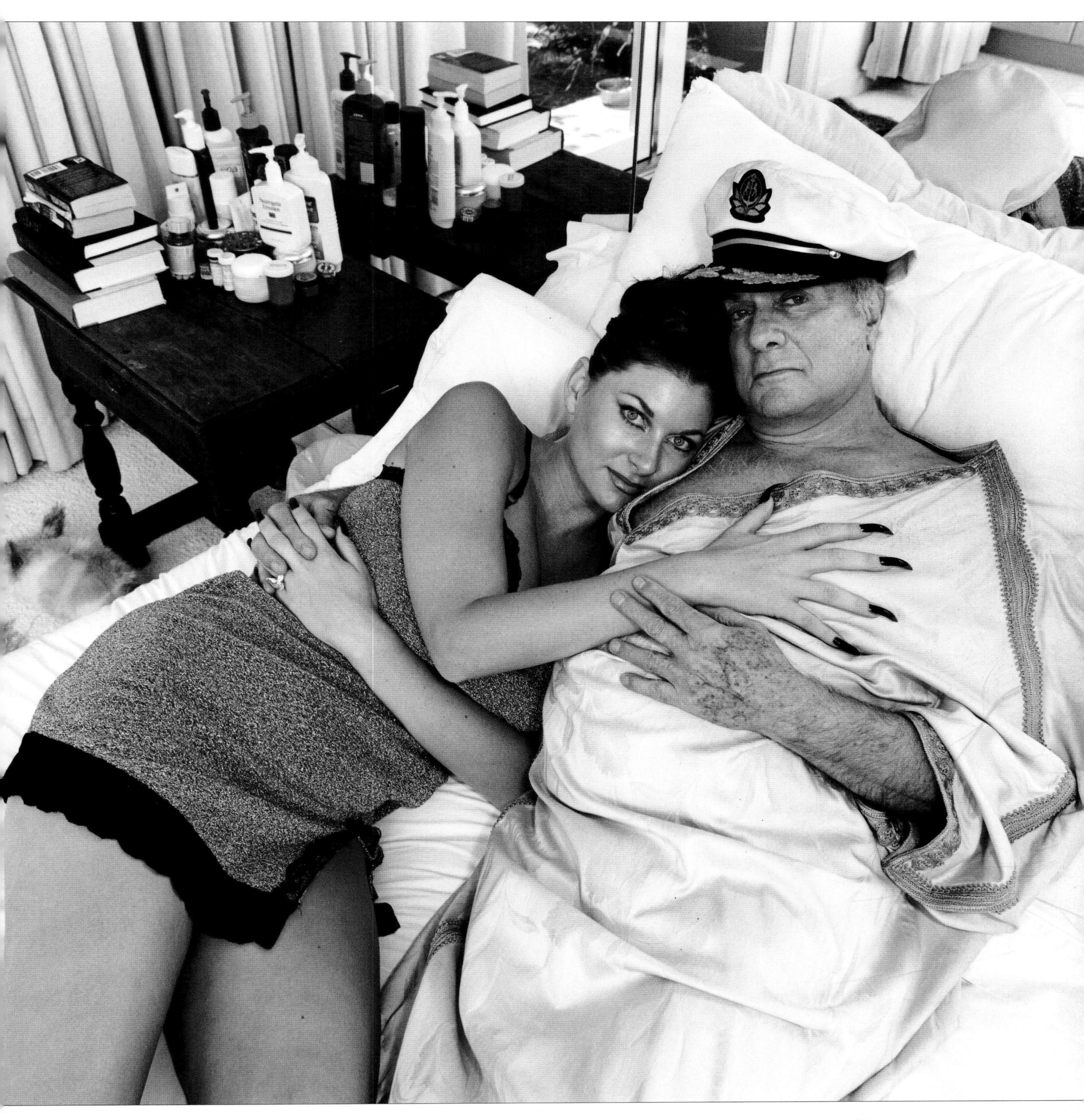

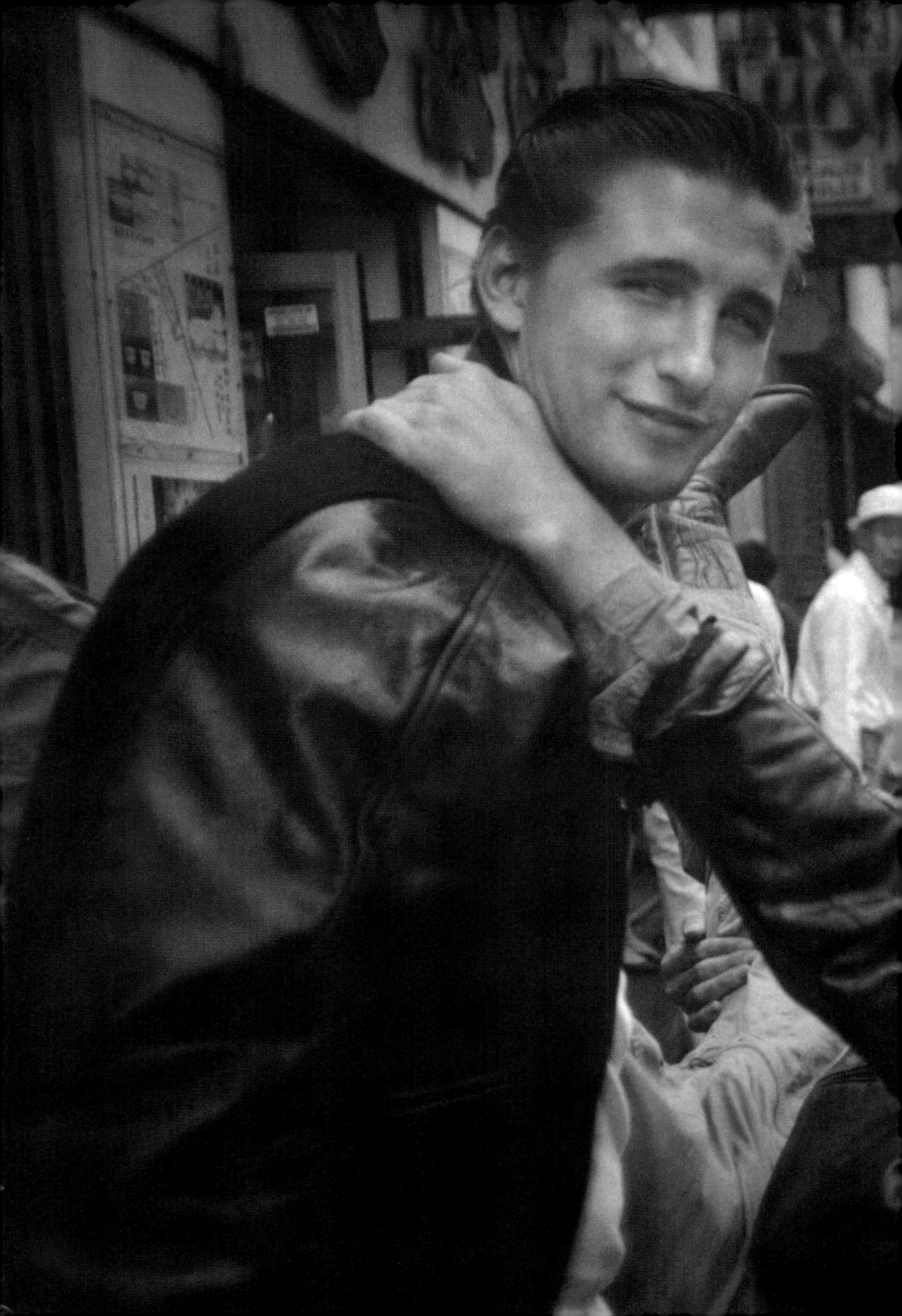

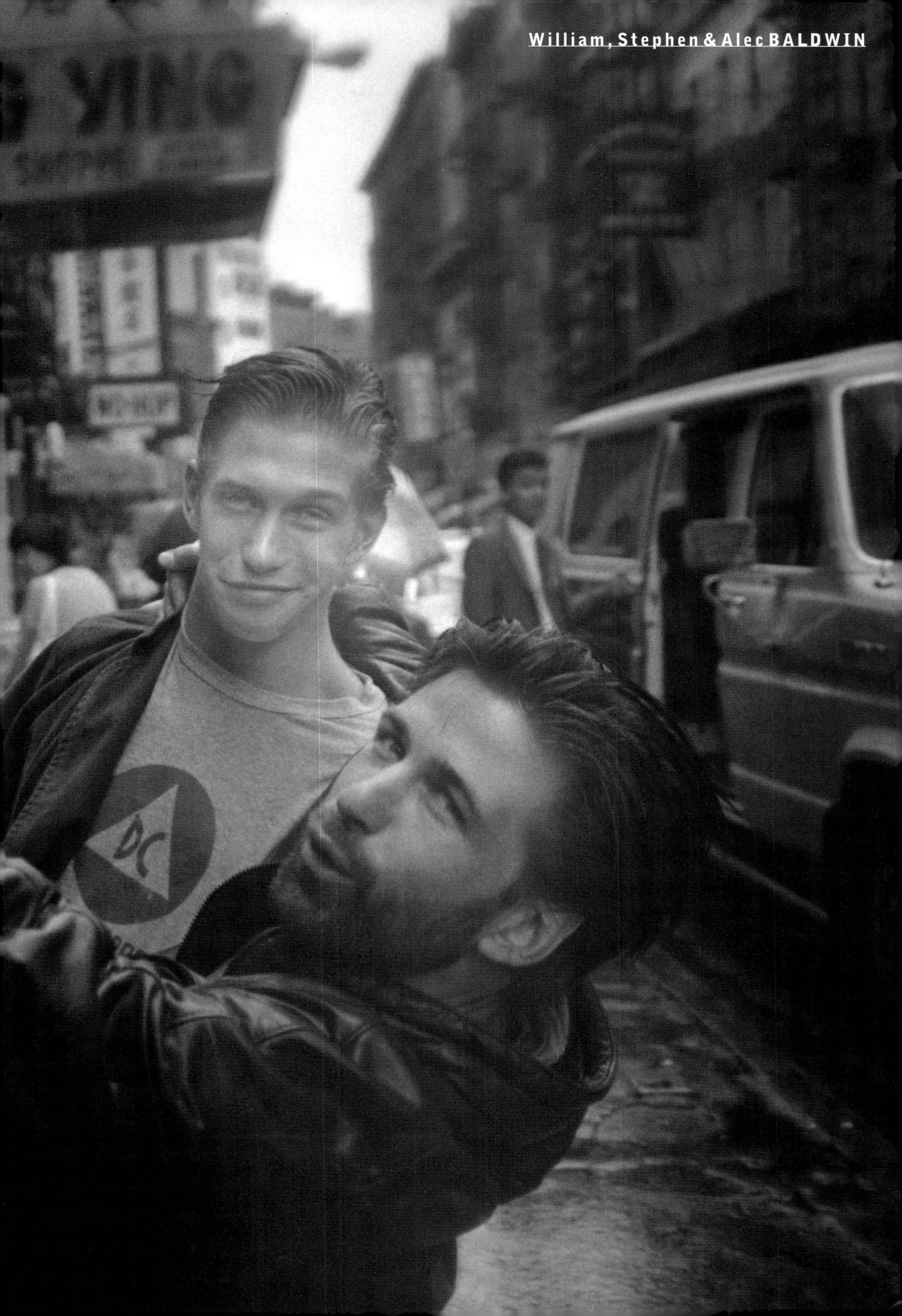

William, Stephen & Alec BALDWIN

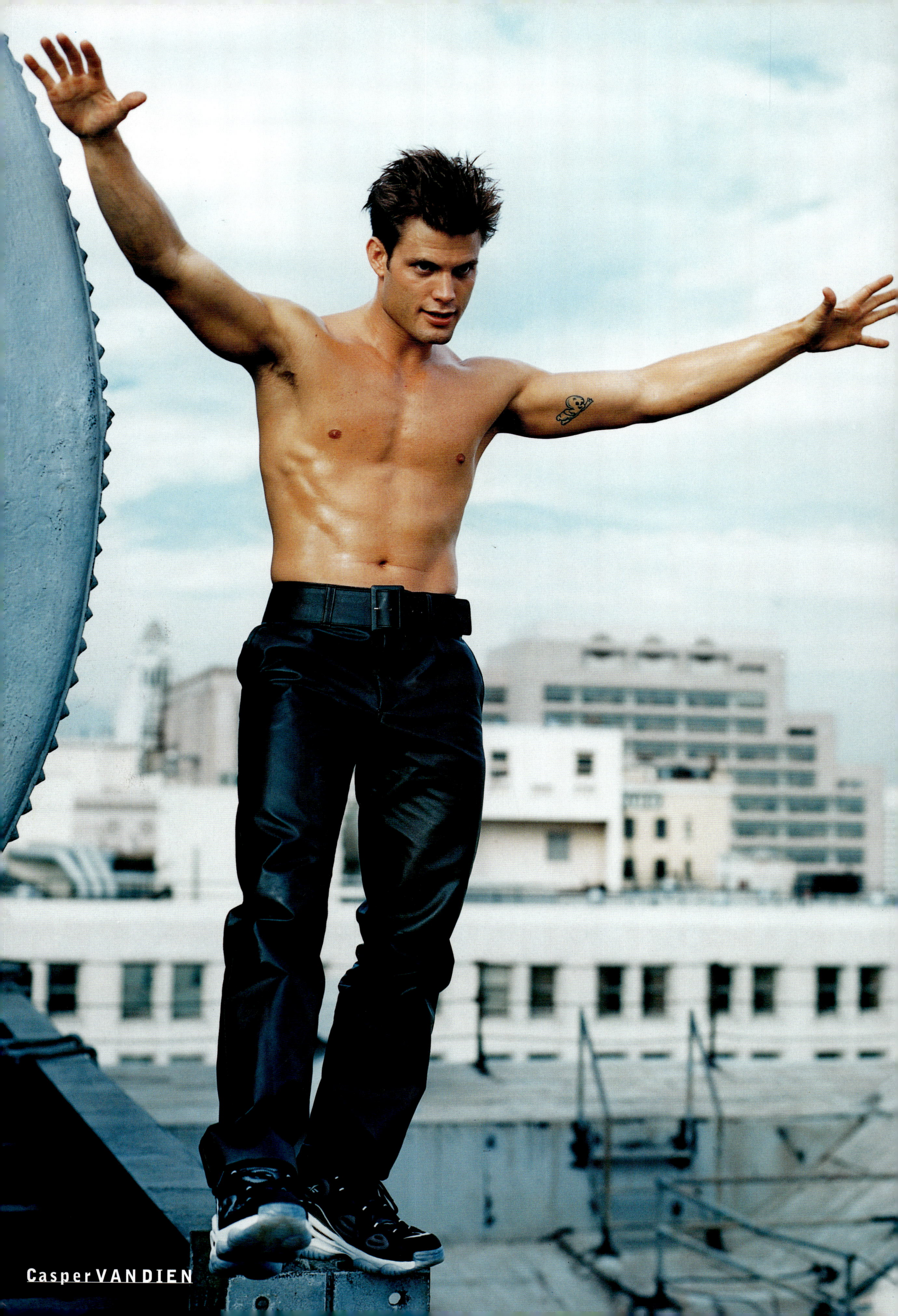

Casper VANDIEN

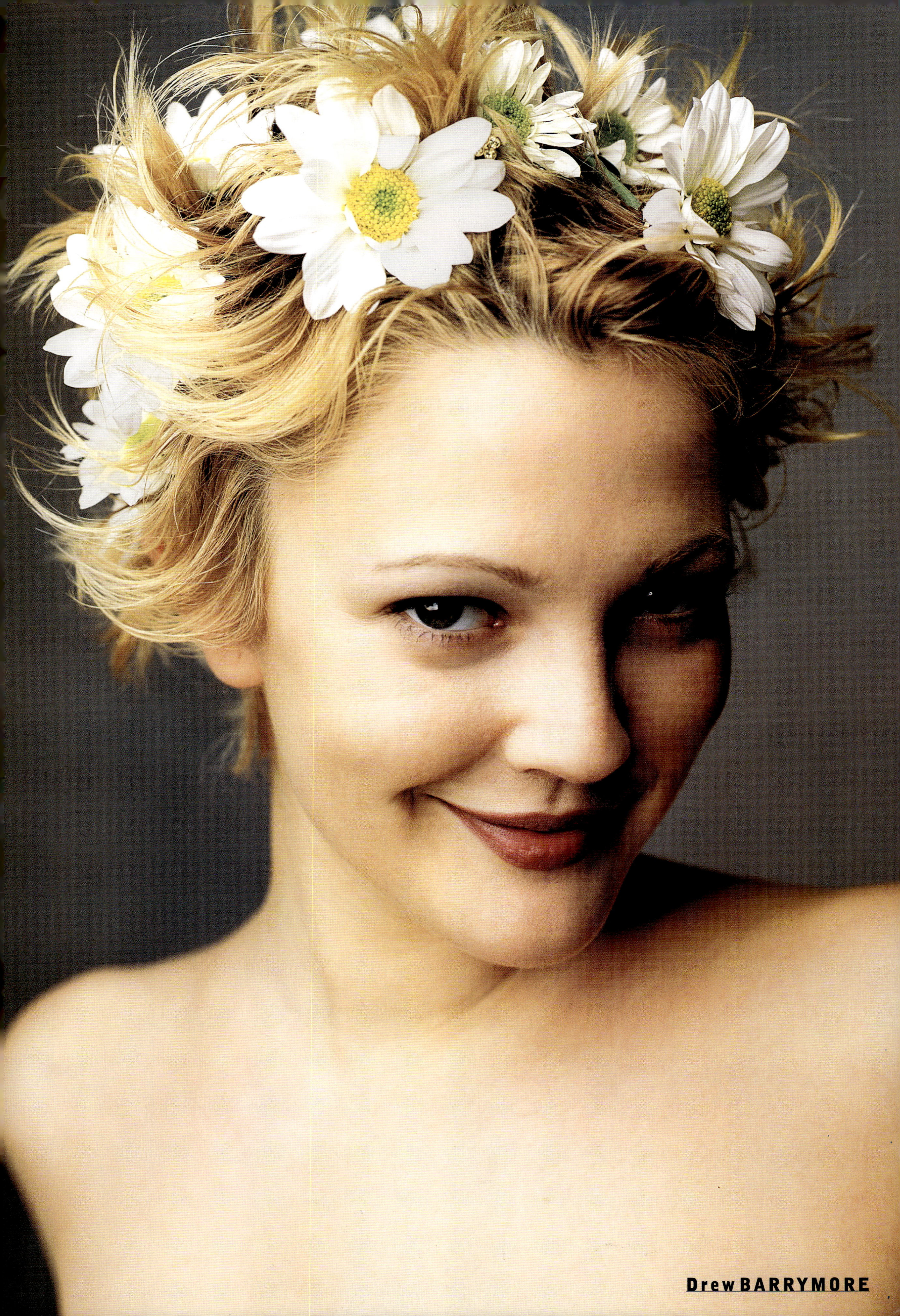

Drew BARRYMORE

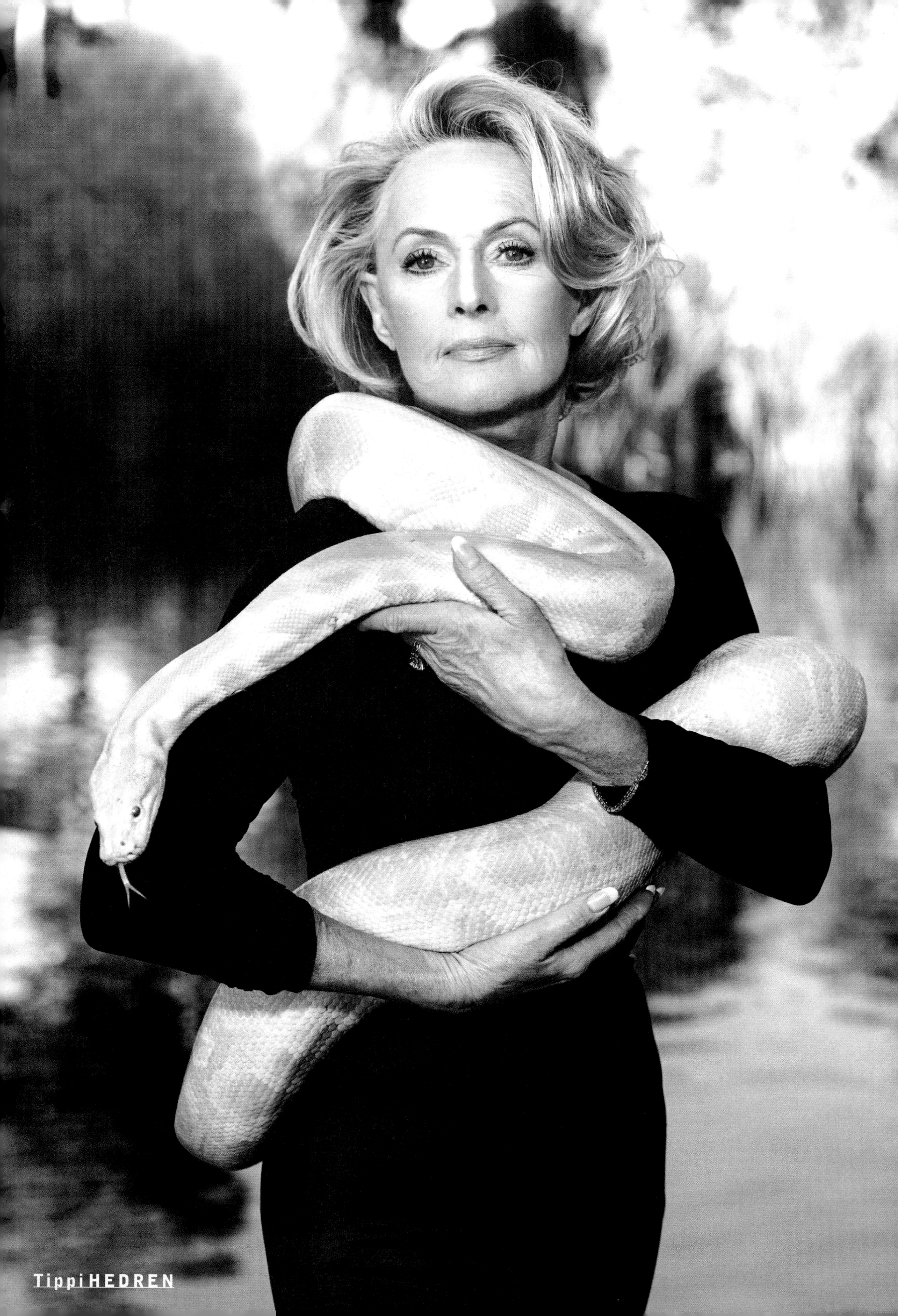

Tippi HEDREN

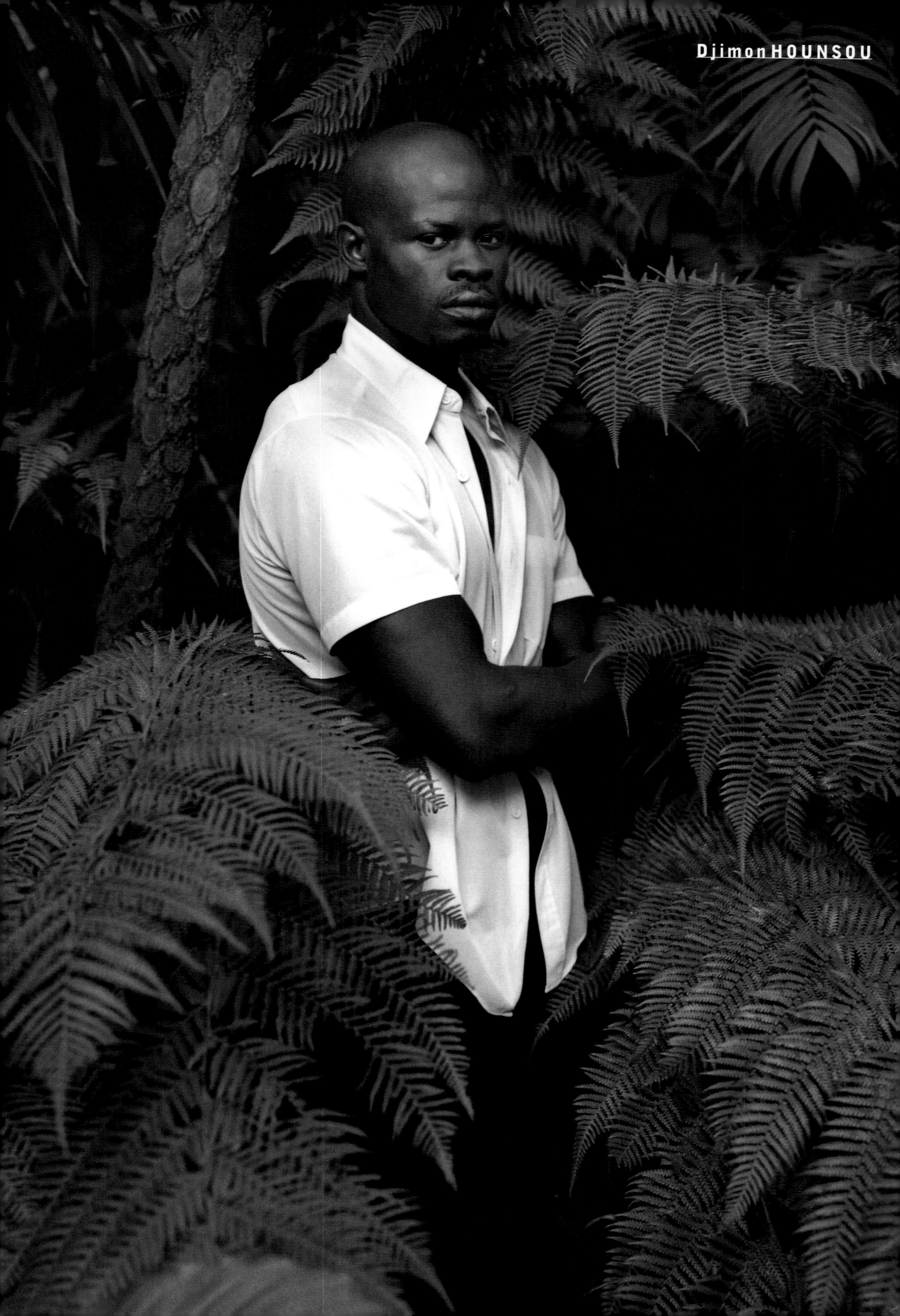

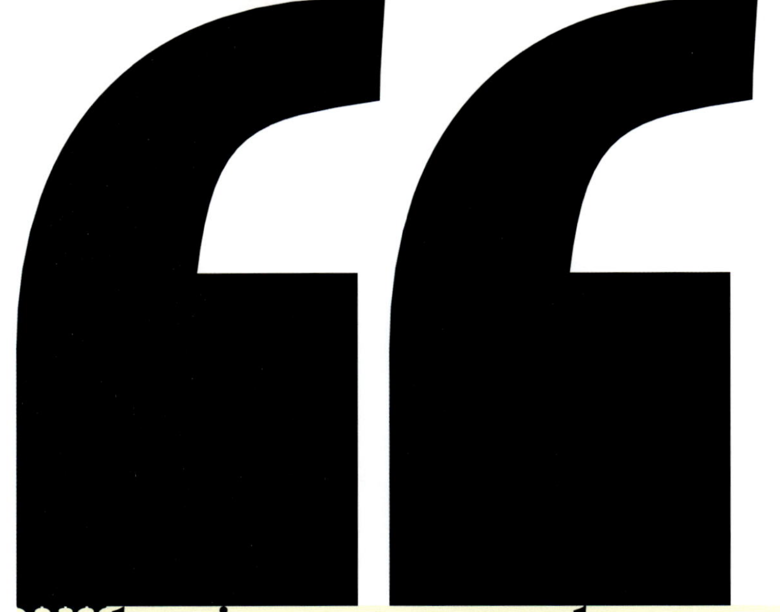

Chris Rock»

Why is race such a potent field for humor?

Like sex, like relationships, it just never dies. People are always going to be racist. You know: silly love songs; always new ways to write about it. Many people think that when you're black and famous, you get above the effects of racism. Actually, you're more in the line of it. Think about it this way: You get money, you're gonna be around more white people. You're gonna be around more white people, you're probably gonna be around more racism. What is new in the way that you talk about race? Well, a black man admitting that sometimes black people do wrong things – this is kind of new. It's not new in the barbershop or at my family reunion. It's new onstage. It's not even new in rap records. [Public Enemy's] Chuck D has said what I've said before.

Has hip-hop influenced you?

Whatever music you listen to is gonna be a huge influence on you. I like hip-hop. [Bill] Cosby likes jazz. Look at our pacing. Cosby works like a jazz musician. He's like Miles Davis, man. He takes so long to get to the joke. It's very cool, and very arrogant. [Laughs.] You said Cosby was the only comedian who made you feel like you were talking to a grown man. He *is* a grown man. You are, too. Yeah, but Cosby's like a real grown man, not to be fucked with. Everybody else, there's a ton of kid in them. When did it dawn on you that you were a man? A man? *Wooooo!* [Pauses] A man. That's a rough one. I don't feel like a man now, a lot of the time. [Pauses] I guess when my dad died. It wasn't, really, I felt like a man. I just knew it was time to be a man. The only time I feel like a man is when I pay my bills.

How did your father die?

My dad died of, basically, having too many kids and not enough money. Ulcer exploded, thus triggering all the other old-black-men diseases: high blood pressure, diabetes... But the ulcer was the kick. He died in November '88. Not long after that, I got 'SNL.' How does your mother feel about your work? That's the beautiful thing about growing up in Bed-Stuy. No one has these dreams of their kids becoming grand things. People just don't want their kids to be on crack. They just want their kids to be good people. Whatever they become, that's all right. Just be a good person.

Do you employ people in your family?

No, man. It's insane, if you ask me. Why? Because then you can't take any time off. And you don't always have something to say. So if your family is working for you, then you know you gotta hit the road. You gotta put food on the table. Yeah. I don't want [them] working for me. I have a flimsy-ass job. I'll pay for them to go to school. And hopefully, if I get fucked up, I can work for them. [Laughs]

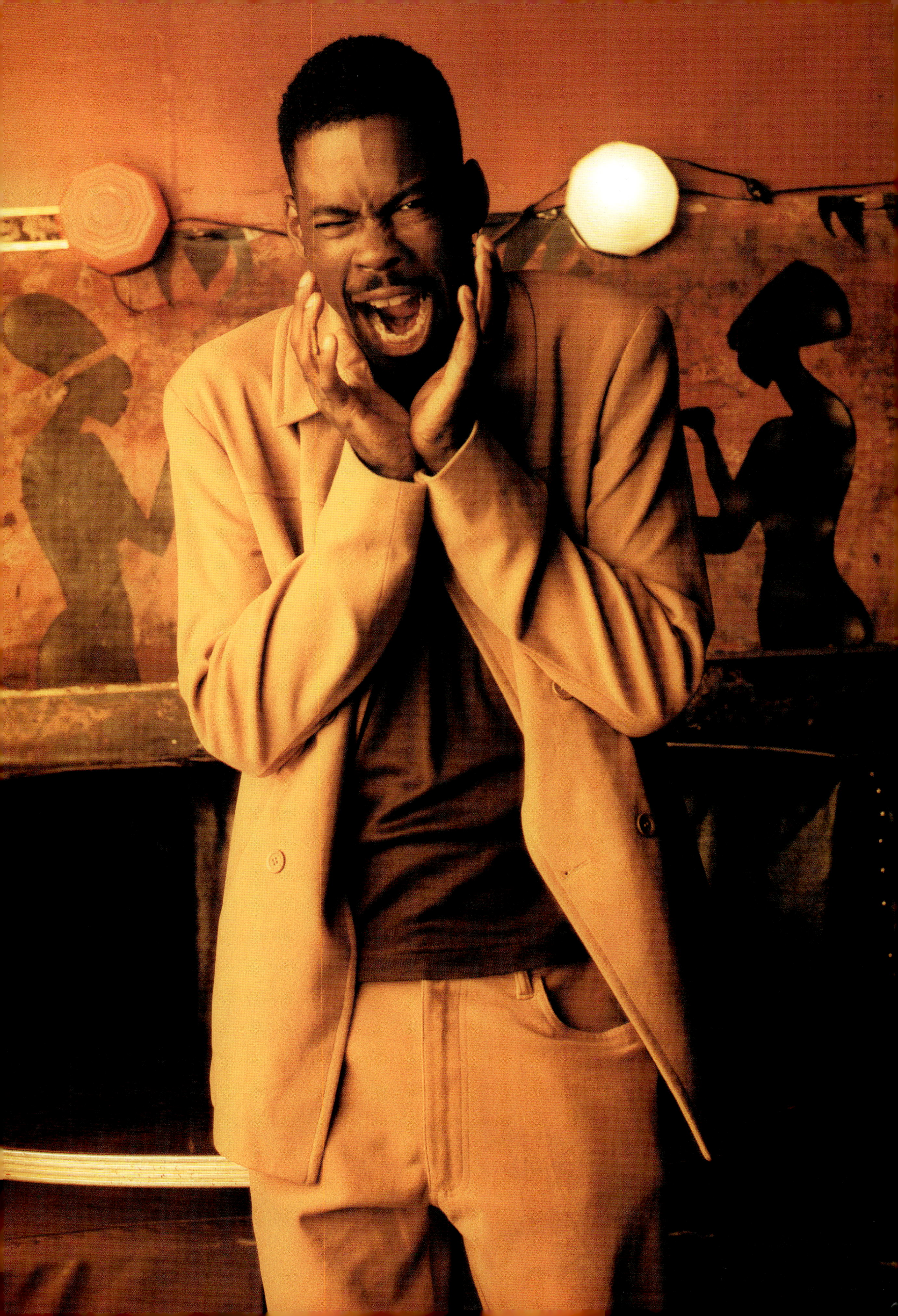

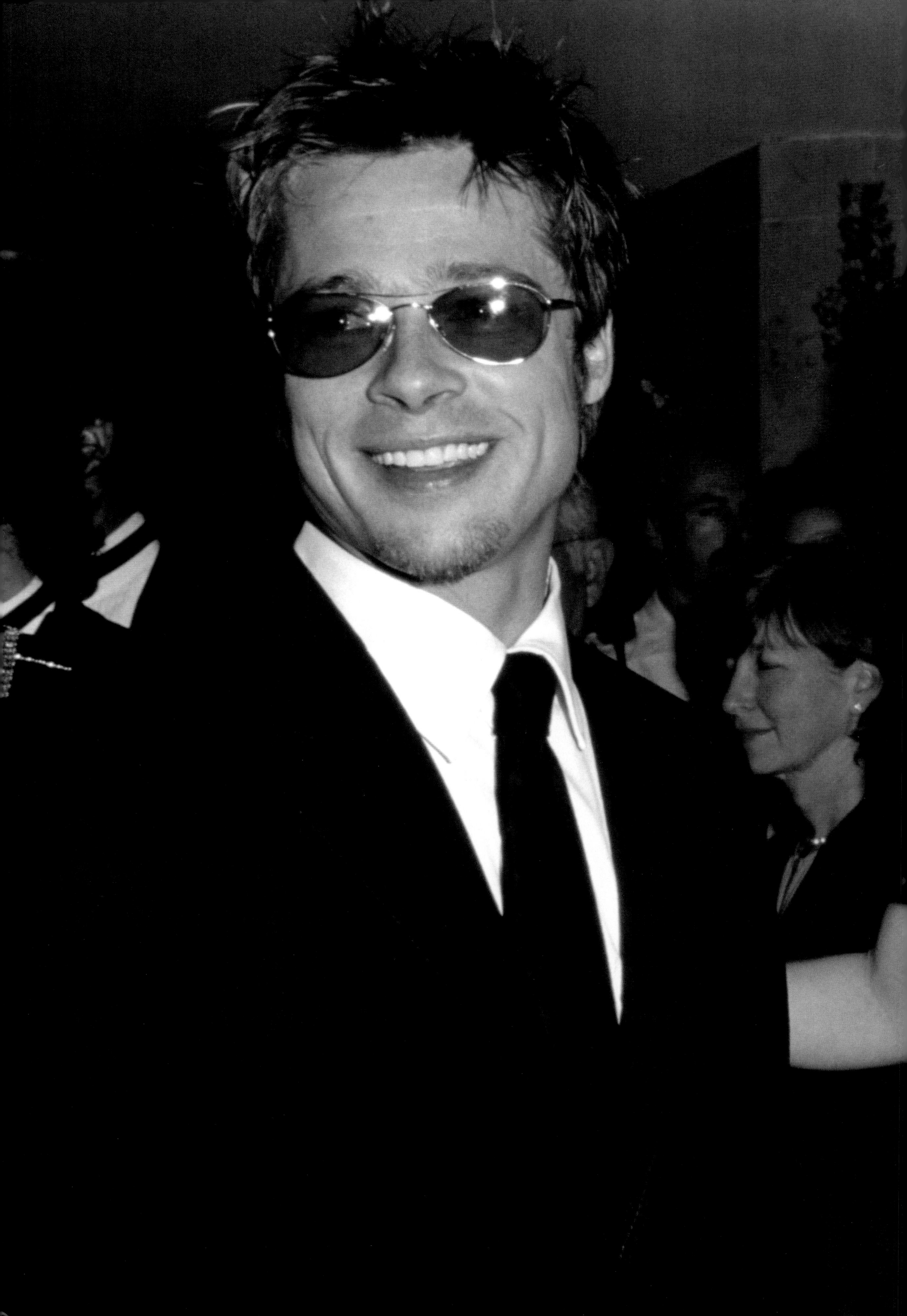

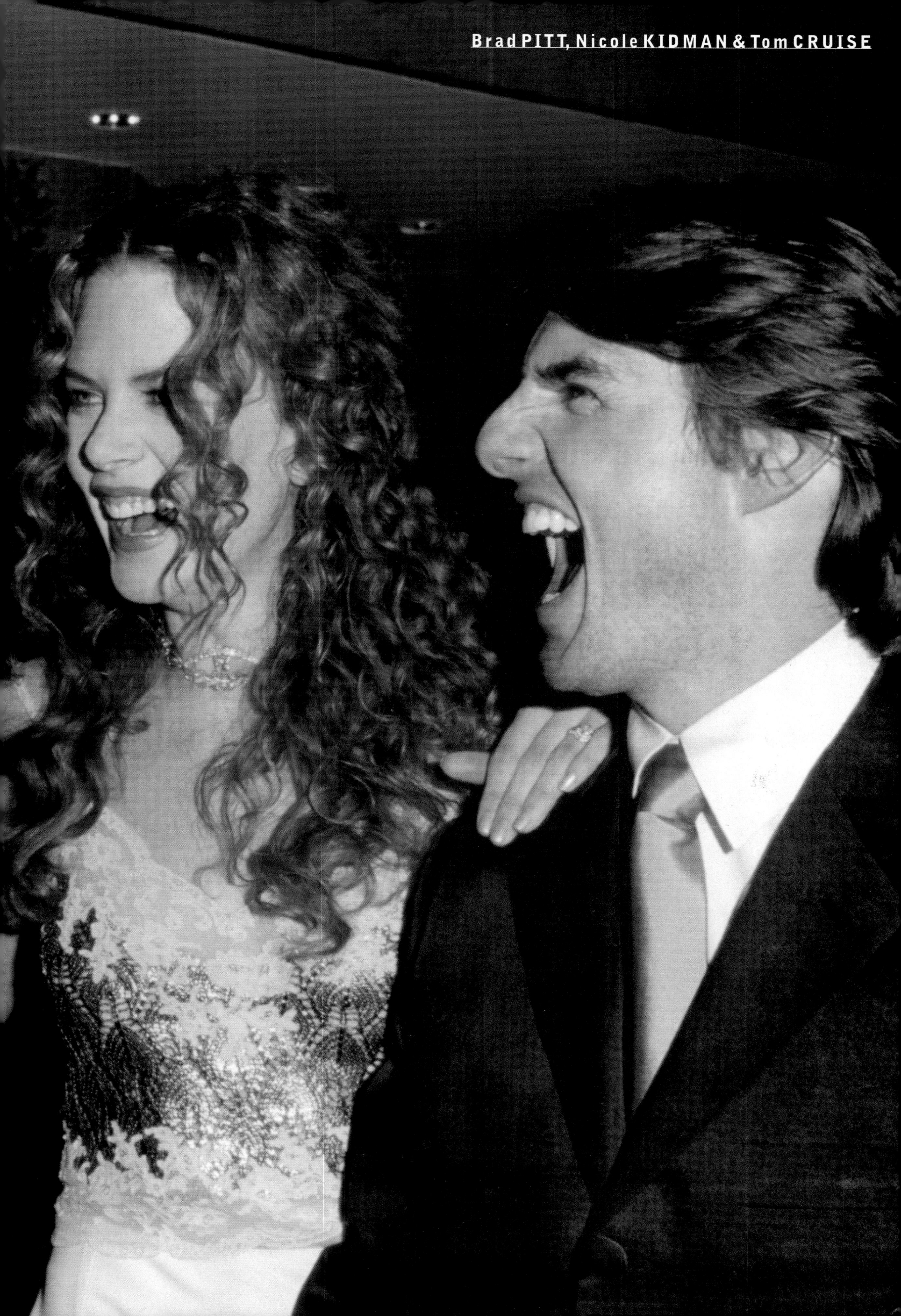

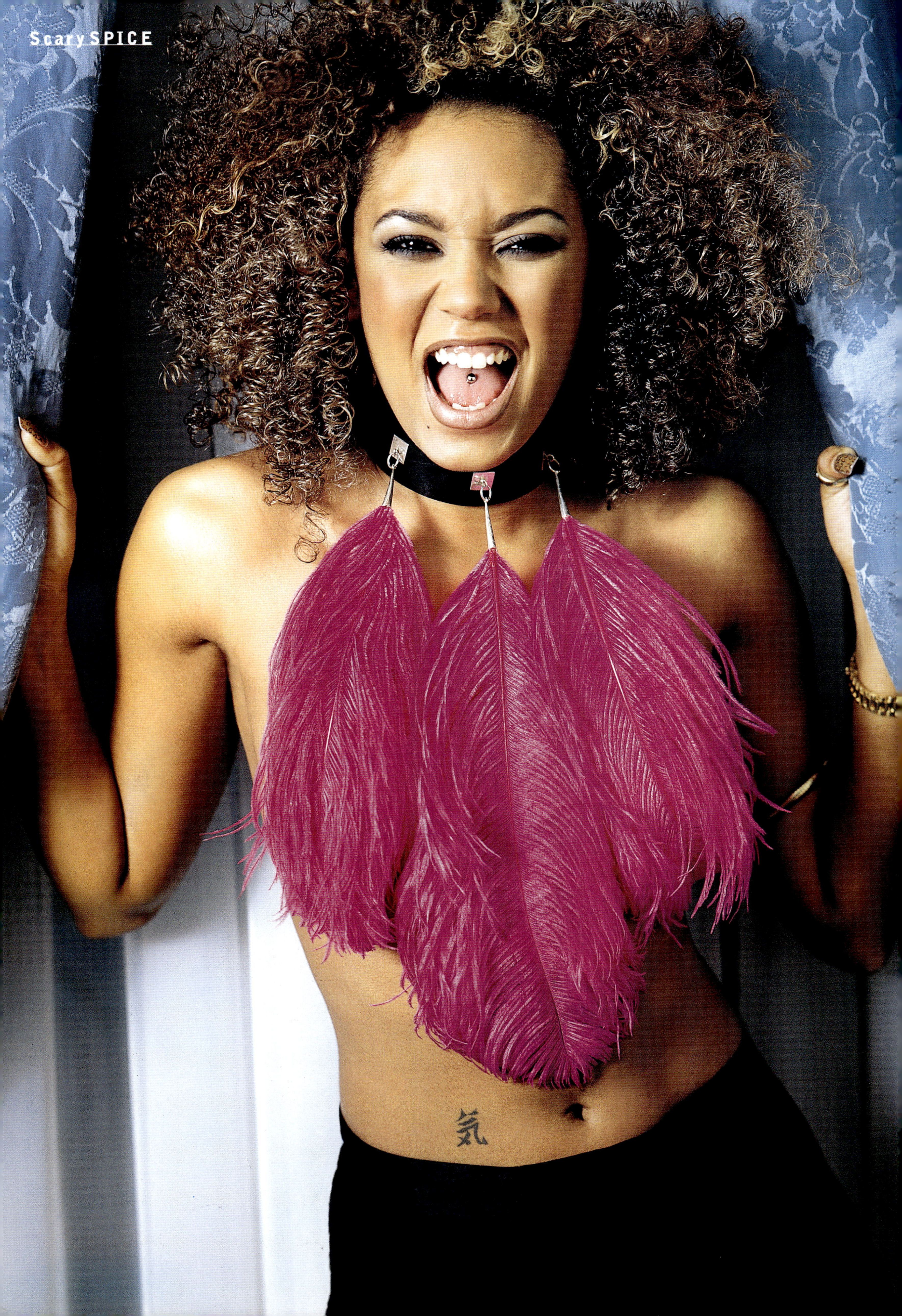

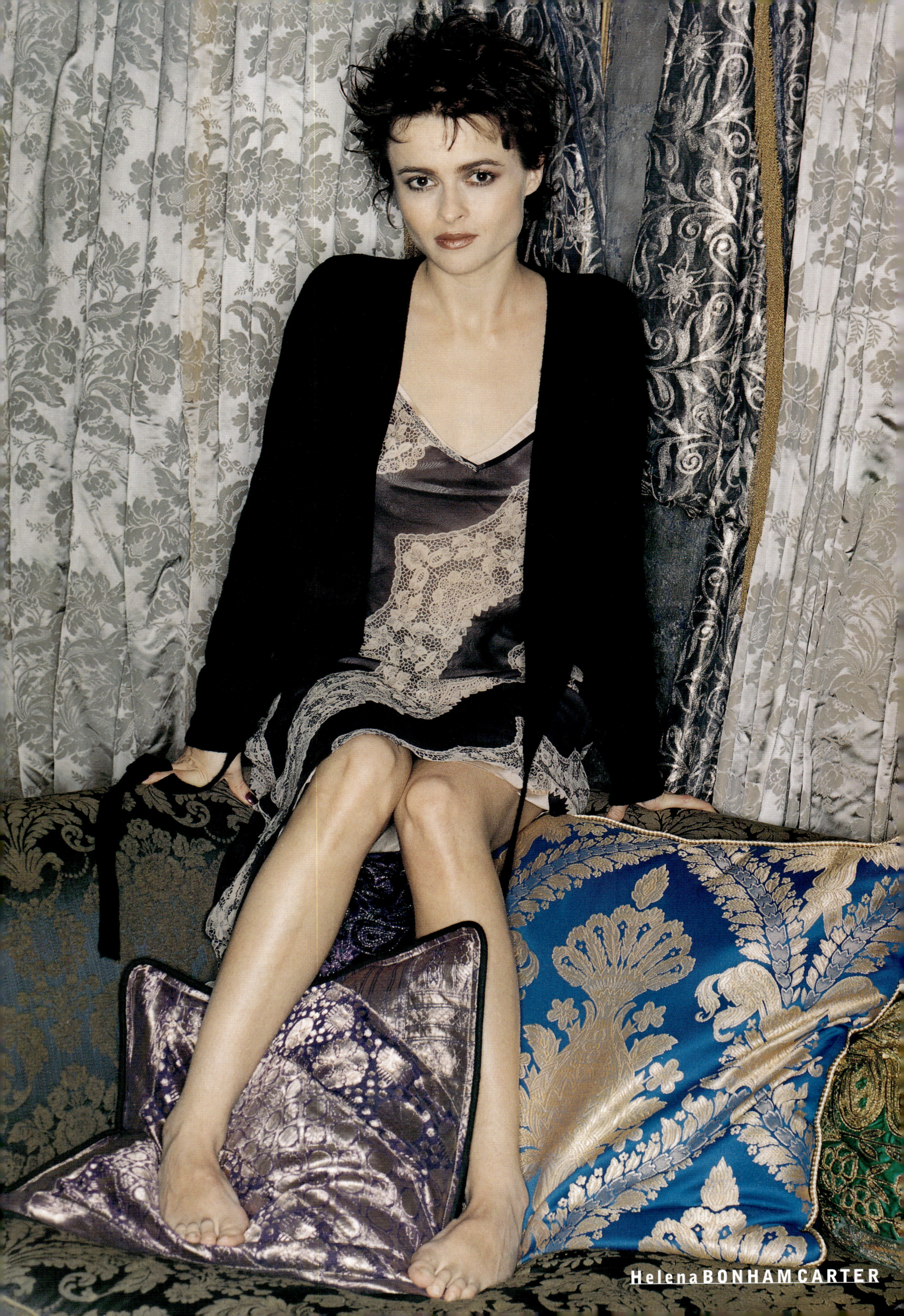

Helena BONHAM CARTER

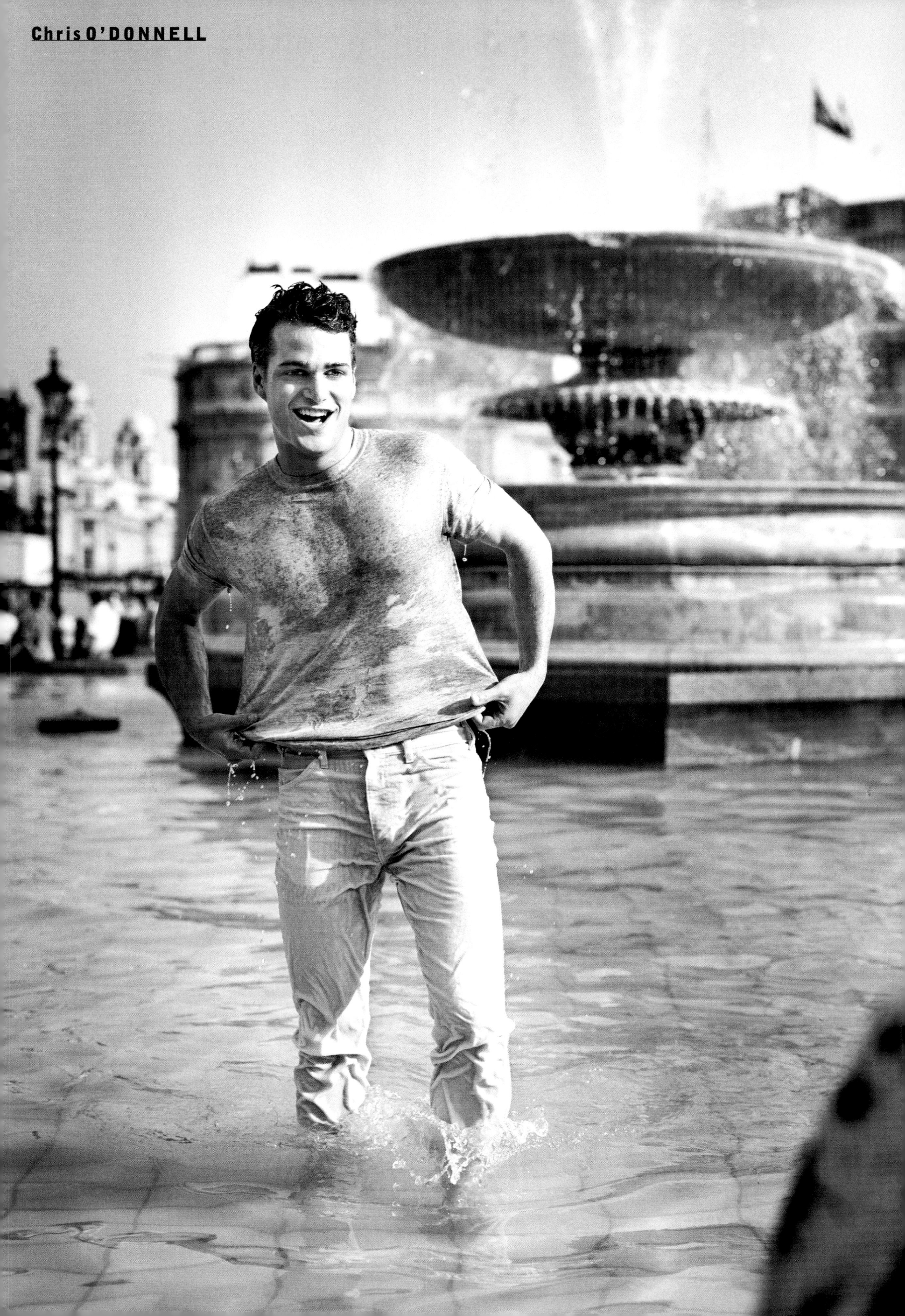

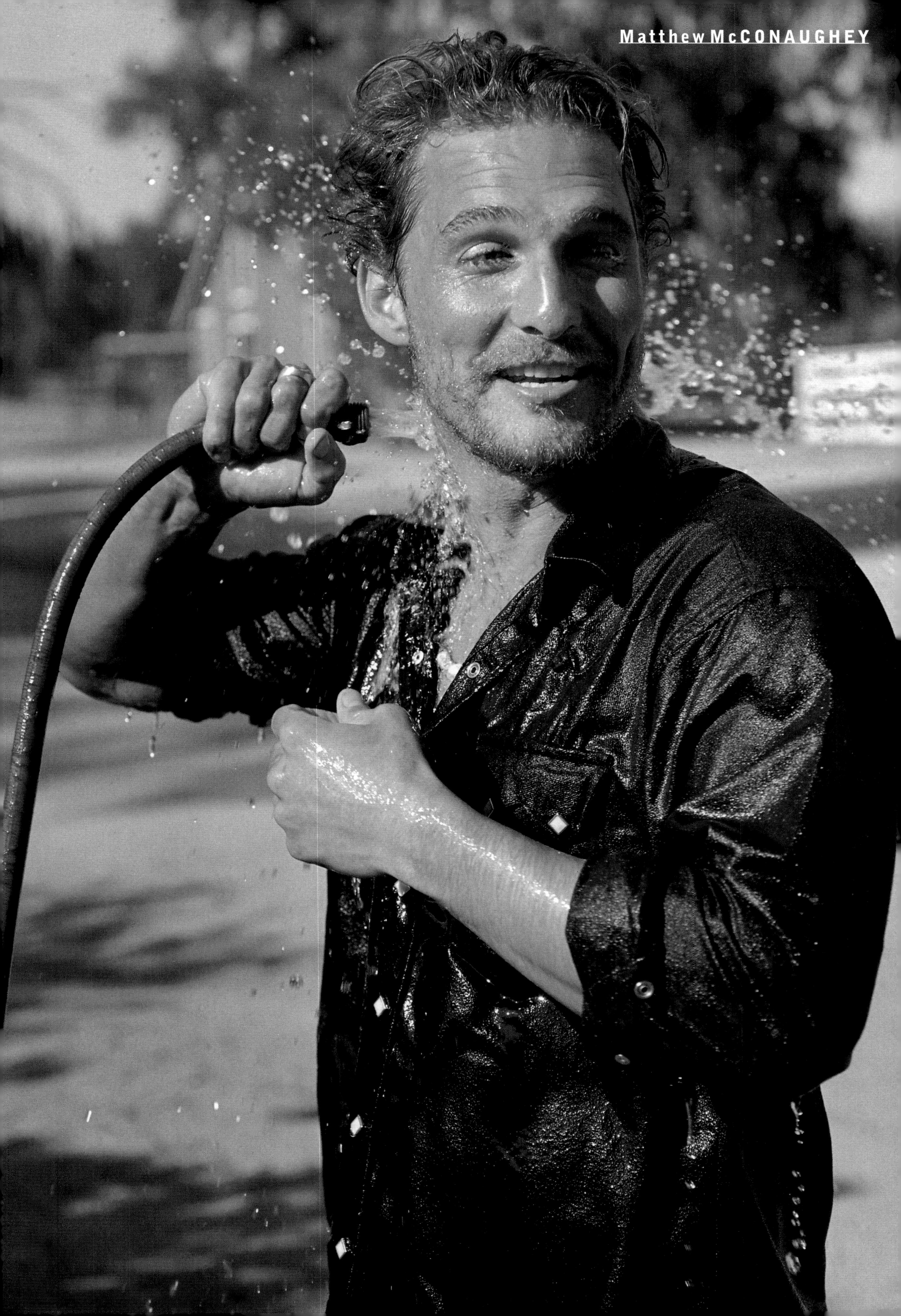

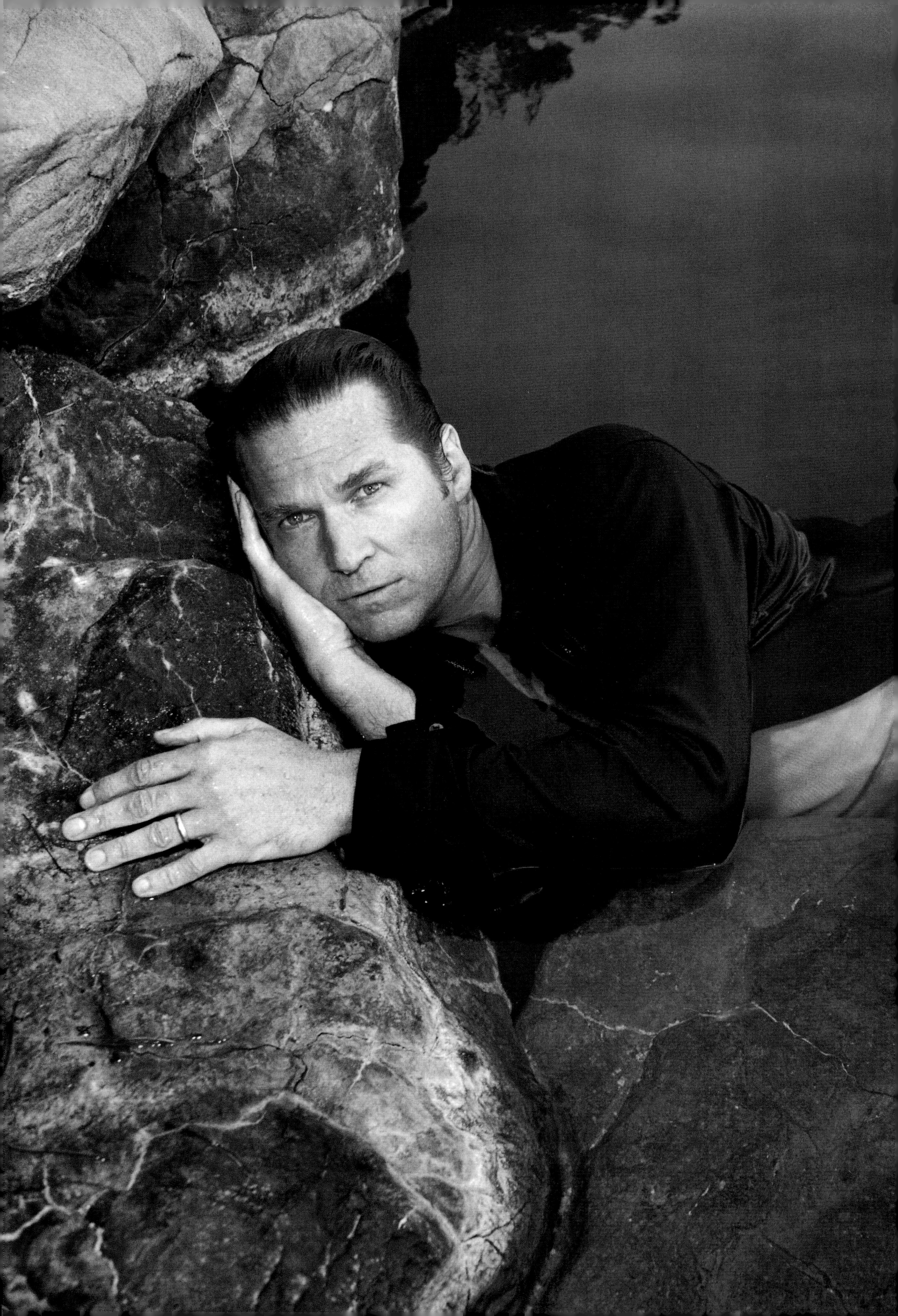

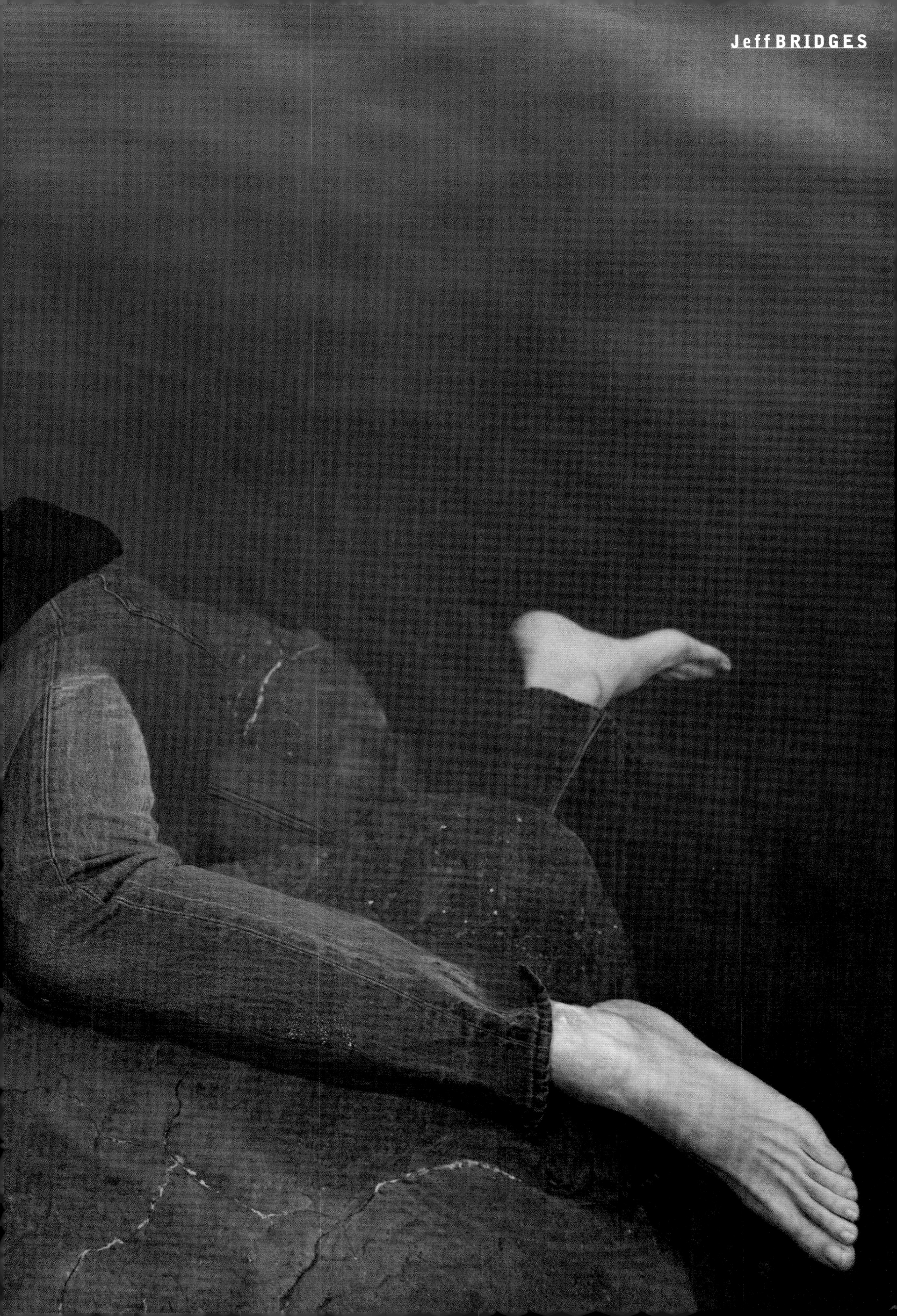

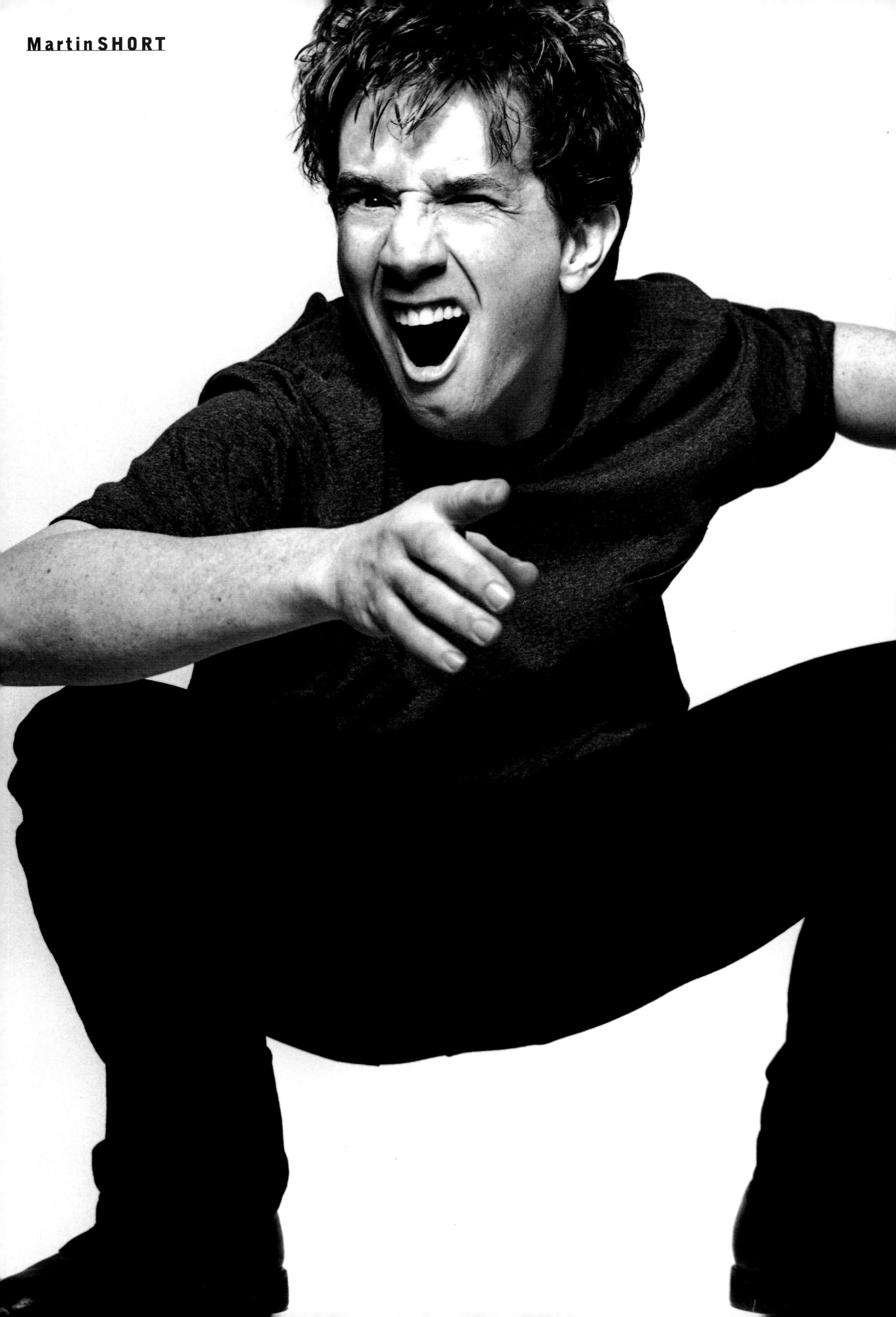
Martin SHORT

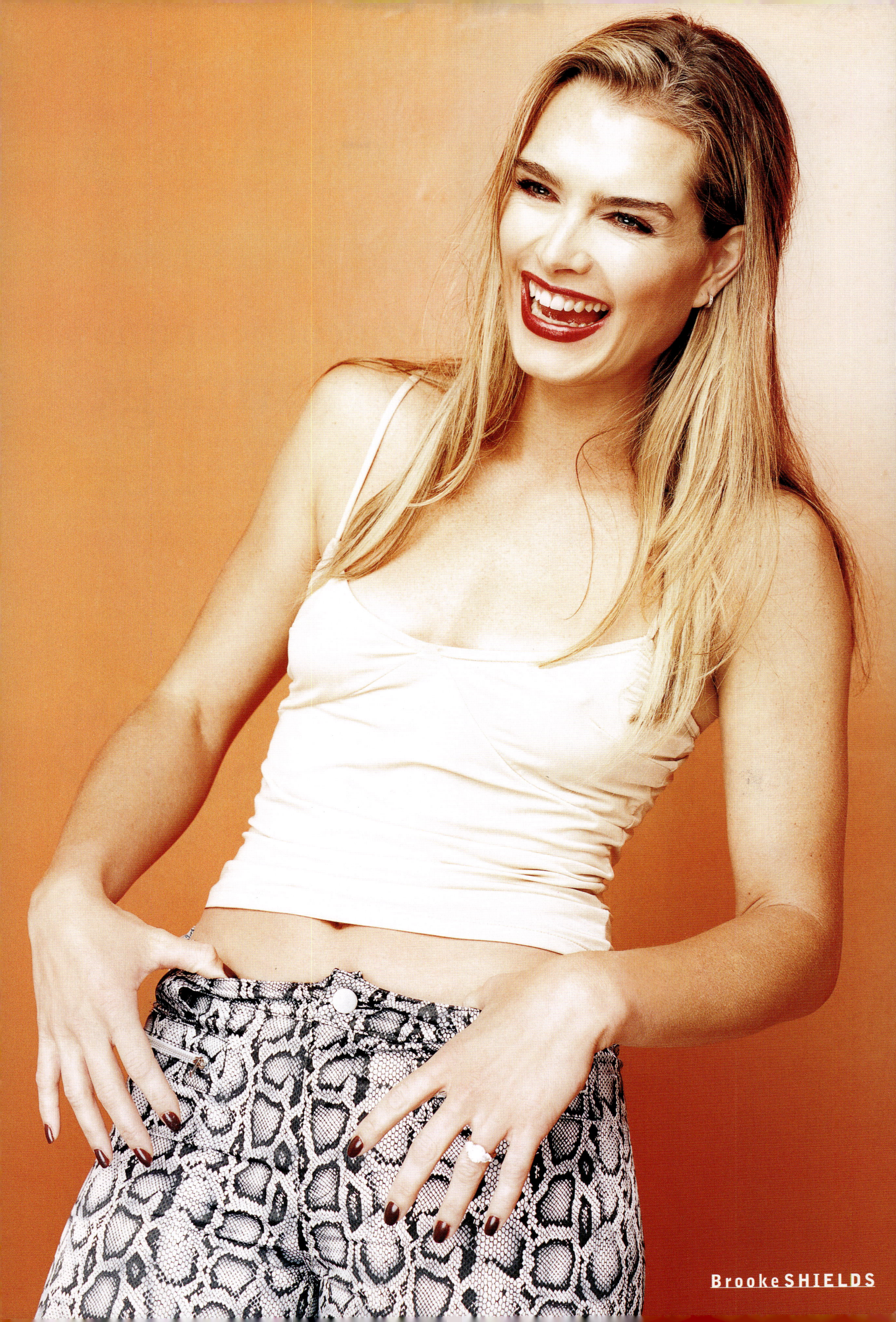

Brooke SHIELDS

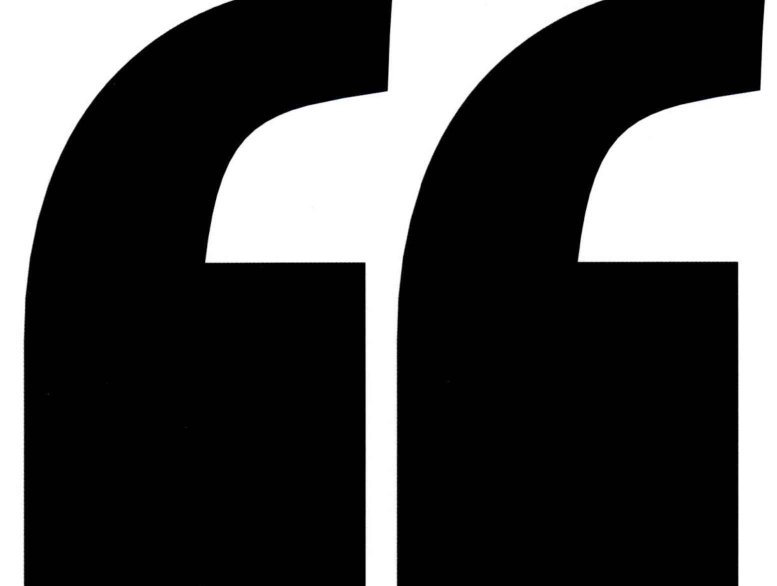

Queen Latifah»

Are you truly a self-confident person now, or is that just the image?

I'm pretty confident, but everyone has some self-doubt. The last four or five years of my life have been the hardest, after my brother died. That screwed me up for real. I thought I was crazy. I felt out of touch with other people on the planet; I was in some zone, and everyone else was here. It wasn't too long after your brother died that your career really took off. Yeah, and I felt real fucked up about that. Because I was always the one getting in trouble. He was, like, the man of the house. And we were as tight as a brother and sister could be. The strange thing is that when my brother died, I lost my grip, the power in my arms. I couldn't make a fist. To this day, it's still not the same. It's been a while — nearly five years — since your last album. What do you think about the state of rap these days? I think hip-hop is back. I really feel good about it. Rap became all this 'keep it real' shit. Rappers thought they couldn't sell a record unless they cursed two thousand times, shooting up this many people, beating my girl, all of this stuff that all sounded the same. The reality that kept getting created was too negative. So much hype. We lost two of the greatest rappers, Biggie [Smalls] and Tupac [Shakur]. They could've changed things and been leaders, you know. I'm sure they're sitting up there now like, 'Ain't this a bitch. This is fucked up.'

What do you think of these girly-girl rappers?

I like some of them. Lil' Kim. Salt-n-Pepa. [But] it's getting a little monotonous, in a way. You know, all these other rappers and artists have had a chance to shine because I haven't had a record out. And I am the Queen. It's time to come back and let them know I'm here. What is the most relentless, untrue rumour about you? I am not Muhammad Ali's daughter. That got started because his daughter was a rapper with a Muslim name and made a record when I did. You seem pretty comfortable with your body image in a town where any given actress is a size two. That, I've actually wrestled with. I was always the biggest girl in my class, until one year, another, bigger girl came. I was so happy! One thing I was self-conscious about was my breasts. I thought they were so big. Then when I was eighteen or nineteen, I dated somebody who just loved my body down. Someone who just praised and adored my body constantly. That really turned me around.

”

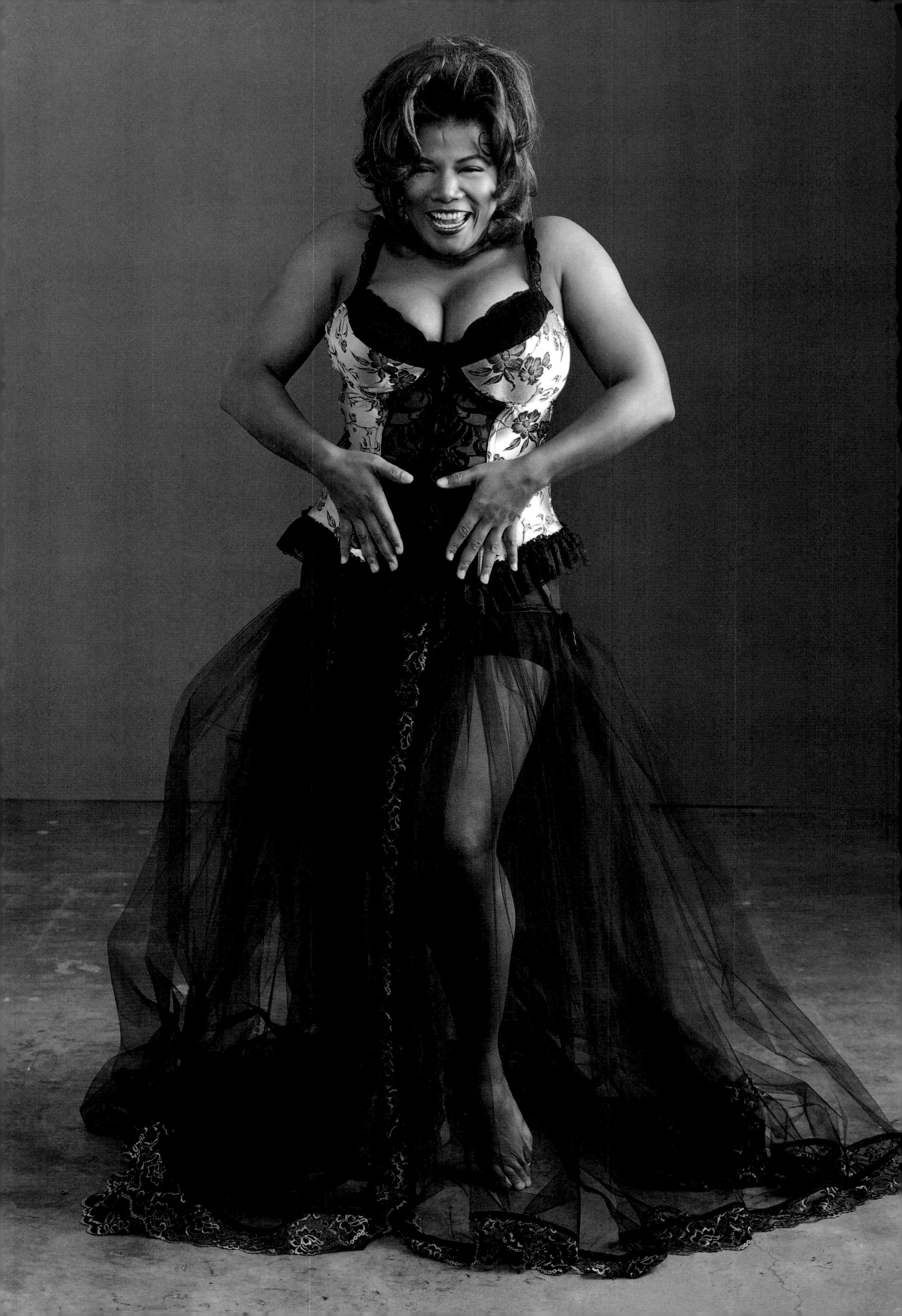

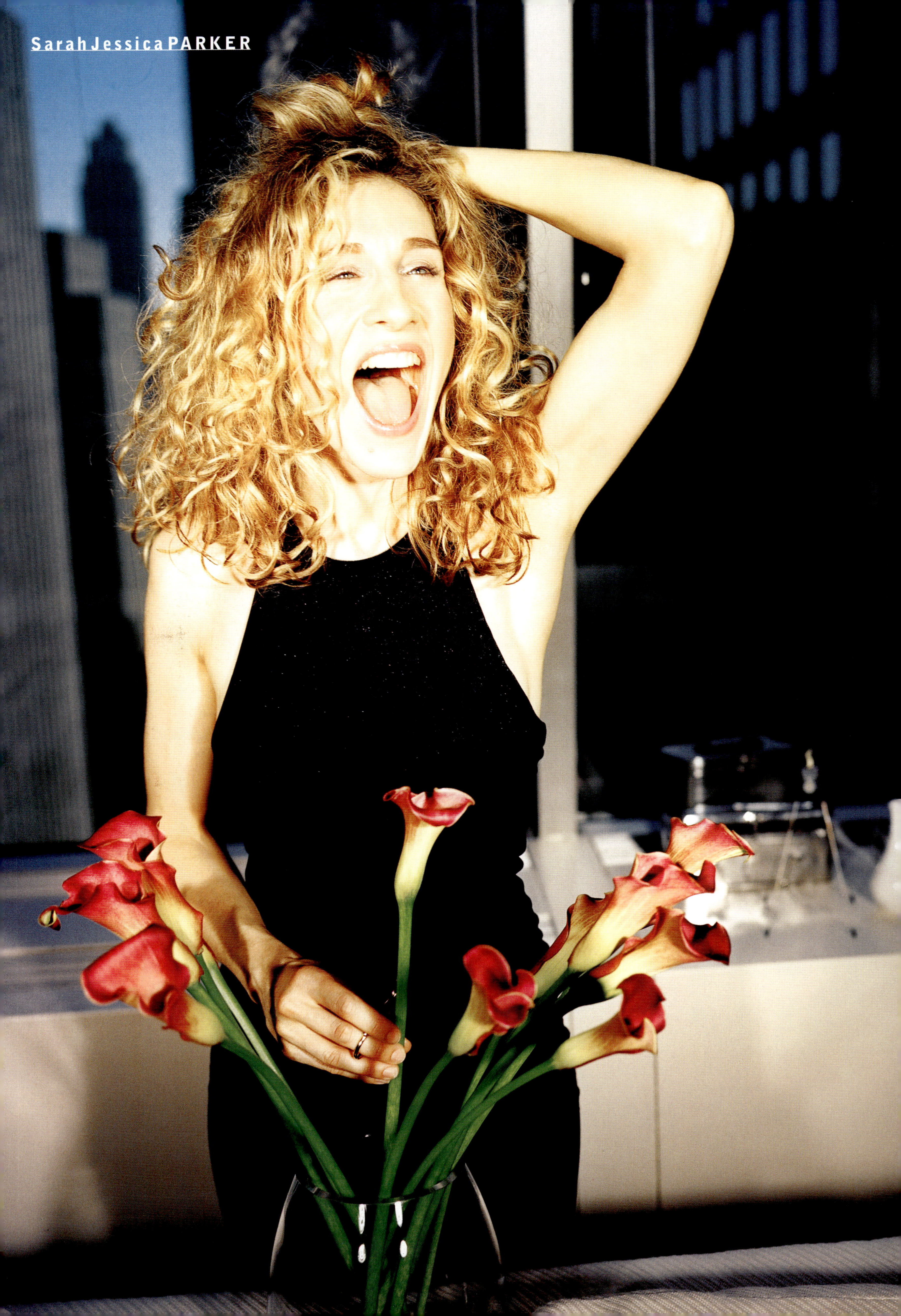

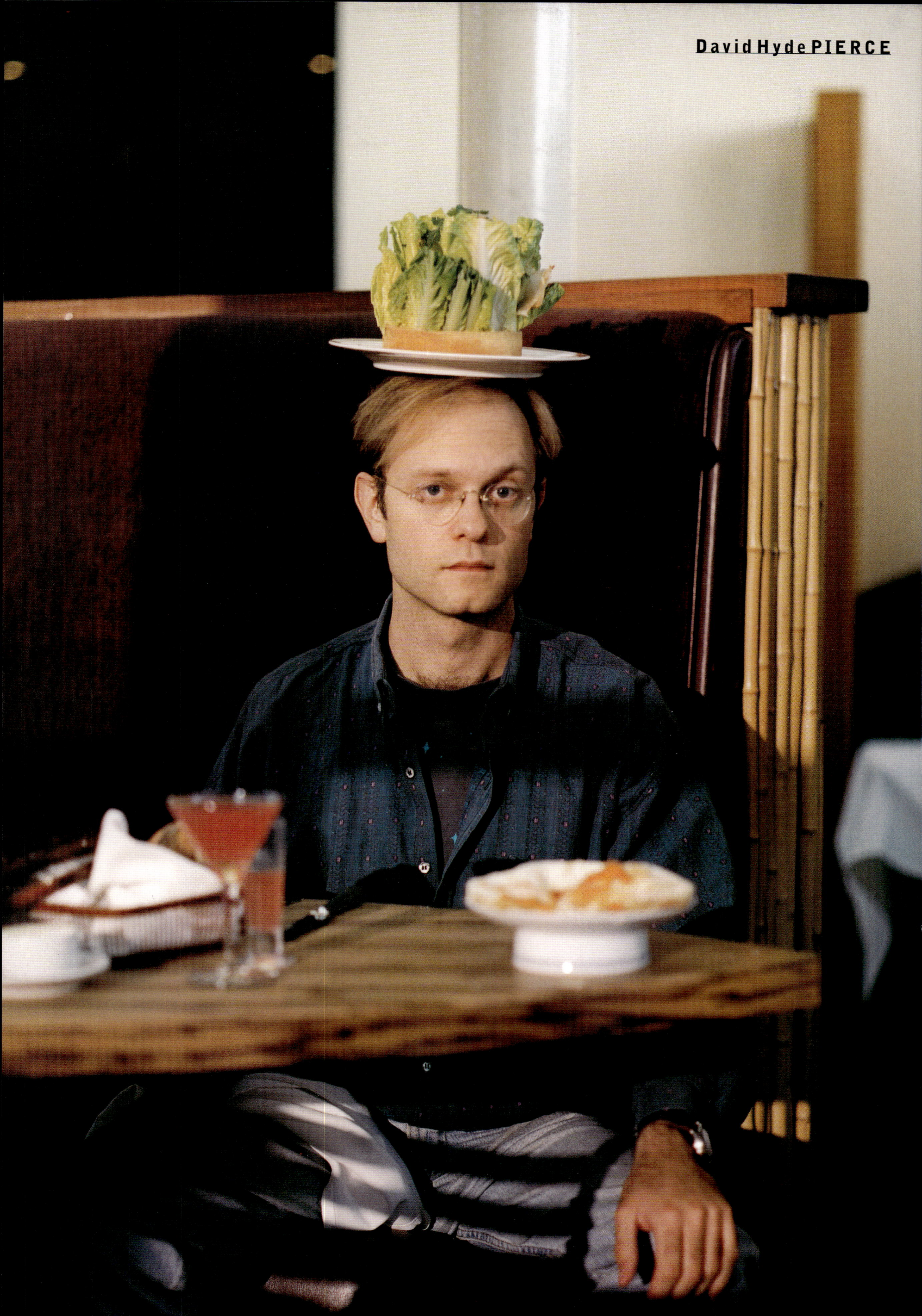

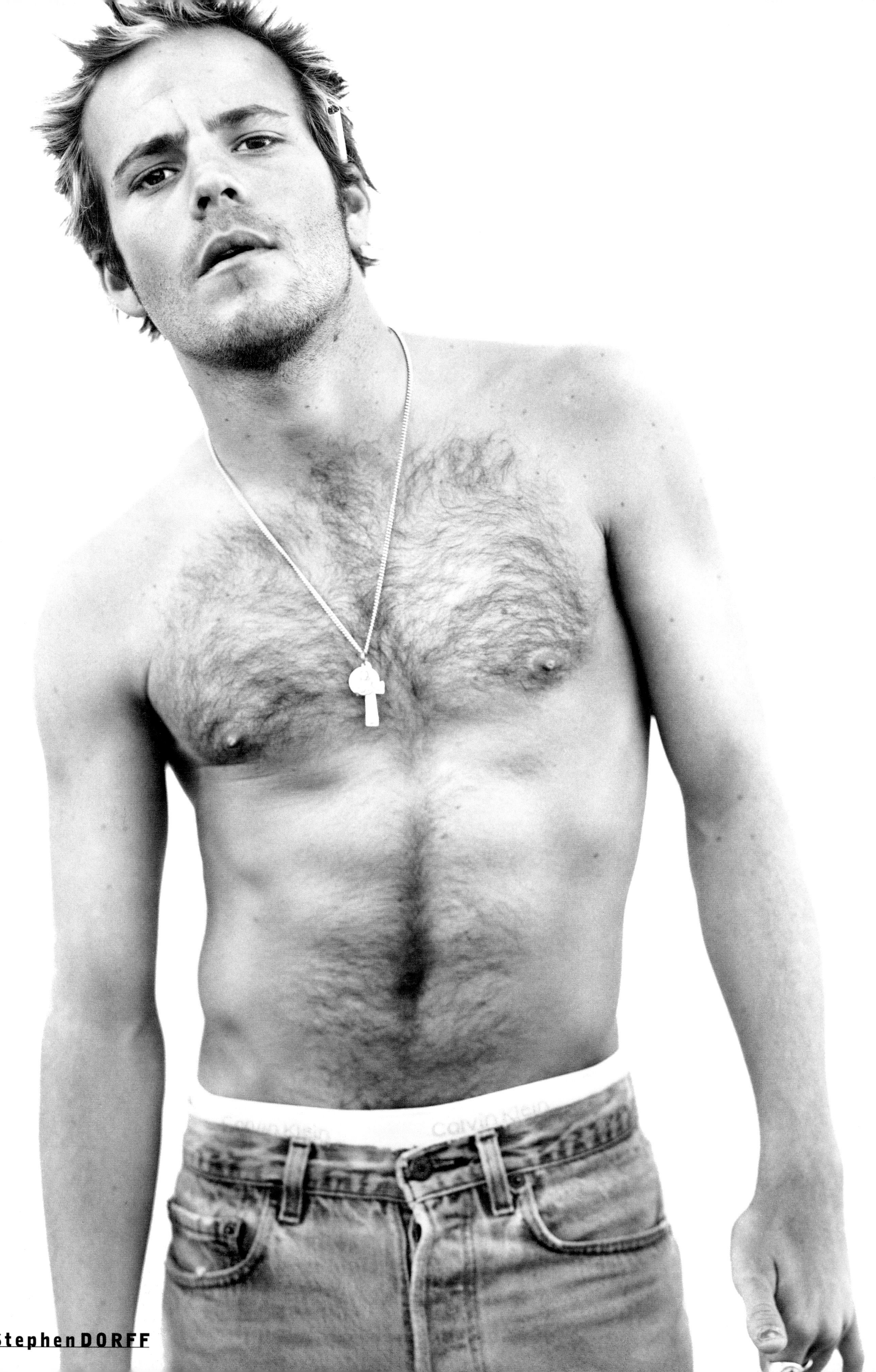

Stephen DORFF

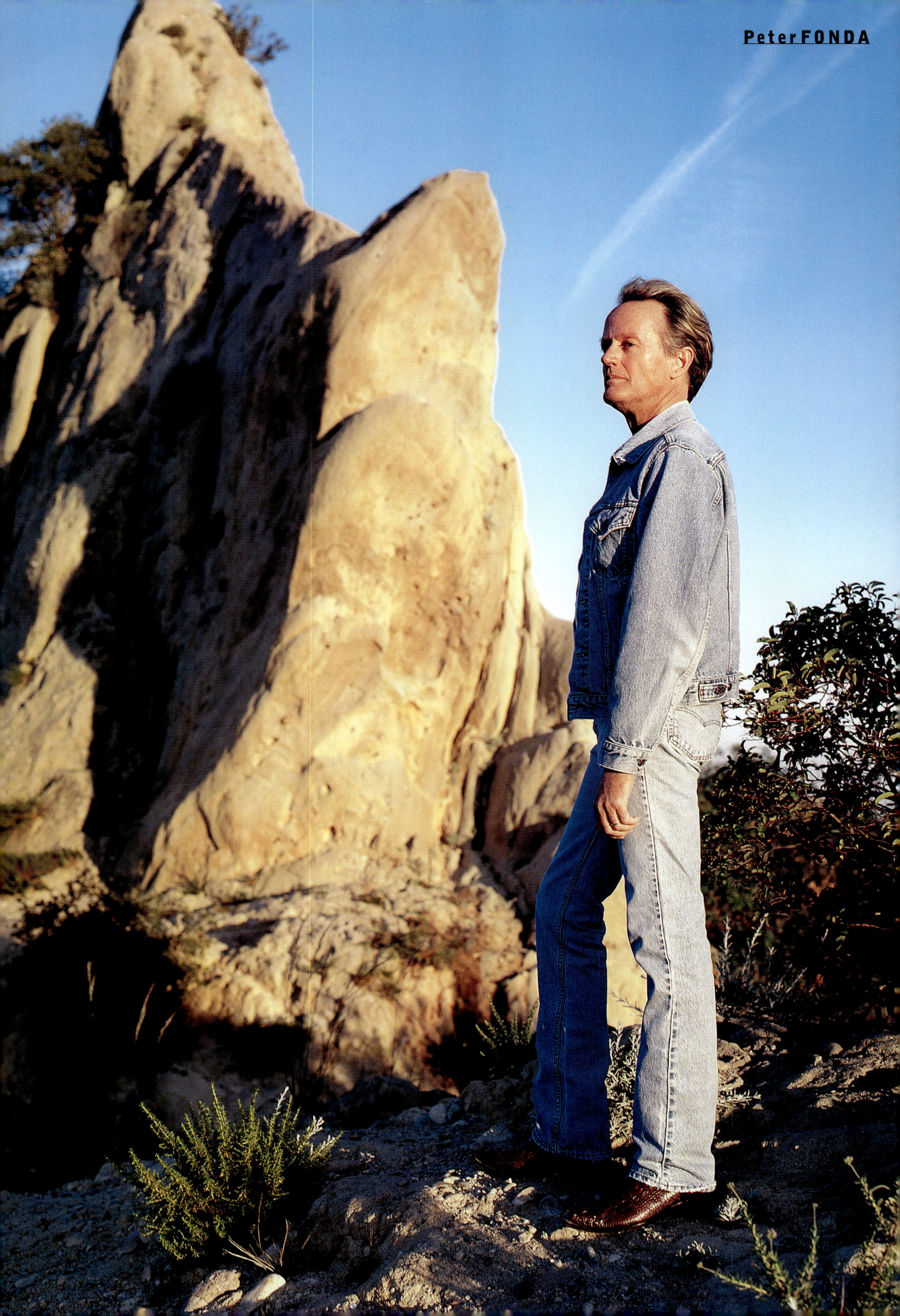

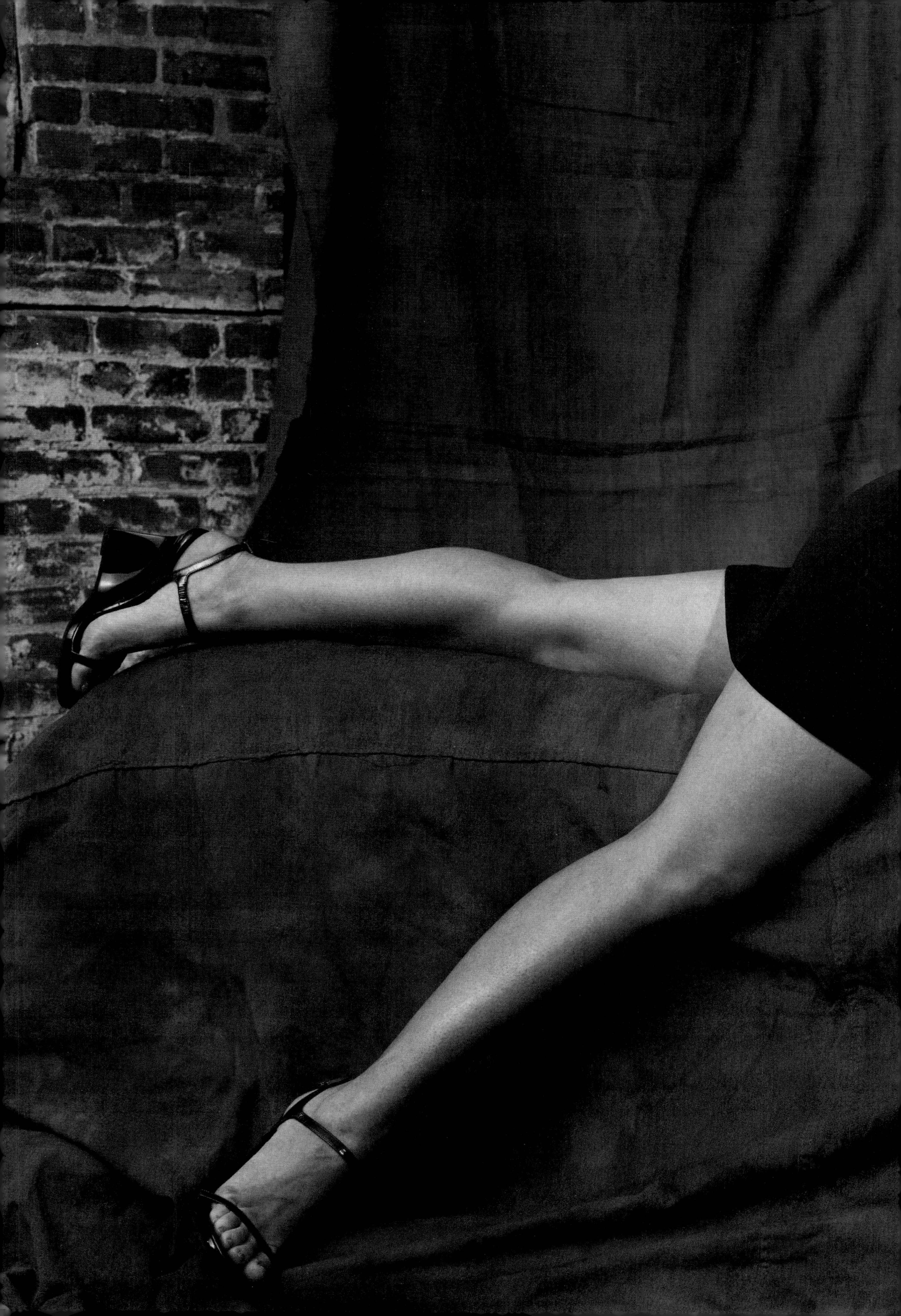

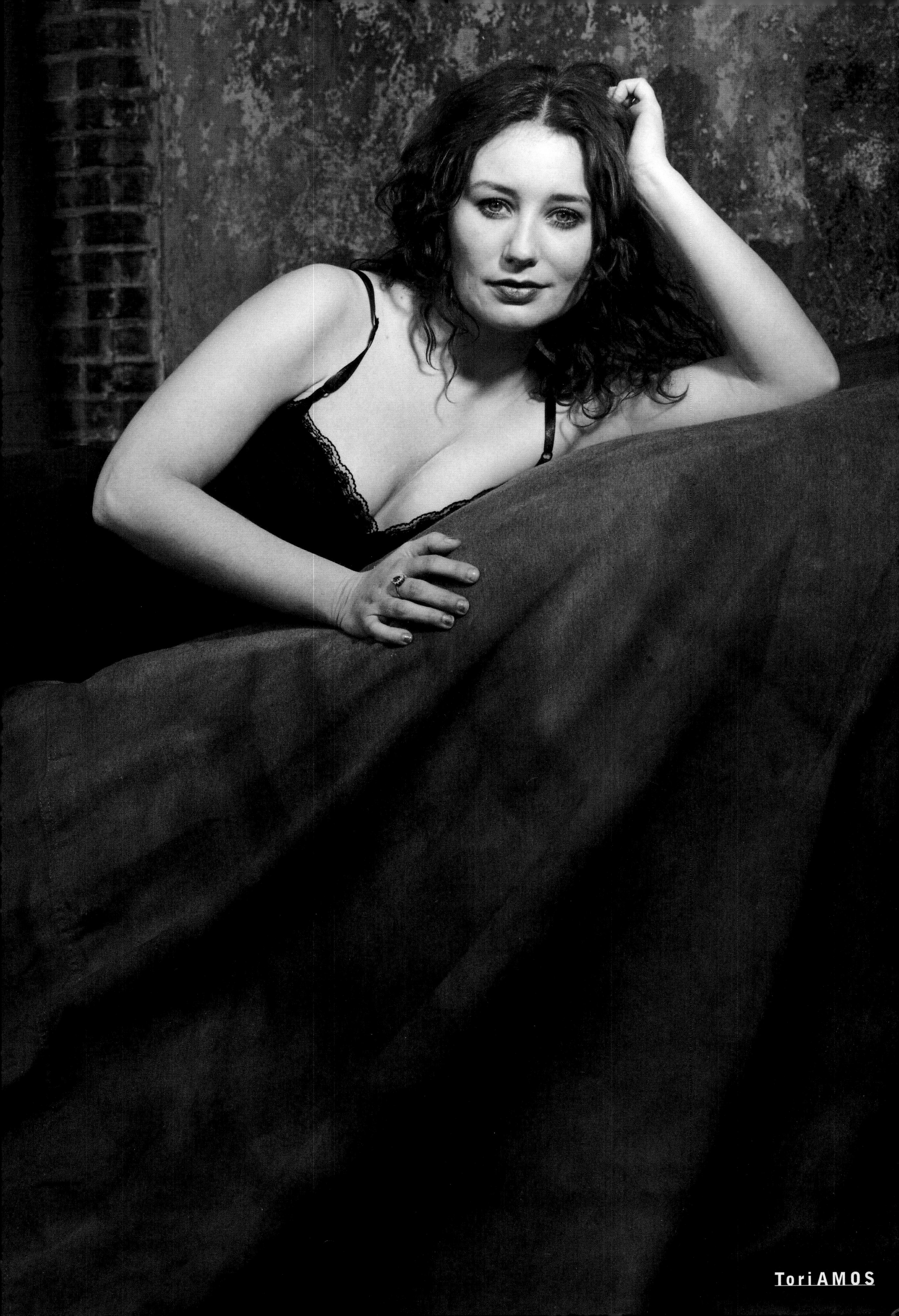

ToriAMOS

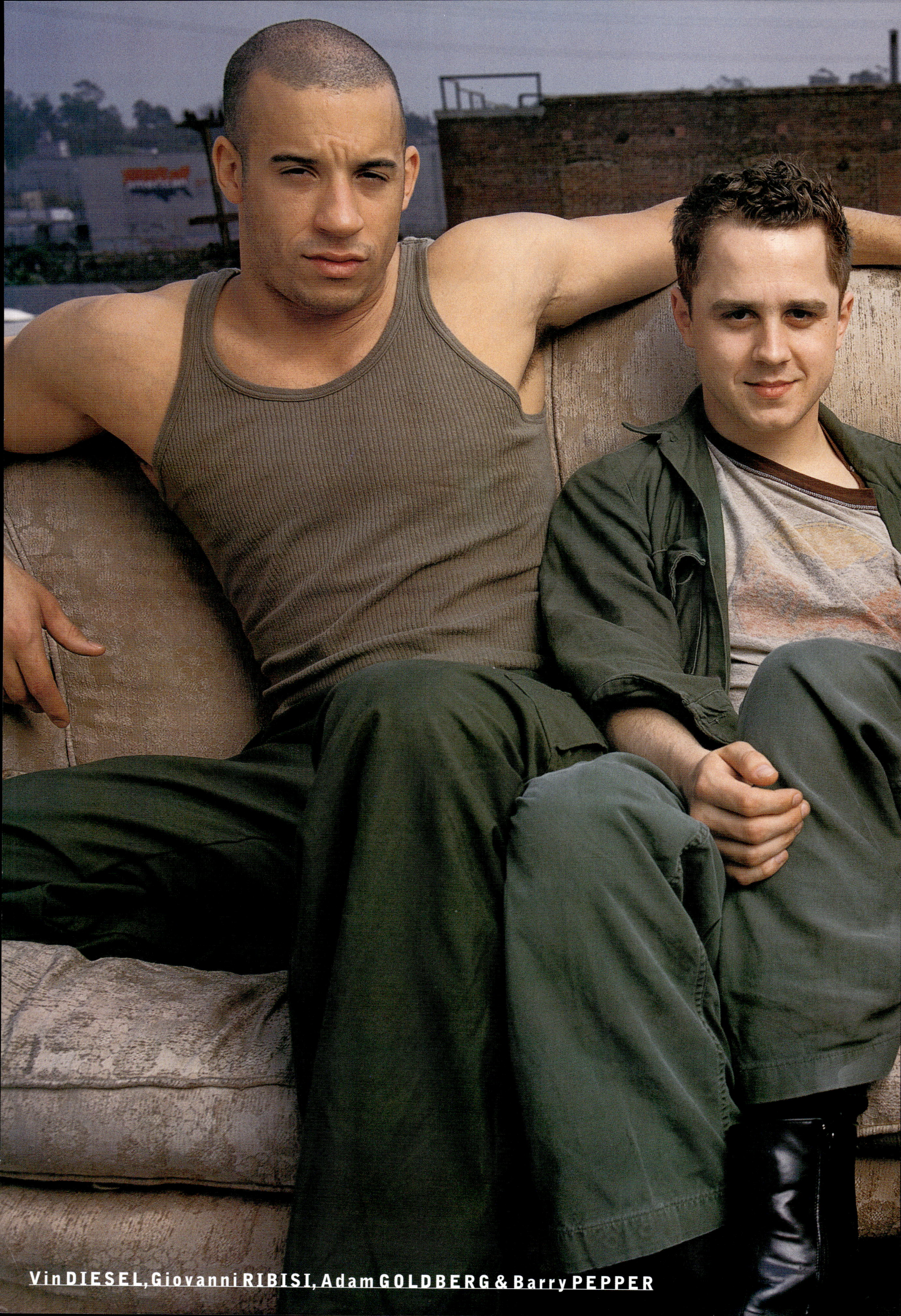

Vin DIESEL, Giovanni RIBISI, Adam GOLDBERG & Barry PEPPER

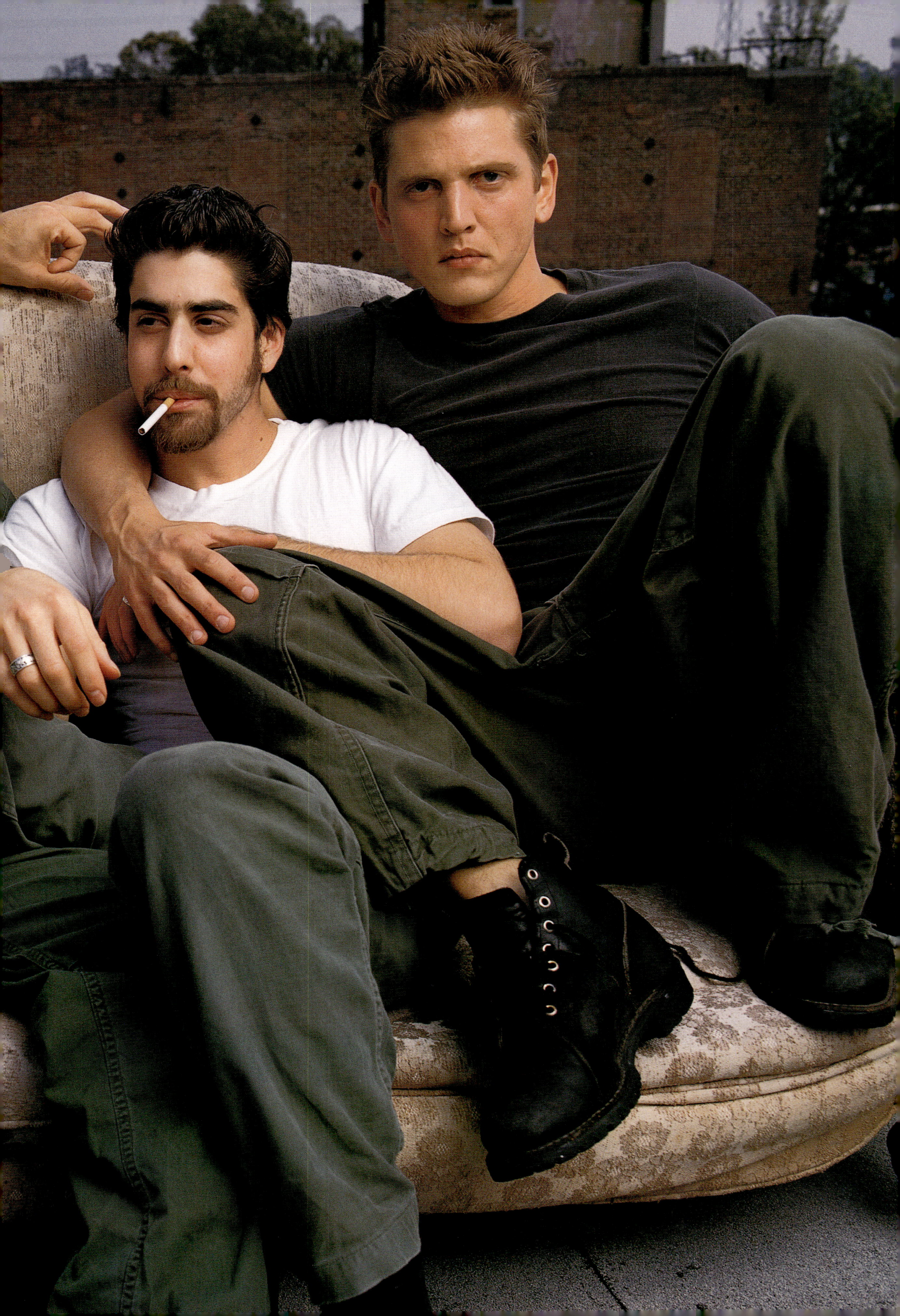

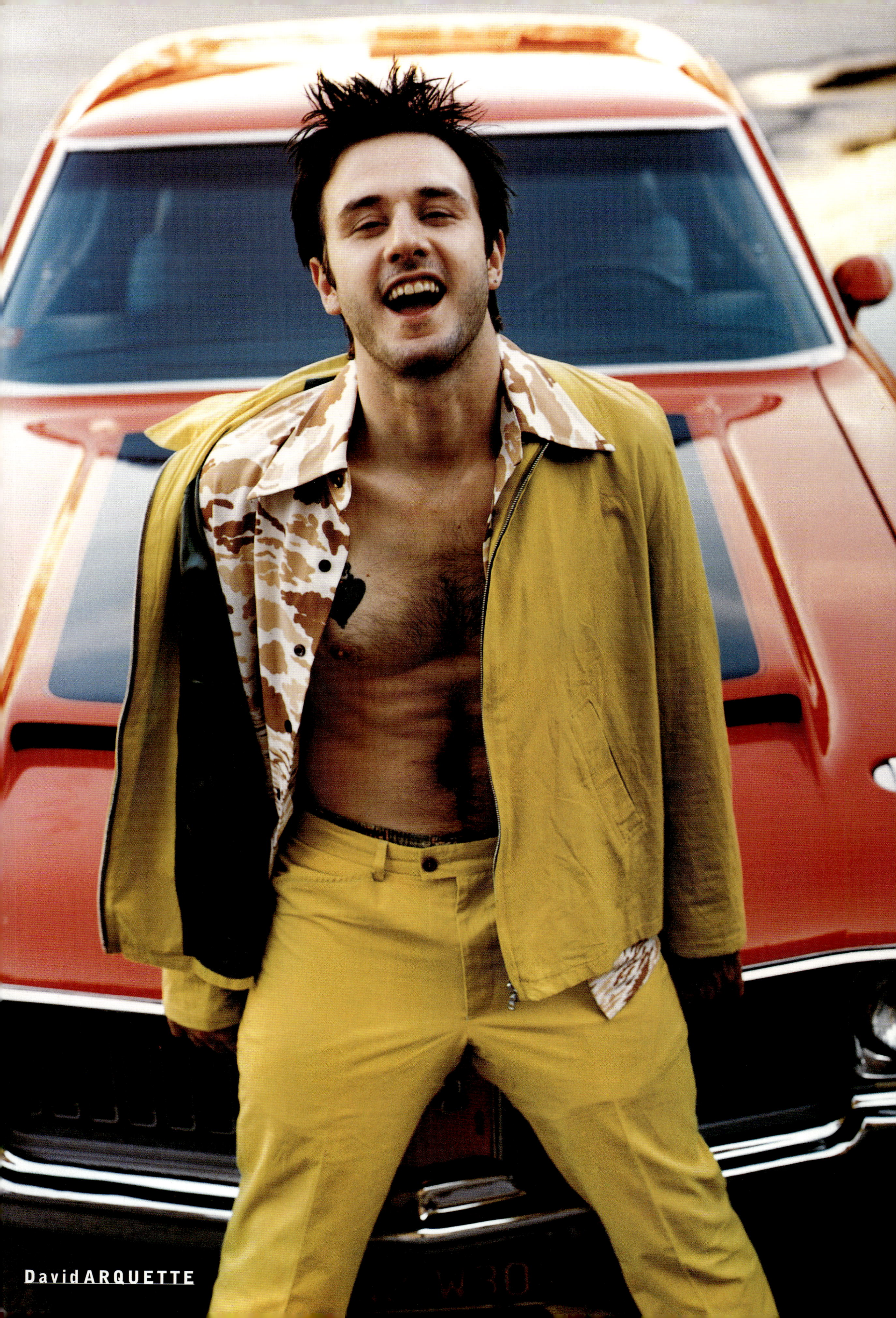

David ARQUETTE

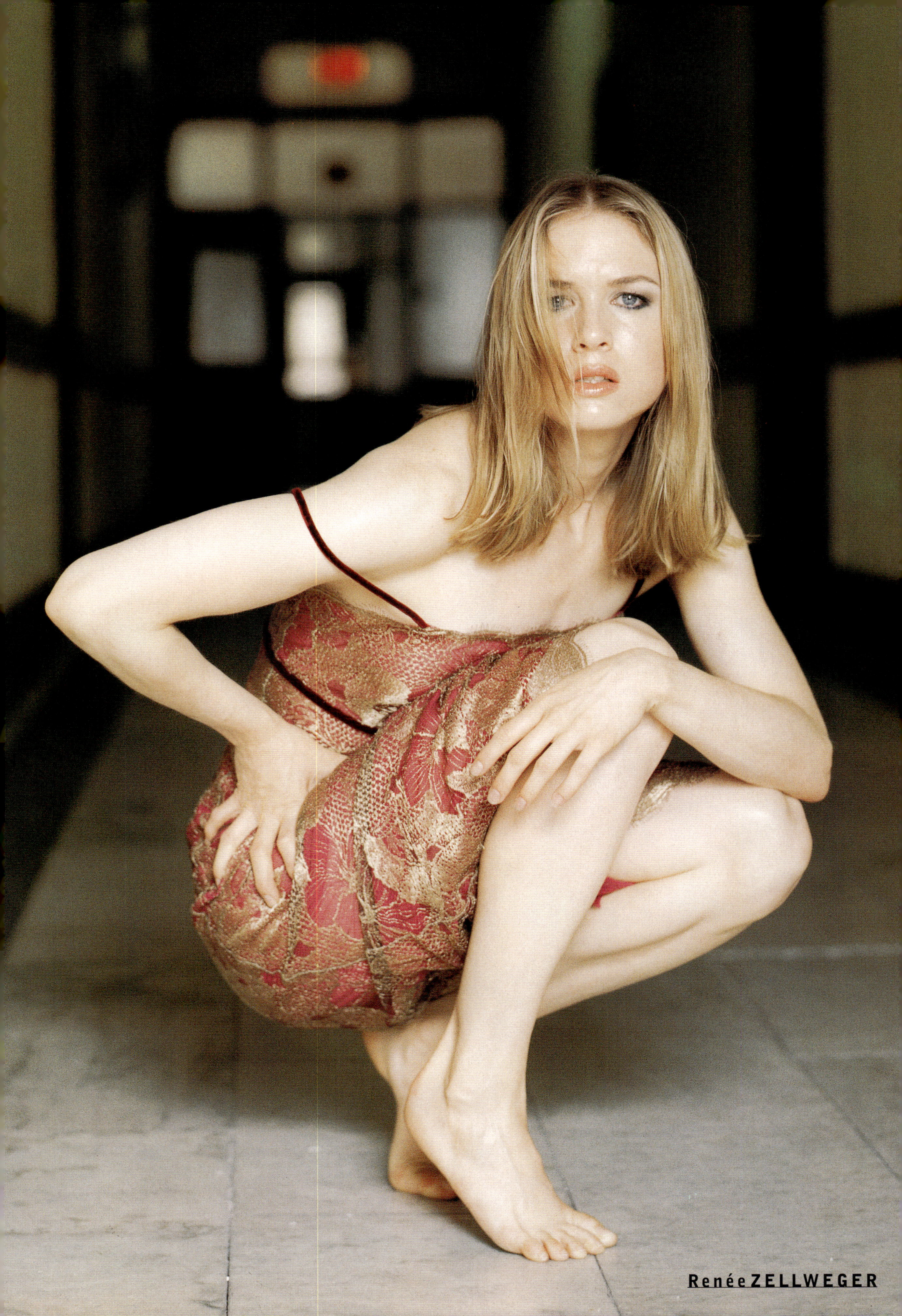

Renée ZELLWEGER

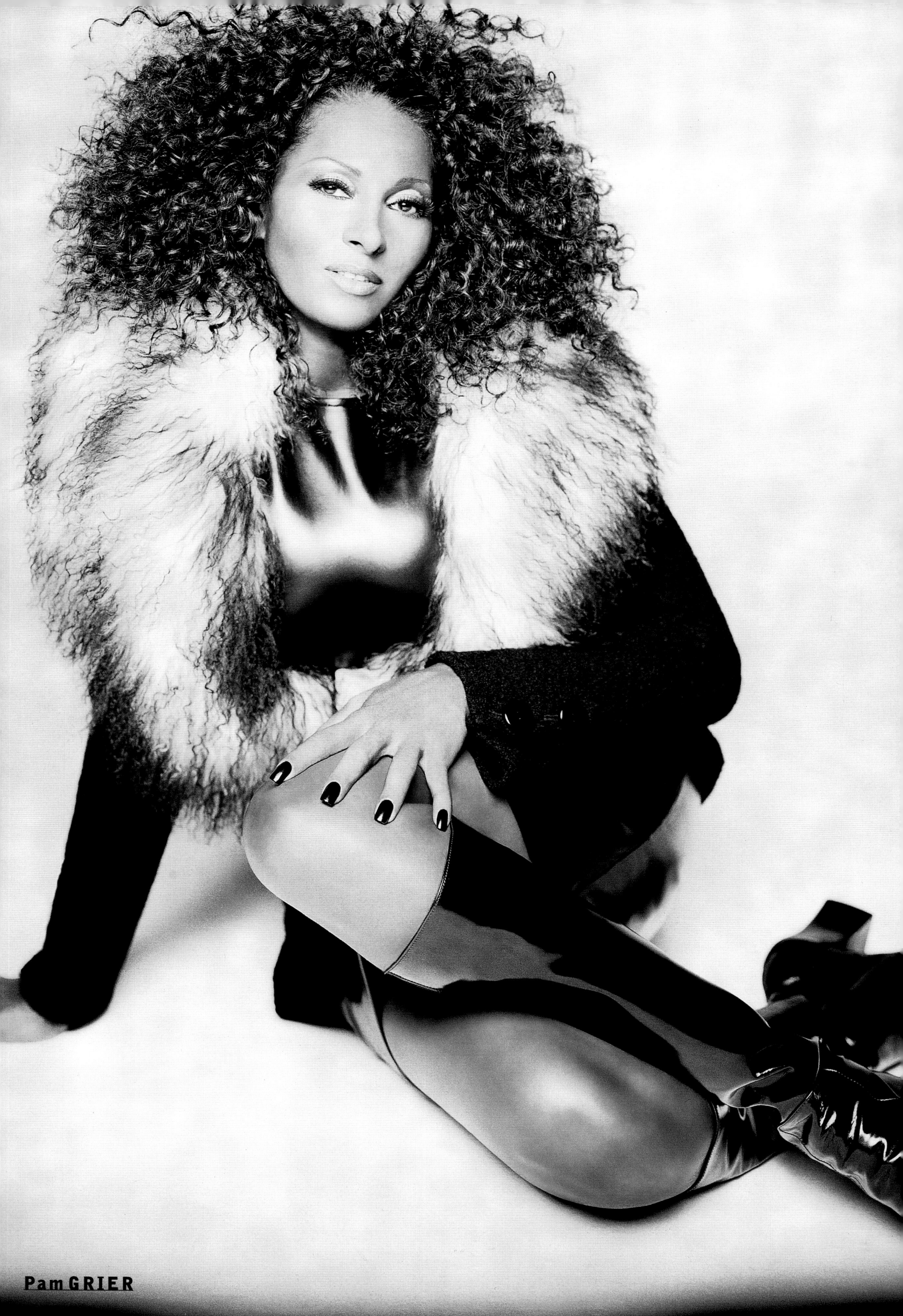

Pam GRIER

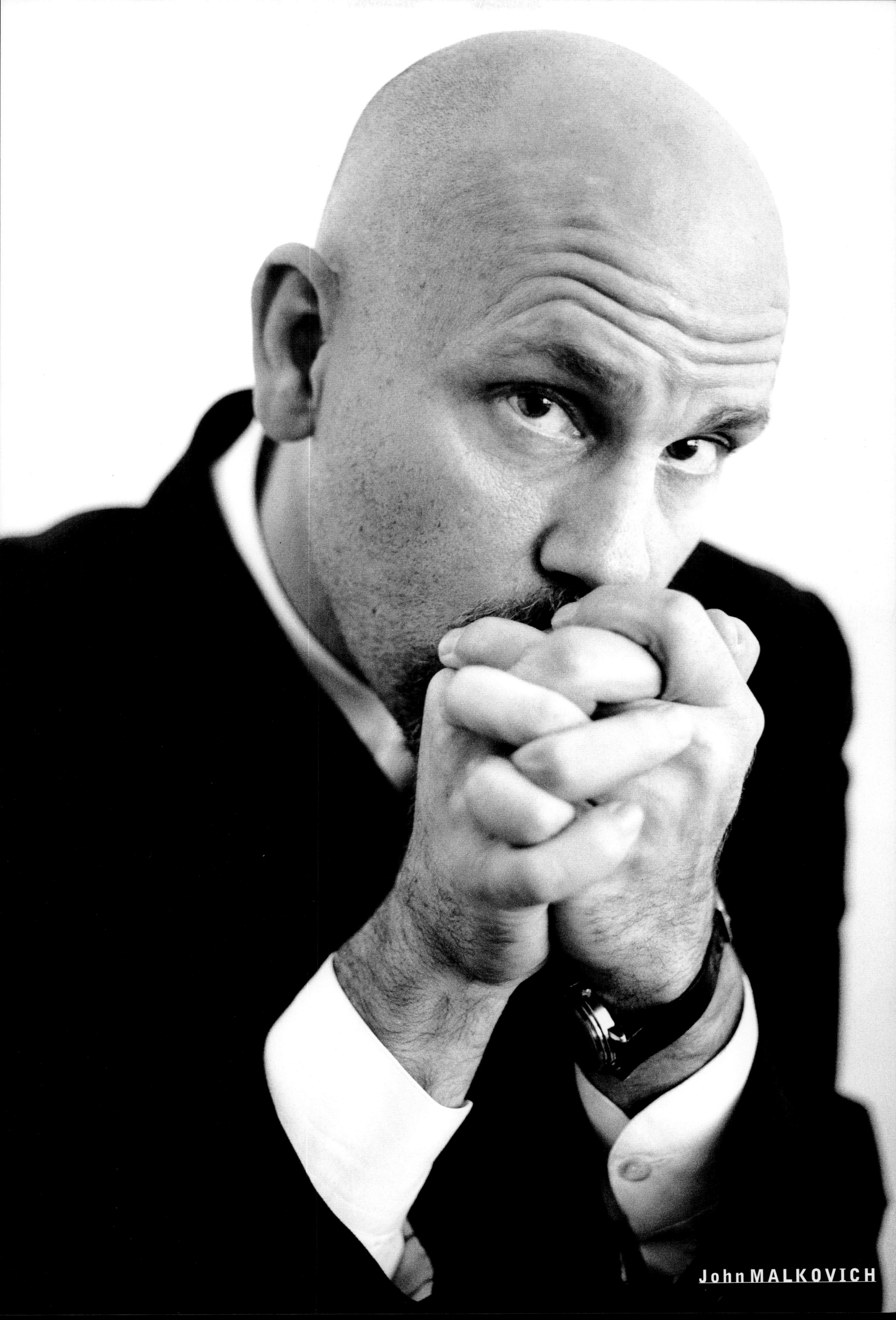

John MALKOVICH

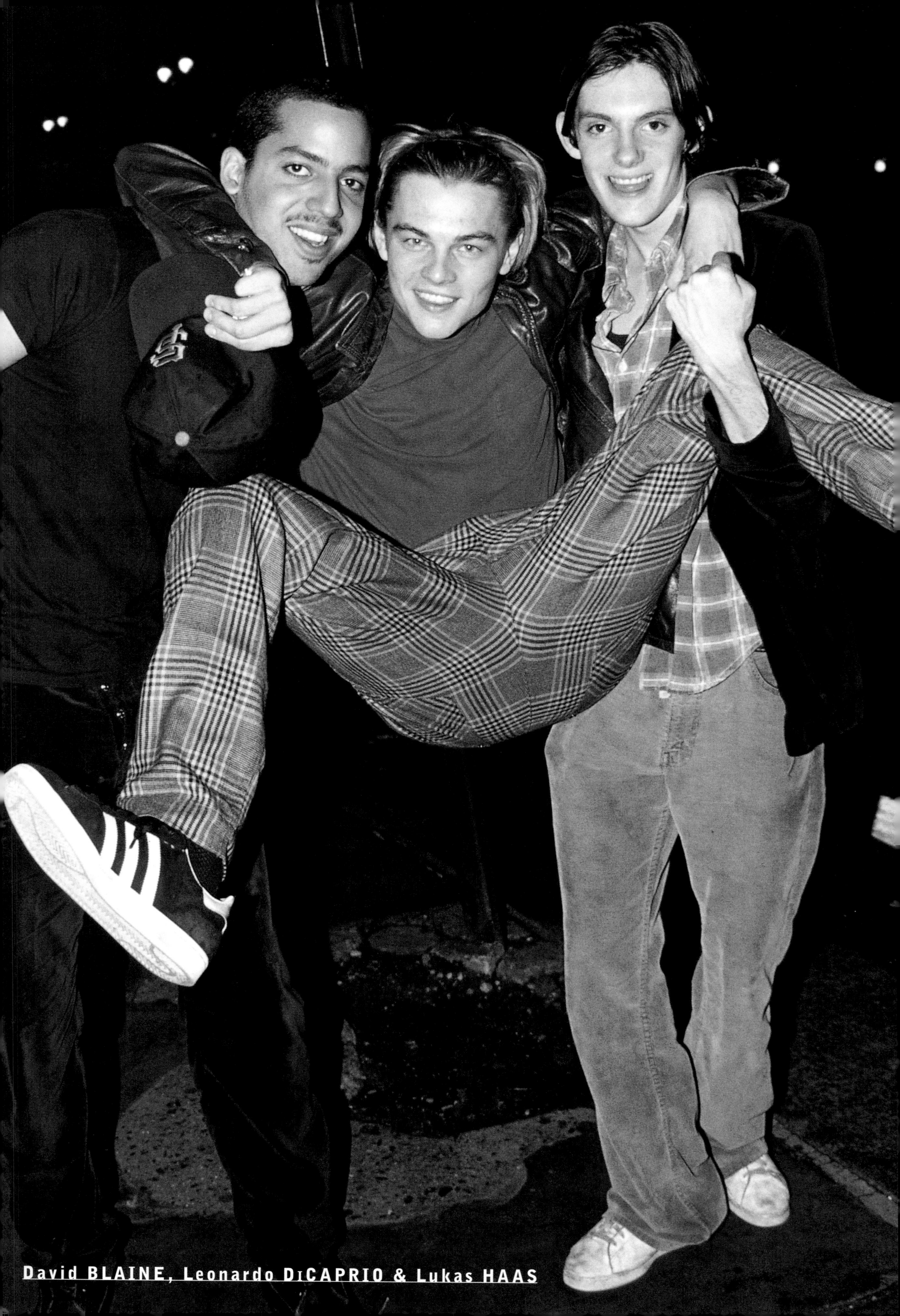

David BLAINE, Leonardo DiCAPRIO & Lukas HAAS

Jason Alexander NIGEL PARRY
Kirstie Alley MARK SELIGER
Tori Amos MARY ELLEN MARK
Gillian Anderson MARK SELIGER
Gillian Anderson & David Duchovny MARK SELIGER
Jennifer Aniston MARK SELIGER
Fiona Apple MARK SELIGER
David Arquette ISABEL SNYDER
William, Stephen & Alec Baldwin DAVID LACHAPPELLE
Drew Barrymore MARK SELIGER
Michael Bergin STEWART SHINING
David Blaine, Leonardo DiCaprio &
Lukas Haas PATRICK MCMULLAN–GAMMA-LIASON
Jon Bon Jovi ROBERT MAXWELL
Brandy MARC BAPTISTE
Benjamin Bratt ISABEL SNYDER
Jeff Bridges MARY ELLEN MARK
Neve Campbell MARK SELIGER
Drew Carey JEFFREY THURNHER
Helena Bonham Carter VALERIE PHILLIPS
David Caruso MARY ELLEN MARK
The Cranberries KATE GARNER
Sheryl Crow BUTCH BELAIR
Tom Cruise LANCE STAEDLER
Tony Curtis & Jill Vanden Berg MARY ELLEN MARK
Claire Danes MARK SELIGER
Danny DeVito MARK SELIGER
Leonardo DiCaprio MAXPPP-RETNA
Vin Diesel, Giovanni Ribisi,
Adam Goldberg & Barry Pepper MARK SELIGER
Stephen Dorff MARK SELIGER
David Duchovny MARK SELIGER
Anthony Edwards MARK SELIGER
Omar Epps ROBERT MAXWELL
Rupert Everett ROBERT MAXWELL
Chris Farley DAN WINTERS
Ralph Fiennes MARK SELIGER
Peter Fonda LANCE STAEDLER
Brendan Fraser EIKA AOSHIMA
Morgan Freeman ROBERT MAXWELL
Sarah Michelle Gellar MARK SELIGER
Richard Gere MARY ELLEN MARK
Mel Gibson BRIGITTE LACOMBE
Ginger Spice MARK SELIGER
Pam Grier MATTHEW ROLSTON
Salma Hayek RUVEN AFANADOR
Anne Heche ROBERT MAXWELL
Tippi Hedren MARY ELLEN MARK
Jennifer Love Hewitt ISABEL SNYDER
Katie Holmes KATE GARNER
Djimon Hounsou MARK SELIGER
Anthony Hopkins LEN IRISH
Elizabeth Hurley BRIGITTE LACOMBE
Jewel EIKA AOSHIMA
Ashley Judd DAVIS FACTOR
Nicole Kidman MARK SELIGER

Kathy Kinney JEFFREY THURNHER
Lenny Kravitz MARK SELIGER
Martin Landau MARY ELLEN MARK
Jonny Lang LEN IRISH
Jude Law ROBERT MAXWELL
Matt LeBlanc FIROOZ ZAHEDI
Sean Lennon LEN IRISH
Jared Leto MARK SELIGER
Courtney Love PEGGY SIROTA
Andie MacDowell MAX VADUKUL
William H. Macy LEN IRISH
Madonna PEGGY SIROTA
John Malkovich BRIGITTE LACOMBE
Lisa Marie & Tim Burton MARY ELLEN MARK
Julianna Margulies JEFFREY THURNER
Matthew McConaughey LANCE STAEDLER
Ewan McGregor DAN WINTERS
Julianne Moore MARK SELIGER
Dermot Mulroney LANCE STAEDLER
Dave Navarro MARK SELIGER
Jack Nicholson WILLY RIZZO
Nick Nolte LEN IRISH
Chris O'Donnell MARK SELIGER
Gwyneth Paltrow & Ben Affleck ALEX BERLINER
Sarah Jessica Parker MICHEL HADDI
Vincent Perez STEWART SHINING
David Hyde Pierce DAN CHAVKIN
Brad Pitt, Nicole Kidman &
Tom Cruise STEVE GRANITZ
Parker Posey ISABEL SNYDER
Queen Latifah MARY ELLEN MARK
Ving Rhames BUTCH BELAIR
Christina Ricci MATTHEW ROLSTON
Michael Richards MARY ELLEN MARK
Julia Roberts SANTE D'ORAZIO
Chris Rock LEN IRISH
Winona Ryder & Matt Damon ALEX BERLINER
Salt-n-Pepa GUY AROCH
Scary Spice MARK SELIGER
Claudia Schiffer & Fiona Apple DANA LIXENBERG
Tom Everett Scott STEPHANIE PFRIENDER
Brooke Shields KATE GARNER
Martin Short LEN IRISH
Christian Slater BUTCH BELAIR
Jada Pinkett Smith ROBERT ERDMANN
Will Smith MARK SELIGER
David Spade JEFFREY THURNHER
Emma Thompson DANA LIXENBERG
Skeet Ulrich RUVEN AFANADOR
James Van Der Beek BUTCH BELAIR
Casper Van Dien ISABEL SNYDER
Vince Vaughn WAYNE MASER
Scott Weiland & His Mother JOHN HUBA
Michelle Williams DEWEY NICKS
Noah Wyle LANCE STAEDLER
Renée Zellweger NEIL DAVENPORT

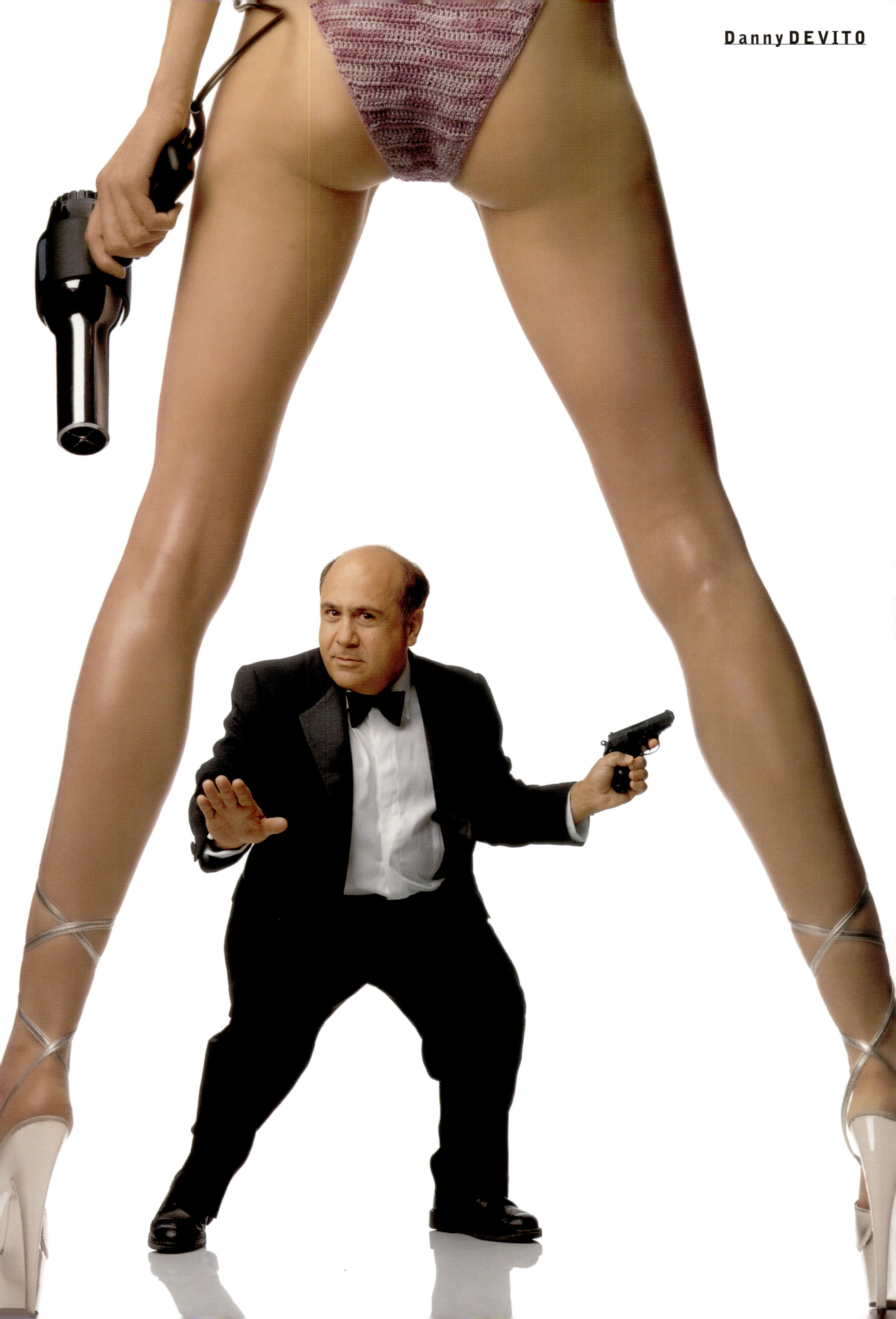

ACKNOWLEDGMENTS

For their help in the creation of *Outrageous,* Rolling Stone Press would like to thank Richard Baker, Jennifer Crandall, Barbara O'Dair, Rina Migliaccio, Bess Wong, Kristin Dymitruk & Lucia Ware. Our gratitude also goes to: the staff of *US,* Jann S. Wenner, Kent Brownridge, John Lagana, Fred Woodward, Rachel Knepfer, Kathy McCarver, Brittain Stone, Steve Best, Tom Worley, Paul Rouse, Pete Rosen, Dennis Wheeler, Janice Borowicz & Hubert Kretzschmar. In addition, we couldn't have done it without the input of Sarah Lazin, Tana Osa-Yande & Alanna Stang; St. Martin's Calvert Morgan, Robert Wallace, Curt Alliaume, Rich Klin & Dana Albarella; & a few others: Tom Gogola, Gretchen Lutz, Peter Kenis, Will Rigby & Tom Soper. Maria Avitabile, Elyse Connolly, Samantha Schwartz, Janet Johnson, Lissette Santiago, Art + Commerce, the Botaish Group, CPI, Michael Ginsburg & Associates, Outline Press Syndicate, Retna, Sygma, Visages & all the photographers whose work appears here is much appreciated. The writers whose Q&A's have been excerpted are: Harry Allen (Chris Rock), Mel Gibson (himself), Chris Heath (David Duchovny), Tom O'Neill (Anthony Hopkins), Chris Mundy (Claire Danes), Margy Rochlin (Gillian Anderson, Nicole Kidman), Johanna Schneller (Richard Gere), Holly Sorensen (Queen Latifah) & Mim Udovitch (Madonna). And, of course, a thank you goes to our *Outrageous* subjects & their staffs.